Sovereignty, RIP

Sovereignty, RIP

DON HERZOG

Yale UNIVERSITY PRESS

New Haven and London

Published with assistance from the Mary Cady Tew Memorial Fund.

Set in type by Newgen North America, Austin, Texas.
Printed in the United States of America.
Library of Congress Control Number:2019948002
ISBN 978-0-300-24772-5 (hardcover : alk. paper)

A catalogue record for this book is available from the British Library.

This paper meets the requirements of ANSI/NISO Z39.48-1992 (Permanence of Paper).

10 9 8 7 6 5 4 3 2 1

For Sam

Contents

Preface

I come not to praise the concept of sovereignty, but to bury it. Well, that's not quite right: I'm in no position to perform the burial myself. But I do want to denounce the concept's role in our politics and law as obsolete, confused, and pernicious. So I want to propose that we retire the concept, that we learn to think and talk and act without relying on it.

If you're instantly alarmed, if you're thinking that surely we need to secure our national borders or to protect state governments against the juggernaut of federal power or to avoid interfering in the internal affairs of other countries, then relax: I have little to say about such questions. I want only to insist that we not appeal to sovereignty in arguing about them. I happen to think that once we remove the worm-eaten strut of sovereignty, the edifices of Eleventh Amendment jurisprudence and sovereign immunity in tort law will collapse, and good riddance. But it's not finally my purpose to pursue those demolition jobs here. There are a host of complicated problems here that can't be settled wholesale, as I'll put it, by an appeal to sovereignty. We have to engage in retail argument, case by case, on the merits. We can do that once we shove sovereignty aside.

There's a daunting theory literature on sovereignty. Scholars have touched on the metaphysics of sovereignty,[1] pursued the ontology of sovereignty,[2] and even invoked the "onto-theological metaphysics of sovereignty."[3] It would be harsh to say that this sort of thing is pernicious nonsense, so I won't say it. (Here we pause for somber contemplation.) Anyway, I take a different approach. I treat sovereignty as a bid to solve contingent but pressing problems thrown up by social change. So here's another reason burial, not praise, isn't quite right: it's plausible that sovereignty was once worth praising. But far-flung legal and political changes have undone even its plausibility. It's time, past time, that we noticed.

My attention to the history of our political problems means that my account is chock-full of concrete political struggles. Not metaphysics, not ontology, but what a wide range of actors have said and done and fought over occupy me. Kings and presidents, legislators and soldiers, pamphleteers

1. For instance, Costas Douzinas, "Speaking Law: On Bare Theological and Cosmopolitan Sovereignty," in *International Law and Its Others*, ed. Anne Orford (Cambridge: Cambridge University Press, 2006), esp. 38; Nicolas Guilhot, "The Kuhning of Reason," *Review of International Studies* (January 2016), 20; Sanford Levinson, "Citizenship and Equality in an Age of Diversity," *Centro Journal* (Spring 2017), 103 n. 16. I have no objection to the substance of the discussion in H. Jefferson Powell, *A Community Built on Words: The Constitution in History and Politics* (Chicago: University of Chicago Press, 2002), 31–37, but I don't see why he says it's about metaphysics, either.

2. For instance, Henry S. Turner, "Francis Bacon's Common Notion," *Journal of Early Modern Cultural Studies* (Summer 2013), 26; Jens Bartelson, *Sovereignty as Symbolic Form* (London: Routledge, 2014).

3. Jacques Derrida, *États d'âme de la psychanalyse: L'impossible au-delà d'une souveraine cruauté* (Paris: Galilée, 2000), 19: "une certaine métaphysique onto-théologique de la *souveraineté*." For an explicitly deconstructionist account of sovereignty, see Elia R. G. Pusterla, *The Credibility of Sovereignty—The Political Fiction of a Concept* (New York: Springer, 2016).

and journalists: all rub shoulders here. Nor am I interested solely in discourse or concepts or ideas. I'm interested in actual practices because I think that's the best way to grasp the stakes of theory. I can help prevent the argument from capsizing in historical detail by stating it baldly up front.

The classic theory of sovereignty, the one I'm keen on burying, holds that every political community must have a locus of authority that is unlimited, undivided, and unaccountable to any higher authority. (If, or so the sources suggest, sovereign authority were legally accountable, the actors exercising that legal authority would qualify as a higher authority. You can put pressure on the spatial metaphor, and I urge you to. But the impulse is clear enough.) Call those the three defining criteria of the concept of sovereignty. Two further thoughts have followed closely on the heels of that theory: first, that sovereign authority is dignified, indeed, immensely dignified; second, that law is the command of the sovereign.

Every one of those commitments was once plausible. Every one of them is now repulsive. Constitutionalism means we've limited state authority. Federalism means we've divided it. The rule of law means we've made it accountable. Bloated dignity and the command theory of law come crashing down, too, in the wake of those changes. We think of state actors as public servants and view them with baleful suspicion instead of prostrating ourselves before them. And we don't think of law as orders barked at us by some boot-camp sergeant to whose will we must submit. Nor are these changes neutral, as in the hemlines-up-hemlines-down or who's-to-say picture of historical variation. They're dramatic improvements in our political arrangements.

So arises a dilemma. If you rely on any of the criteria of the classic concept, you're appealing to a view that's not just obsolete, but also bad. If you renounce all the criteria, you've got a vacuous or meaningless concept on your hands. (Imagine saying, "This is a bachelor, but not an unmarried male.") You can always propose different criteria for the concept. You're free to stipulate that by *sovereign* you mean, oh, an actor with jurisdiction or authority: concepts not without their own difficulties, but not in the desperately bad working order that the concept of sovereignty now is. But if you say that—don't flinch—you have to agree that parents and surgeons and Boy Scout patrol leaders all enjoy sovereignty. The weirdness of such locutions underlines immediately what a radical reconstruction of the concept of sovereignty that would be. Or you might use *sovereign* as a synonym for *state* or as a vacuous adjective suitable for trotting out on formal occasions, without staking out any further commitments on what's distinctive about states. Consider the UN Charter's declaration that "the organization is based on the principle of the sovereign equality of all its Members."[4] What would change if we deleted *sovereign* and shifted the sentence to something like "of the equality of all member states"? Maybe nothing, right?

"Straw man alert! No one believes in that classic theory anymore." I agree that it's hard to find people willing explicitly to defend the view that political authority should be unlimited, undivided, and unaccountable, though easy enough to find celebrants of sovereign dignity, easy too to find defenders of the command theory of law. But I think many people rely, however furtively or unthinkingly, on the classic theory. Pay attention—now and then I'll cheerfully prompt you with recent examples—to how often people defend political and legal views by brandishing an incantation of the form "because

4. United Nations Charter, chap. 1, art. 1.1.

sovereignty," and how often that peremptory appeal must rely on the classic theory to make sense.

That's the boldly drawn or cartoonish account of my argument. I'll turn it into a more detailed and I hope compelling painting by mustering historical evidence. The history is not, in Poohbah's immortal words, "merely corroborative detail, intended to give artistic verisimilitude to an otherwise bald and unconvincing narrative." It's where the action is: not, again, in metaphysics or ontology, not in discourse, but in the efforts of actual people to solve actual problems.

The magicians of the University of Michigan law library once again effortlessly produced one elusive source after another: I'm deeply grateful. I presented part of the argument at Duke, Fordham, Harvard, Northwestern, Notre Dame, St Andrews, UCLA, and Yale: thanks to workshop participants and audience members for probing questions. I also sketched the argument in giving the 2018 MacDermott Lecture at Queen's University Belfast: thanks to the locals for asking great questions with disarming hospitality. As always, I've relied on friends for incisive comments on the manuscript: thanks to John Turquet Bravard, Kristina Daugirdas, Daniel Fryer, Monica Hakimi, Scott Hershovitz, John Hudson, Caroline Humfress, Hillary John, Ellen Katz, Daryl Levinson, Hallie Lipsey, Emily Minton Mattson, Gabe Mendlow, Bill Miller, Julian Davis Mortenson, Sasha Natapoff, Richard Primus, Jonathan Simon, Andy Stark, and Lauren Stotts. Thanks, too, to Robin DuBlanc for pitch-perfect copyediting and to Margaret Otzel for exemplary production editing.

Sovereignty, RIP

1
Sovereignty

"Oh what a bloody age is this!" lamented one observer.[1] Country after country riven by combat, abashed by unabashed cruelty: and this on a continent serenely confident it was civilized. Millions were killed. Contemporaries shrank from telling the tale—"unspeakable,"[2] thought one; "no words can sufficiently describe it, nor tears bemoan it,"[3] thought another; "no tongue can express the barbarous usage," thought a third[4]—but still they told plenty.

1. *The Blovdy Persecution of Protestants in Ireland* (London, 1641), sig. A2 recto. I've modernized spelling (not capitalization) and cleaned up punctuation in quotations throughout, but kept the original spellings of titles in footnotes to make it easier to track down the sources.

2. "The Most Humble Supplication of Certaine of the States of Lower Austria Made vnto the Emperor," in *Two Very Lamentable Relations* (n.p., 1620), n.p. I owe the reference to *The Thirty Years War: A Sourcebook*, ed. Peter H. Wilson (New York: Palgrave Macmillan, 2010), 29.

3. Otto von Guericke's eyewitness account in *The Thirty Years War: A Documentary History*, ed. Tryntje Helfferich (Indianapolis: Hackett, 2009), 109.

4. A 20 September 1644 letter from E.H., in G.S., *A True Relation of the Sad Passages, between Two Armies in the West* (London, 1644), 9. Likewise the poet Schiller on the Siege of Magdeburg: Johann Christoph Friedrich von Schiller, *The History of the Thirty Years' War*, trans. A. J. W. Morrison

Yes, that was Europe—in the sixteenth and seventeenth centuries. If you had a certain kind of high school education, you can, if dimly, recall that the crumbling Holy Roman Empire wasn't particularly Holy or Roman or imperial, and you can recall some of the names of the wars of religion, some comic, some anodyne: the Schmalkaldic War, the Eighty Years' War, the War of the Jülich Succession, the Thirty Years' War, the Wars of the Three Kingdoms, and so on, and on, and on; some of them invasions of foreign troops, some of them, to use the familiar piquant oxymoron, civil wars. If your teacher was fond of France, you might remember the St. Bartholomew's Day Massacre, August 1572, when Catholics slaughtered tens of thousands of Huguenots (French Protestants) in the streets of Paris, elsewhere around France too. Voltaire counted nine civil wars in France alone.[5] The sheer scale of chaos invites you to imagine yourself as a strategic genius playing Risk. Like that board game, the casualty counts are invidiously abstract. We have better things to do than dope out just how many millions were killed.[6] Instead let's gaze unflinchingly at "this horror of

(n.p.: Floating, 2008), 251; [François de La Noue], *The Politicke and Militarie Discovrses of the Lord de la Novve*, trans. E.A. (London, 1587), 36–47. And then, of course, shrinking authors rely on ominous abstractions: "all manner of whoredom, ravishments, violences and worse, were committed by those infernal hellhounds, villains, and savage robbers" (Antony Colynet, *The True History of the Ciuill Warres of France* (London, [1591]), 205); "strange cruelties," "burning, spoiling, and making havoc after a strange and cruel manner," "horrible cruelties," "outrageous cruelty," "killing, spoiling, and murdering the inhabitants in most cruel and horrible manner, and making havoc of all things without pity or mercy," and so on (*The Mutable and Wauering Estate of France, from the Yeare of Our Lord 1460, vntill the Yeare 1595* (London, 1597), 24, 26, 32, 42, 57).

5. Voltaire, *Traité sur la tolérance* ([Genève], 1763), chap. 3.

6. The aptly named necrometrics.com (last visited 28 February 2018) offers a range of estimates with the sources they come from.

blood and massacre,"[7] at some unspeakable tales of life—no, death—on the ground.

Here's Spain's Duke of Alba smashing rebellion in the Netherlands. Naarden, 1572: the locals dutifully respond to a summons to the hospital chapel. "All these poor and miserable inhabitants being thus assembled, the Spanish soldiers were commanded to murder them all." So they did, though they paused to rape the women first. Then they headed out to the rest of the town. "The children had their throats cut, and in some houses some were tied to posts with cords, then the houses were fired, and they burnt alive." The troops killed everyone and razed the town. The chronicler thought future ages wouldn't believe that a man, a Christian, could even think of such atrocities.[8] But the duke proudly contemplated his sanguinary years in the Netherlands. "Ransacking, spoiling, ruining, expelling, destroying, imprisoning, chaining, banishing, and confiscating of men's goods, burning, hanging, beheading, breaking upon wheels, hanging men alive by the feet," and more: the duke "bragged" over dinner that he'd ordered eighteen thousand executions over and above those his soldiers had killed.[9] No wonder he earned the nickname "the iron duke." No wonder a contemporary engraving shows him

7. [Anthony Nixon], *The Warres of Swethland* (London, 1609), n.p.

8. Likewise for the St. Bartholomew Day's Massacre, [Ambrosius de Bruyn], *A Narration, Briefely Contayning the History of the French Massacre, Especially That Horrible One at Paris, Which Happened in the Yeare 1572* (London, 1618), 25: "Good God, can these things enter into the hearts of *Christians*?"; and James Howell, *A German Diet: or, The Ballance of Europe* (London, 1653), 54: "Is it possible that a Christian people trusting in the same Redeemer, govern'd by the same Laws, eating the same bread, breathing the same air, should prove such tigers?"

9. Ed[ward] Grimeston, *A Generall Historie of the Netherlands* (London, 1608), 496–97, 533–34.

eating a child.[10] No wonder that when a furious Leiden soldier found a fallen Spanish soldier, he "plucked the heart out of his body, as he lay half dead, and when he had gnawn it with his teeth, he cast it away from him."[11]

Pomerania, 1630[12]: the Count of Tilly and Albrecht von Wallenstein's soldiers tied burning matches to residents' "noses, tongues, jaws, cheeks, breasts, legs, and secret parts." They also lit satchels of gunpowder on people's genitals. They tied cords around victims' necks and twisted hard enough for their ears and noses to bleed and for their eyes to pop out of their heads. They skinned people, as if they were seeking leather. They burned some in ovens, some in fires—and kept others alive over smoldering fires, relieving them now and then with cold drink, "lest in their torment they should die too soon." They castrated men in front of their wives and children, raped daughters in front of their parents. They forced the dying to pray to the devil. They pried open victims' mouths, "then poured down their throats water, stinking puddle, filthy liquids, and piss itself." And "they made the people by force to eat their own excrements."[13]

Hochstatt, Swabia, 1634: too impatient to wait for the residents to open the gates, Croats and Polish soldiers "furiously

10. There's a reproduction in James Tanis and Daniel Horst, *Images of Discord: A Graphic Interpretation of the Opening Decades of the Eighty Years' War* (Grand Rapids, MI: Bryn Mawr College Library and William B. Erdmans, 1993), 67. Or see http://historynet.com/wp-content/uploads/image/2013/MHQ/EXTRAS/Netherlands.jpg (last visited 25 July 2018).

11. T[homas] S[tocker], *A Tragicall Historie of the Troubles and Ciuile Warres of the Lowe Countries* (London, [1583]), 124 verso.

12. I think that's the right year for the narrative I'm relying on here, thanks to *Chronologische taafelen* (Amsterdam, 1709), 28. For a stunning wealth of information on (especially but not only) the German military, see Fritz Redlich, *The German Military Enterpriser and His Work Force: A Study in European Economic and Social History*, 2 vols. (Wiesbaden: Franz Steiner Verlag GmbH, 1964–65).

13. [Philip] Vincent, *The Lamentations of Germany* (London, 1638), 11–14.

plundered" the city. They also raped and killed the women; "poured dunghill water and vinegar into the throats of seven men"; "some they hanged up by the privy members, sawed off the legs of some"; stripped people and marched them through the streets, beating them with axes and hammers along the way. They "roasted alive" the director of the hospital and made off with the city's food supply and everyone's clothing.[14]

Some brevity is in order. Cabrières, 1545: pursuing the forcible conversion of the Waldensians, more patient than those soldiers at Hochstatt would be, the president of Aix's parliament persuaded the residents to open the city gates—and killed all of them. Shut up in a barn full of hay and straw, forty women were incinerated: the president's troops used pikes and spears to keep the women from jumping out.[15] Paris, 1572: "Living Infants were torn out of the Wombs of their newly dead Mothers, for fear some Accident should help them into the World before they should send them out of it."[16] Antwerp, 1576: Spanish troops "slew infinite numbers of people," "17,000 men, women, and children," "great numbers of young children, but many more women more than fourscore years of age." "I refrain to rehearse the heaps of dead Carcasses which lay at every Trench where they entered: the thickness whereof, did in many places exceed the height of a man."[17] Lower Austria, 1620: Cossack and Walloon troops raped not just women, but also boys. They roasted pregnant women on the fire until

14. [N.C.], *The German History Continued: The Seventh Part* (London, 1634), 50–51.

15. John Sleidan [Johannes Sleidanus], *The General History of the Reformation of the Church* (London, 1689), 347.

16. *A Season[a]ble Warning to Protestants; from the Cruelty and Treachery of the Parisian Massacre, August the 24th 1572* (London, 1680), 28.

17. [George Gascoigne], *The Spoyle of Antwerpe* (London, [1576]), n.p. See too Thomas Churchyarde, *A Lamentable, and Pitifull Description, of the Wofull Warres in Flaunders* (London, 1578), 61–62.

men could see the fetuses.[18] Magdeburg, 1631: a fire lit to terrify the residents consumed the city. Embers and ash reached a town seventeen miles away. Twenty thousand corpses, swirling aimlessly in an eddy, clogged the Elbe River.[19] The Piedmont, 1655, another assault on the Waldensians: "Some women had their breasts cut off, some men had their members cut off, some were starved to death with cold, and some were forced to eat their own excrement,"[20] all because they wouldn't convert to Catholicism. Poitou, 1681: troops dragged women by their hair, by ropes around their necks; they "put them to the torture with screws, by clapping their fingers into a vice" and squeezing; they beat eighty-year-old men; they hauled people into Catholic churches, splashed them with holy water, and told them they were now Catholics.[21]

These decades were strewn with beheaded corpses with penises jammed into their mouths;[22] corpses dug out of graves "to be hanged or burnt" (Alba strikes again);[23] corpses dug out of graves to be devoured by wolves and ravens;[24] corpses

18. "Humble Supplication," in *Two Very Lamentable Relations*, n.p. For a contemporary engraving, see http://www.alamy.com/stock-photo-atrocities-against-the-people-of-lower-austria-committed-by-polish-104897467.html (last visited 28 February 2018). For a contemporary publication, see Joh[ann] Lodew[ig] Gottfried, *Historische kronyck*, 3 vols. (Leyden, 1698–1700), 2:1295–96.

19. Von Guericke in *Thirty Years War*, ed. Helfferich, 109, 111.

20. L.P., *The Christians Calamities: or, The Protestants Complaint* (London, 1655), 10.

21. [Roger L'Estrange], *An Apology for the Protestants of France* (London, 1683), 27.

22. A Gentleman, Who Was an Eye Witnesse, *A True and Credible Relation of the Barbarovs Crveltie and Bloudy Massacres of the English Protestants* (London, 1642), sig. A3 verso.

23. Grimeston, *Generall Historie*, 535.

24. [Elie Benoist], *The History of the Famous Edict of Nantes*, 2 vols. (London, 1694), 1:111–12; and see 1:261–62.

dug out of graves to be devoured by famished humans;[25] besieged Parisians eating "rats, mice, and other filthy and unaccustomed things"—and each other;[26] soldiers eating children alive ("one was known to take a small Infant, and holding it by one leg with his left hand to tear it in sunder with his right, and so to eat and suck the blood of it");[27] mothers killing and devouring their own children, even selling some of the flesh to their neighbors.[28] We should then envy those in 1635 Ulm who, unlike thousands of their peers, survived by munching on weeds.[29] There are degradations worse than having to imitate livestock.

Are these numbers too high? the parade of horribles too mind-numbing? Let's zero in on the plight of staunch Protestant Sir Patrick Dunson. In 1641, Catholic rebels surrounded his house in Armagh, Ireland. Knowing what was coming, he summoned the household to prayer. The rebels burst in and threatened him with death if he didn't convert. Dunson wouldn't budge. "I had rather be a doorkeeper in the house of my God," he announced, "than to live in the richest tents of the wicked." The rebels reciprocated this cheery gambit with one of their own: they raped his wife, killed his children, and again demanded that he convert. Dunson laughed and told them that such cruelty would send his family to heaven. They tied him to a board so tightly that his eyes burst out of his head. "They cut off his ears, then his nose, then seared off both his cheeks; after that they cut off his arms, after that his legs"; still he survived; they finished him off by

25. Vincent, *Lamentations*, 59.

26. *The Miserable Estate of the Citie of Paris at Present* (London, 1590), 4.

27. Eusebius Nieremberg, S.J., *A Treatise of the Difference b[e]twixt the Temporal and Eternal*, trans. Vivian Mullineaux (n.p., 1672), 299.

28. Vincent, *Lamentations*, 53, 55–56.

29. Hans Zeberle's diary in *Thirty Years War*, ed. Helfferich, 320.

cutting out his tongue and ramming "a red hot iron into his bowels."[30]

Eat shit and die: whatever you make of rapturous martyrdom, that was the literal plight of many in early modern Europe, just one horror of many more. Even when you review the long list of wars and try to get in focus the millions of deaths, you might miss that those living in times and places of relative quiet couldn't feel secure. Disorder had been unleashed. Nothing comic or anodyne about what these people were up against, nothing metaphysical or ontological, and lots more than a history of discourse could capture.

We call them wars of religion; so, occasionally, did contemporaries.[31] No wonder that in 1566, Protestants desecrated one splendid Catholic church after another in the Low Countries: altars overturned, sacred images broken, organs shattered, the host trampled on the floor.[32] Maybe we should tread more cautiously.[33] They weren't *only* wars of religion. Contemporaries were aware of even more skeptical views: take the imagined dialogue in which a Huguenot lawyer, confronting the massacre of St. Bartholomew's Day and France's civil wars

30. *Blovdy Persecution*, sig. A3 recto ff. For more from 1641 Ireland, see [Thomas Ashley], *Prosperovs Proceedings in Ireland* (London, 1642), 3–4. For Jesuits assaulting a Protestant rector, see Eleazar Gilbert, *Newes from Poland* (London, 1641), 20–21. For Irish Catholics as "inhumane butchers," Richard Harrison, *Irelands Misery since the Late Cessation* (London, 1644), 6.

31. For instance, Gidion [Gédéon] Pontier, *A New Survey of the Present State of Europe*, trans. J.B. (London, 1684), 62, 147–48; Edmund Bohun et al., *A Geographical Dictionary* (London, 1693), 84, 273, 279, 284, 299.

32. Famianvs [Famiano] Strada, *De Bello Belgico: The History of the Low-Countrey Warres*, trans. Rob[ert] Stapylton (London, 1650), 121–25.

33. For a blunt polemic, see William T. Cavanaugh, *The Myth of Religious Violence: Secular Ideology and the Roots of Modern Conflict* (Oxford: Oxford University Press, 2009), chap. 3. Thanks to Sue Juster for the reference.

more generally, insists, "these Wars were not originally Wars of Religion, but Wars of State."[34] Of course there were dynastic rivalries, geopolitical maneuvering, and the like. You can't make sense of the German Peasants' War of 1524–25 without saying something about grievances of class and status. And yes, Martin Luther famously denounced the peasants. But it matters too that Thomas Müntzer championed them: think about what it takes for a Protestant theologian to join in combat and earn torture, execution, and the forbidding display of his head for his troubles.[35] We can and should flip the skeptical scrutiny. You can't make sense of the decision of Spain's King Philip II to send the Armada to invade England without noticing his desire to please the pope by toppling that Protestant Jezebel, Queen Elizabeth, from the throne.[36] You can't make sense of the English effort to relieve the French siege at La Rochelle in 1628 without noticing that the residents were Huguenots and England was a Protestant power; and that remains true even if you agree that trade and diplomatic interests were also involved.[37] (Then too, the episode is a useful reminder that England's Charles I was suspicious of Puritans, Spain's Philip IV of Calvinists: so the endlessly fissiparous nature

34. [Pierre Jurieu], *The Last Efforts of Afflicted Innocence* (London, 1682), 194.

35. For a workmanlike overview, see Paul P. Kuenning, "Luther and Muntzer: Contrasting Theologies in Regard to Secular Authority within the Context of the German Peasant Revolt," *Journal of Church and State* (Spring 1987). On Müntzer's end, Eric W. Gritsch, *Thomas Müntzer: A Tragedy of Errors* (Minneapolis: Fortress, 1989), 107–9.

36. Garrett Mattingly, *The Armada* (Boston: Houghton Mifflin, 1959), remains indispensable.

37. Simon L. Adams, "The Road to La Rochelle: English Foreign Policy and the Huguenots, 1610 to 1629," *Proceedings of the Huguenot Society of London* (May 1975).

of Protestantism opens possibilities trickier than a simple Protestant-against-Catholic mapping could capture.) For that matter, you should think about why France would be besieging one of its own cities in the first place—and in turn why that city, and the region more generally, might be rebelling against royal authority. That religious conflict is routinely entangled with other issues doesn't begin to show that religious conflict isn't real, isn't important.[38]

But then we might wonder about the veracity of some of these accounts. These writers aren't exactly patron saints of objectivity. Some of them are propagandists devoted to inspiring horror and hatred of the enemy. Not all these sources claim to be based on eyewitness testimony; I suppose some tales grew in the telling. And there might be literary or pictorial license: I rather doubt that the Duke of Alba literally ate a child, but I'm inclined to believe that some soldier did, and the difference is not that I've got any mystified reverence about aristocrats—more like supercilious contempt—but that the duke's doing it would be better attested. Or again, look at the eyebrow-raising claim of that indefatigable Protestant, John Foxe, that the pope celebrated the massacre of St. Bartholomew's Day.[39] That too might inspire disbelief. But Foxe was right, even if his details are a bit spotty: Pope Gregory XIII ordered an annual Te Deum to celebrate the great event; he commissioned a special medal depicting an angel holding a cross over Protestants being murdered; and he added some frescoes to the Sistine

38. On the religious motivation and structure of popular violence, see Natalie Zemon Davis, "The Rites of Violence: Religious Riot in Sixteenth-Century France," *Past and Present* (May 1973). See too Mack P. Holt, "Putting Religion Back into the Wars of Religion," *French Historical Studies* (Fall 1993).

39. John Foxe, *Actes and Monuments*, 2 vols. (London, 1583), 2:2153.

Chapel's antechamber.[40] Discount liberally for propaganda's lurid exaggerations and still it would be irrational to deny the casualties, the torture, across the board.

If you want to explain why such violence erupted in Europe in the early sixteenth century, you'd better be able to say something not just about religious conflict, but also about its contingency. Even if you have a suitably baleful view of the ubiquitous human potential for grave evil, even if you think history is essentially the history of war, you need to be able to come to terms with the scale and shape of these unbearable decades. Nor will it do to inveigh against religious enthusiasm. Even if evil and enthusiasm are timeless features of the human condition, we need to know why they exploded so spectacularly in early modern Europe.

So a plausible explanation needs to appeal to contingent historic developments, to culture, society, politics, and law, not to allegedly timeless features of the human condition. Here's the obvious candidate: the Reformation shattered the unity of Christendom. The latter had been the common currency of public philosophy for centuries. Whatever one made of disputes between church and state, Christianity glued Europe together, and Christianity was Catholicism, period. The Catholic Church had repeatedly faced challenges—in England alone, Lollards and Hussites—and more or less successfully vanquished them. Don't think of church inquisitors as weird sadists gratuitously torturing others; think of them as entrusted with the grim duty of safeguarding a modicum of

40. Robert M. Kingdon, *Myths about the St. Bartholomew's Day Massacres, 1572–1576* (Cambridge, MA: Harvard University Press, 1988), 45–46; Carter Lindberg, *The European Reformations*, 2nd ed. (Chichester, UK: Wiley-Blackwell, 2010), 279.

doctrinal constancy and so maintaining social order.[41] Many contemporary Catholics indicted Luther as the snake in the grass. Queen Mary's chaplain and confessor, for instance, blamed the German Peasants' War on "the devil and Luther together" and reviled Luther for branding the emperor "a sack of worms" without authority over the gospel. He wrote just after the suppression of Wyatt's Rebellion, motivated in large part by horror at Mary's insistence on marrying Philip II of Spain: the worry was not just that he was a foreigner, though the House of Commons urged her to marry someone English, but that both were Catholic.[42] Convenient, I suppose, to have a villain on hand; but it's the collision between the success of Protestantism and that older commitment to the unity of Christendom that set Europe ablaze. Likewise, the familiar mandate charging the state with leading subjects to salvation became a recipe for violence after people no longer agreed, even roughly, on how to do that. It became crucial to seize control of the state, lest your religious rivals harness its might to consign thousands to hell.

I don't want even to flirt with the thesis that the wars of religion somehow caused the classic theory of sovereignty. Life would be easier if problems magically solved themselves, but

41. On torture, see, for instance, [Luke Beaulieu], *The History of the Romish Inquisition and Inquisitors* (London, 1700), 137–40. For a typical polemic against inquisitors, see James Salgado, *The Slaughter-House, or A Brief Description of the Spanish Inquisition* (London, [1682]), esp. 54–57, 60–62. Carlo Ginzburg, *The Cheese and the Worms: The Cosmos of a Sixteenth-Century Miller*, trans. John Tedeschi and Anne C. Tedeschi (Baltimore: Johns Hopkins University Press, 1980), is rightly celebrated.

42. [John Christopherson], *An Exhortation to All Menne to Take Hede and Beware of Rebellion* (n.p., [1554]), n.p.; *DNB*, s.v. "Christopherson, John." On this rebellion, see Anthony Fletcher and Diarmaid MacCulloch, *Tudor Rebellions*, 4th ed. (London: Longman, 1997), 81–93.

they don't. It takes creativity, agency, to hammer out solutions, especially when the problems depend on deeply entrenched views and practices. In his cruder moods Marx sometimes writes as if underlying forces and relations of production automatically secrete ideas that legitimate them, however ideologically; that won't do.[43] And social theorists have puzzled over the dialectic of structure and agency, as if it's mysterious how individuals could act freely when they are inescapably caught up in, produced by, society.[44] But I don't see any profound explanatory or ontological mysteries here. "The tradition of dead generations" may "weigh like a nightmare on the brains of the living," as Marx said in a happier moment;[45] but if we're stuck, it's for lack of creativity or because we face intractable problems, not because we are in society. Where else would we be? What but society would have equipped us with the powers of critical reflection and imagination? And where but in society would actual possibilities for new and improved practices be?

If you shift your organizing framework from cause/effect to problem/solution, it's harder to be distracted by obscure conceptual pyrotechnics, easier to see what's going on. So one familiar script about the wars of religion is that the international unity of Christendom, now a problem, gets replaced by *cuius regio, eius religio*: the ruler of each realm decides what its religion is. Think of each country as a distinct, brightly colored patch on the globe; give up the aspiration to have all of

43. I'm thinking especially of the preface to *A Contribution to the Critique of Political Economy*.

44. For a typically recondite account, see Anthony Giddens, *Central Problems in Social Theory* (London: Macmillan, 1979); Giddens, *The Constitution of Society* (Cambridge: Polity, 1984).

45. *The Eighteenth Brumaire of Louis Napoleon*, in *The Marx-Engels Reader*, ed. Robert C. Tucker, 2nd ed. (New York: Norton, 1978), 595.

Europe united and borders take on dramatically new significance. Not all social groups and institutions are spatially organized: think of King Crimson fans, the Society for Molecular Biology and Evolution, or your own family or kin group. But the sovereign state emphatically rules over a distinct territory. We associate *cuius regio* with the 1555 Peace of Augsburg; you can find intimations of it in the 1526 Diet of Speyer; but in fact the view takes decades to crystallize.[46] Still, the trajectory is clear enough. Martin Luther nails his ninety-five theses to the church door in 1517; Henry VIII splits with the pope in 1532. No longer would attacks on the Catholic Church be successfully suppressed.

Nothing wrong with this script, as far as it goes. But we can go further. It's no accident that the classic theory of sovereignty is articulated in the sixteenth and seventeenth centuries. The theory then articulated is not brand new, not created ex nihilo,[47] but you won't find it in Plato or Aristotle, Augustine or Aquinas, Marsilius or Machiavelli. And so I want to reject the habit of some theorists to translate all kinds of terms for political authority or leadership as *sovereignty*, to conscript authors scattered across centuries and continents as theorists of sovereignty. Ancient Greek *basileus* and *kyrion*, Latin *auctoritas*, Hebrew *kavod*; Chrétien de Troyes, Boethius, and de Sade: Giorgio Agamben enlists them all.[48] The infinitely more sober

46. Craig Harline, *A World Ablaze: The Rise of Martin Luther and the Birth of the Reformation* (New York: Oxford University Press, 2017), 265; Richard Andrew Cahill, *Philipp of Hesse and the Reformation* (Mainz: Verlag Philipp von Zabern, 2001), 141–50; Peter H. Wilson, *The Thirty Years War: Europe's Tragedy* (Cambridge, MA: Belknap Press, Harvard University Press, 2009), 42 and *passim*.

47. Walter Ullmann, "The Development of the Medieval Idea of Sovereignty," *English Historical Review* (January 1949).

48. *The Omnibus Homo Sacer* (Stanford, CA: Stanford University Press, 2017), 29, 226–27, 1083, 237–38, 551, 433, 487, 1111. See too Jacques Derrida,

and discerning Quentin Skinner is willing to take Mario Salomonio's 1514 reference to *principatu* as sovereignty, and that's just one of the difficult issues about translation confronting him as he ranges over five languages and several centuries.[49] You can treat sovereignty as a catch-all category for all kinds of competing conceptions of political authority. But then you have an invidiously flabby concept on your hands. It's hard to see what the payoff could be. Maybe I'm finicky in shrinking from Agamben's outlandish gluttony. Regardless, I'll be focusing on a particular understanding of sovereignty. And I will largely restrict my attention to English-language materials to sidestep some difficulties raised by translation.[50]

The etymology is worth noting. The word *sovereign* in English goes back to the fourteenth century, a cognate for terms in Old French and Italian.[51] It indicates high or supreme authority, and that's a more capacious, less finicky category than what I'm calling the classic theory. Especially with earlier

---

Voyous: Deux essais sur la raison (Paris: Galilée, 2003), 192, translated as Derrida, *Rogues: Two Essays on Reason*, trans. Pascale-Anne Brault and Michael Nass (Stanford, CA: Stanford University Press, 2005), 138.

49. *The Foundations of Modern Political Thought*, 2 vols. (Cambridge: Cambridge University Press, 1978), 1:131. For more probing of issues raised by translation in the context of Skinner's work, see my chapter on *Foundations* in *The Oxford Handbook of Classics in Modern Political Theory*, ed. Jacob T. Levy (Oxford: Oxford University Press, online 2015). But contrast Quentin Skinner, "A Genealogy of the Modern State," *Proceedings of the British Academy* (2009), 325, with which I entirely agree. I have the same worries about Daniel Lee's equally erudite and impressive book, *Popular Sovereignty in Early Modern Constitutional Thought* (Oxford: Oxford University Press, 2016), which despite its title goes all the way back to Roman law.

50. Some, not all. Some English-speaking contemporaries of course read—and sometimes misread—foreign texts and translations.

51. *OED*, s.v.v. "sovereign" and "sovereignty." On French literary treatments of the old notion, see Peggy McCracken, *In the Skin of a Beast: Sovereignty and Animality in Medieval France* (Chicago: University of Chicago Press, 2017).

invocations of sovereignty, then, it can be tricky or downright impossible to tell whether the classic theory is being invoked. And if we switch the frame to contemporary and later reader receptions, different readers or onlookers might well have picked up different understandings.

Regardless, I take the early modern wars of religion as the decisive context for the emergence of the theory of sovereignty.[52] Again, this view of sovereignty isn't metaphysical or ontological, isn't some timeless or necessary bit of conceptual furniture in appraising politics. It always has to be an open question whether it does a decent job orienting people toward their world, whether it helps them solve their problems. But if you want to see it at its best, and I do, it's most illuminating to see the early modern theorists of sovereignty as grappling with the unutterably cruel bloodbaths of their day, trying to hammer out a way of restoring social order.

The Classic Theory

Jean Bodin first published *Les six livres de la République* in 1576; an expanded Latin translation followed in 1586; an English translation in 1606 was based mostly on the Latin version. This complicated textual history aside, I'm interested in the popular uptake of Bodin's work. It matters that the French version came out just four years after the St. Bartholomew's Day Massacre, in the midst of the French wars of religion. It matters because context bestows meaning: we can grasp and evaluate Bodin's views as a bid to put an end to grotesque social and political turmoil.

52. So does Dieter Grimm, *Sovereignty: The Origin and Future of a Political and Legal Concept*, trans. Belinda Cooper (New York: Columbia University Press, 2015), 5.

Bodin is explicit, emphatic, about the commitments that comprise what I'm calling the classic theory of sovereignty. "Majesty or Sovereignty," he declares, "is the most high, absolute, and perpetual power over the citizens and subjects in a Commonweale." "Sovereignty is not limited either in power, charge, or time certain."[53] Nor can sovereign power be divided: "such states as wherein the rights of sovereignty are divided, are not rightly to be called Commonweales, but rather the corruption of Commonweales." That sounds like a verbal quibble, but Bodin is pressing an empirical claim: "where the rights of sovereignty are divided betwixt the prince and his subjects: in that confusion of the state, there is still endless stirs and quarrels, for the superiority, until that some one, some few, or all together have got the sovereignty."[54] The sovereign is accountable only to God: "he only is to be called absolute sovereign, who next unto God acknowledgeth none greater than himself." The sovereign, then, doesn't answer to any earthly power: "if he be enforced to serve any man, or to obey any man's command (be it by his own good liking, or against his will) . . . he loseth the title of majesty, and is no more a sovereign." So Bodin shrugs aside feudal dependencies: "whereby a man may easily judge, that there are few or none absolute sovereign princes." So too he denies the possibility of holding the sovereign legally accountable. Law is the command of the sovereign, and it doesn't make sense to imagine the sovereign commanding himself, since he can as readily unbind himself, "which is a necessary reason to prove

53. Jean Bodin, *The Six Bookes of a Commonweale: A Facsimile Reprint of the English Translation of 1606 Corrected and Supplemented*, ed. Kenneth Douglas McRae (Cambridge, MA: Harvard University Press, 1962), 84, 85.

54. Bodin, *Six Bookes*, 194. See too P. Dormer, *Monarchia Triumphans: or, The Super-Eminency of Monarchy over Poliarchy* (London, 1666), 9.

evidently that a king or sovereign prince cannot be subject to his own laws."[55]

Thomas Hobbes published *Leviathan* in 1651; his account of sovereignty is strikingly similar to Bodin's. (In another work Hobbes even quotes Bodin on "the corruption of Commonweales" in insisting that it's an error to think that sovereignty can be divided.[56] But I've no interest in whether Hobbes got his views from Bodin. Even if I were fond of intellectual history, I would hope we could do better than epidemiology. "Who'd they get the ideas from?" and "Who'd they transmit them to?" are enervating questions.) No surprise: one needn't run roughshod over the differences between sixteenth-century France and seventeenth-century England to note the similarities. "The Sovereign Power," holds Hobbes, "whether placed in One Man, as in Monarchy, or in one Assembly of men, as in Popular and Aristocratical Commonwealths, is as great, as possibly men can be imagined to make it."[57] "Power Unlimited, is absolute Sovereignty."[58] So sovereignty can't be limited. Nor can it be divided: Hobbes reviles a "doctrine, plainly, and directly against the essence of a Common-wealth; and 'tis this, '*That the Sovereign Power may be divided*.' For what is it to divide the Power of a Common-wealth, but to Dissolve it; for Pow-

55. Bodin, *Six Bookes*, 86, 114, 128, 92.

56. Tho[mas] Hobb[e]s, *De Corpore Politico: or The Elements of Law, Moral & Politick* (London, 1650), 167.

57. Thomas Hobbes, *Leviathan* (London, 1651), 106–7. Quentin Skinner, "From the State of Princes to the Person of the State," in his *Visions of Politics*, 3 vols. (Cambridge: Cambridge University Press, 2002), 2:413, urges that we see Hobbes's "state as a purely impersonal authority": "it is Hobbes who first speaks systematically and unapologetically in the abstract and unmodulated tones of the modern theorist of the sovereign state." Nothing for my purposes is at stake in that claim.

58. Hobbes, *Leviathan*, 115.

ers divided mutually destroy each other."[59] Again we see not a quibble about the meaning of a term, but a substantial claim about the conditions of social and political order. Nor can the sovereign be held legally accountable: it's an "opinion, repugnant to the Nature of a Common-wealth . . . *That he that hath the Sovereign Power, is subject to the Civil Lawes*."[60] Hobbes is adamant that every commonwealth must have a sovereign.[61]

Here's Grotius, originally from 1625: that power, which he immediately glosses as sovereign, "is called Supreme, whose Acts are not subject to another's Power, so that they cannot be made void by any other human Will."[62] Pufendorf, 1672: "that sovereignty or supreme command, which appears in every state," has to "be acknowledged *unaccountable*," "exempt from human laws, or, to speak more properly, *above* them," and has to be indivisible too: "there is so near and so necessary a connection between all the parts of the sovereignty, as that not one of them can be separated from any other, but the regular frame of the commonwealth must be destroyed."[63]

59. Hobbes, *Leviathan*, 170.

60. Hobbes, *Leviathan*, 169. For an important echo of the view, see John Austin, *The Province of Jurisprudence Determined* (London, 1832), 268–69.

61. For instance, *Leviathan*, 115; *De Corpore Politico*, 74–81. Compare Thomas Hob[be]s, *Behemoth: or An Epitome of the Civil Wars of England, from 1640, to 1660* (London, 1679), 140, where the speakers reviewing the history wonder where sovereignty lay once Charles I was imprisoned.

62. Hugo Grotius, *The Rights of War and Peace*, ed. Richard Tuck, 3 vols. (Indianapolis: Liberty Fund, 2005), 1:259.

63. Samuel Pufendorf, *The Law of Nature and Nations*, trans. Mr. Carew, 5th ed. (London, 1749), 650, 687, 688, 661. See too A Person of Quality [Pufendorf], *The Present State of Germany* (London, 1690), 150: "all kinds of mixture can produce nothing at last but a monstrous deformed Government." For more on irregular government, *Present State*, 152–54, and especially *The Pufendorf Lectures: Annotations from the Teaching of Samuel Pufendorf, 1672–1674*, ed. Bo Lindberg (Stockholm: Kungl. Vitterhets Historie och

Burlamaqui, 1747: "Sovereignty can admit of no share or partition." It's "a supreme and independent power [that] acknowledges no other superior power on earth." "That in every government there should be such a supreme power, is a point absolutely necessary."[64]

Vattel, 1758, has the same sort of view: "Every nation that governs itself, under what form soever, without any dependence on a foreign power, is a *sovereign state*." He hammers away at the dignity of sovereign powers: "Nations and sovereigns, are then, at the same time under an obligation, have a right to maintain their dignity, and to cause it to be respected as of the utmost importance to their safety and tranquillity." And he's especially insistent on the link between dignity and unaccountability: "The majesty of a sovereign will not suffer his being punished like a private person." Even an ambassador, "a public minister representing the person and dignity of a sovereign," warrants "particular honours."[65] In his analysis of the English constitution, de Lolme cranked up the volume: "the constitution has invested the man whom it has made the sole head of the state, with all the personal privileges, all the pomp, all the majesty, of which human dignities are capable. . . . He is

---

Antikvitets Akademien Handlingar, 2014), 193–95. For a helpful overview of competing conceptual frames for understanding the Holy Roman Empire, and further illumination of Pufendorf's use of *monstrous* and *irregular*, see Peter H. Wilson, "Still a Monstrosity? Some Reflections on Early Modern German Statehood," *Historical Journal* (June 2006).

64. Jean-Jacques Burlamaqui, *The Principles of Natural and Politic Law*, trans. Thomas Nugent, ed. Peter Korkman, 2 vols. (Indianapolis: Liberty Fund, 2006), 2:32, 44–45. See too [Chevalier Ramsay], *An Essay upon Civil Government* (London, 1722), 38.

65. [Emer] de Vattel, *The Law of Nations; or Principles of the Law of Nature*, trans. from the French, 2 vols. (London, 1759), 1:10, 133, 22, 2:140; see too 1:137, 2:158.

not to be addressed but with the expressions and outward ceremony of almost eastern humility."[66] In the presence of royalty, "bow down unto the ground in token of subjection and humility," James Cleland instructed his noble reader.[67] It's tempting to overlook fawning and scraping as weird bits of trivia. Don't. Even when wholly conventionalized, they speak volumes. "Royal Sovereignty," insisted another writer, is "the highest Dignity among mortal men"; "nothing in the World ought more to oblige the Subject to . . . perfect awe and reverence."[68]

I could pile on (a promise or a threat?) with less august or canonical figures—and, crucially, with figures across the political spectrum. Robert Filmer, 1680: "There can be no laws without a Supreme Power to command or make them. . . . [I]n a Monarchy the King must of necessity be above the Laws; there can be no Sovereign Majesty in him that is under them."[69] Halifax, 1688: "There can be no Government without a *Supreme Power* . . . wherever it is lodged, it must be *unlimited*:

66. J. L. de Lolme, *The Constitution of England*, new ed. (London, 1817), 198.

67. James Cleland, *Hero-Paideia, or The Institvtion of a Yovng Noble Man* (Oxford, 1607), 173. I owe the reference to Markku Peltonen, *The Duel in Early Modern England: Civility, Politeness and Honour* (Cambridge: Cambridge University Press, 2003), 66.

68. *Fundamental Law the True Security of Sov'reign Dignity* (London, 1683), 71, 70.

69. Robert Filmer, *Patriarcha: or The Natural Power of Kings* (London, 1680), 99–100. See too [Robert Filmer], *The Necessity of the Absolute Power of All Kings: and in Particular, of the King of England* (London, 1648), 6–7; R[obert] Filmer, *Observations concerning the Original and Various Forms of Government* (London, 1696), 299–300; [John Humfrey], *A Peaceable Resolution of Conscience Touching Our Present Impositions* (London, 1680), 41–42; Philip Warwick, *Memoires of the Reign of King Charles I* (London, 1701), 75, echoed in Richard Bulstrode, *Memoirs and Reflections upon the Reign and Government of King Charles the 1st* (London, 1721), 66; A Person of Honour [Philip Warwick], *Rules of Government* (London, 1710), 38.

It hath a jurisdiction over every thing *else*, but it cannot have it above *it self*."[70] Matthew Tindal, 1694: "every Supreme Power is at liberty to act in his own Dominions as he has a mind to" and "there cannot be *Imperium in Imperio*, or more than one Sovereign in the same Society."[71] That last is worth pausing over. Anxious denunciations of *imperium in imperio* go back to at least the seventeenth century and figure centrally in debates about church and state.[72] Even some ostensible critics of sovereignty are struggling only over where sovereignty is lodged. So, for instance, in 1689 Samuel Masters bitterly as-

70. [George Savile, Marquess of Halifax], *The Anatomy of an Equivalent* (n.p., [1688]), 10–11.

71. Mat[thew] Tindal, *An Essay concerning the Law of Nations, and the Rights of Soveraigns* (London, 1694), 10, 11.

72. For instance, [Dudley Diggs], *The Vnlawfvlnesse of Subjects Taking Up Armes against Their Soveraigne, in What Case Soever* (n.p., 1643), 67–69; *England's Universal Distraction in the Years 1643, 1644, 1645* (n.p., 1659), 3–4; Gloria Italiano Anzilotti, *An English Prince: Newcastle's Machiavellian Political Guide to Charles II* (Pisa: Giardini, [1988]), 98–99; [Anthony Ashley Cooper, Earl of Shaftesbury], *A Letter from a Person of Quality, to His Friend in the Country* (n.p., 1675), 24; Miles Barne, *A Sermon Preached before the King at White-Hall, October 17 1675* (London, 1675), 33–34; [Samuel Thomas?], *The Presbyterians Unmask'd: or, Animadversions upon a Nonconformist Book, Call'd The Interest of England in the Matter of Religion* (London, 1676); *Debates of the House of Commons* (Sir Thomas Meres, 4 November 1678); Tho[mas] Hunt, *An Argument for the Bishops Right in Judging Capital Causes in Parliament* (London, 1682), 216–17; Timothy Tickle, Esq., "A Whip for the American Whig," *New-York Gazette; and the Weekly Mercury* (14 November 1768); *Parliamentary Register* (Sir Roger Newdigate, 10 March 1779); *Parliamentary Register* (John Wilkes, 8 December 1783); *Parliamentary Register* (Earl of Radnor, 17 December 1783). The flurry of discussion around 1675 arises from Parliament's considering imposing an oath on members of Parliament and other officers of church and state that they would not "endeavour to alter the Protestant Religion or the Government either of Church or State." For concerns about the oath and *imperium in imperio,* see *History and Proceedings of the House of Lords* (13 April 1675).

sailed a "false principle to be dismissed . . . which asserts the *English Monarchy* to be *absolute* and *unlimited*, at least that in its *Original* and *Essential* Constitution it is so, and cannot be otherwise." But, he added easily, "any impartial unprejudiced person will certainly conclude, that our *English* Government, according to its *Essential Constitution,* is a mixture of Three Forms of Government; for he observes a *Monarchy* in the *King,* an *Aristocracy* in the *Peers,* and a *Democracy* in the *Commons;* all which share in *that Part* of the Sovereignty which consists in making Laws."[73]

Not every one of these writers embraces every criterion of the classic concept. Grotius, for instance, maintains that sovereignty can be divided, though in the way he puts it you can see the strain between the classic concept and his awareness of historical variation: "Though the sovereign Power be but one, and of itself undivided . . . yet it sometimes happens, that it is divided."[74] Nothing to stop Grotius, or anyone else, from articulating an account of sovereignty as unlimited and unaccountable, but divisible. So too Burlamaqui holds that the people can grant the sovereign absolute authority or hedge him in: "These regulations, by which the supreme authority is kept within bounds, are called, *The fundamental laws of the state.*"[75] Nothing to stop Burlamaqui, or anyone else, from articulating

73. Samuel Masters, *The Case of Allegiance in Our Present Circumstances Consider'd* (London, 1689), 7, 10.

74. Grotius, *War and Peace,* 1:305–306. Compare Pufendorf's remark on the sovereign's authority over the church in Samuel Puffendorff, *Of the Nature and Qualification of Religion, in Reference to Civil Society* (London, 1698), 167.

75. Burlamaqui, *Principles,* 2:55. Compare, for instance, [Thomas Rymer], *A General Draught and Prospect of Government in Europe, and Civil Policy* (London, 1681), 48: "One of the Rights of Soveraignty is to be above the Law, and to give Laws to the people.

an account of sovereignty as indivisible, but limited and even accountable.[76] But if you renounce *all* the criteria of the classic concept and put nothing in their place, it becomes entirely mysterious what you could be talking about.

The classic concept, however glorious or inglorious, appears over and over again in actual historical settings, in political and legal struggles, not just in learned tomes. My claim is not that Bodin, with or without an assist from Hobbes and the rest, launched a concept with a decisively important historical trajectory. I've no confidence in what the world would look like had Jean and Thomas each died of the flu at age eight, any more than I do in what today's boundaries of Poland would be had Napoleon and Marx died as children. What matters here are political actors' appeals to the classic theory, not who originated it or even whether it has an originator. That theory motivated some of the feints toward absolutism of the Stuart monarchs—and shaped how they were received. Ponder why in 1610 James I would instruct Parliament, "The State of MONARCHIE is the supremest thing upon earth: For Kings are not only GOD's Lieutenants upon earth, and sit upon GOD's throne, but even by GOD himself they are called Gods."[77] Ask what has to be true for a king to imagine this is a choicewor-

---

"Neither of these Royalties belong to the Emperour; he may be call'd to account for violating the Laws." The point is perhaps tied to Rymer's suggestion that the Germans "never trusted the Soveraignty out of their own hands" (46), which raises complications I set aside for now.

76. See too, for instance, William Tooker, *Of the Fabriqve of the Church and Church-mens Living* (London, 1604), 99–100.

77. "A Speech to the Lords and Commons of the Parliament at *White-Hall*," 21 March 1609/10, *The VVorkes of the Most High and Mightie Prince, Iames* (London, 1616), 529; and see James's speech, *Journal of the House of Lords* (9 November 1605).

thy, even intelligible, thing to say. Before Hobbes had gotten around to publishing his more narrowly political books, Charles had demanded the prosecution of John Lord of Balmerino for seditious libel: "by the Law of God and Laws of all Nations, the Person of the supreme and sovereign Prince is and ought to be sacred and inviolable, and he ought to be reverenced, honoured, and feared, as God's Lieutenant on Earth: and that all Subjects are bound and tied in Conscience to content themselves in humble Submission to obey and reverence the Person, Laws, and Authority of their supreme Sovereign."[78] (If your instinct is to figure out how Bodin's text made its way to Charles's hands or, less implausibly, those of his tutors or advisers, notice that there might be no such transmission. Sometimes there is: Hobbes presented the future hapless Charles II, perched in Paris during the interregnum, with a prepublication copy of *Leviathan*, beautifully bound with vellum pages. There's direct transmission for you! but it made Hobbes unwelcome at court, perhaps because someone figured out that

78. Francis Hargrave, *A Complete Collection of State-Trials*, 4th ed., 11 vols. (London, 1776–81), 1:430. On the king (and not the pope) as Christ's vicegerent, see, for instance, H. Johnsen, *Anti-Merlinus: or A Confvtation of Mr. William Lillies Predictions for This Year 1648* (n.p., 1648), 41; William Towers, *A Thanksgiving Sermon: For the Blessed Restauration of His Sacred Majesty Charles the II* (London, 1660), 7; [Johann Amos Comenius], *A Generall Table of Europe* ([London], 1670), 236. James I also referred to "God and Christ, in whose Throne we sit" (*His Maiesties Speech in the Starre-Chamber, The XX of Ivne Anno 1616* (London, [1616]), n.p.; also in *VVorkes of the Most High*, 550), and see his close echo in *Journal of the House of Lords* (19 February 1624). On such language, see especially Walter Rale[i]gh to Prince Henry, 12 August 1611, in *The Works of Sir Walter Ralegh*, 8 vols. (Oxford, 1829), 8:665–66; and *The Tryal of Sir Henry Vane, Kt. at the Kings Bench, Westminster, June the 2d and 6th, 1662* (n.p., 1662), 123–24, allegedly Vane's reflections from his prison cell.

the theory seemed to yield the decidedly unwelcome judgment that Cromwell was the sovereign.)[79] By 1830, the U.S. Department of State library included editions of Pufendorf, Vattel, Burlamaqui, and Grotius.[80] When an impoverished Jefferson sold his library, the U.S. Library of Congress came into possession of all of those—of Hobbes too.[81] It's an open question who read them, there and elsewhere, and to what uses and abuses they were put. But there was no firewall between these theories of sovereignty and the conceptual repertoires of legal and political actors.

You can think of sovereignty as an abstract rendition or idealization of divine authority—so arises the sadly overheated tradition of political theology[82]—or of monarchy. There are countless references to God as lord in the King James Bible. Hobbes must have known full well that he was engaged in mystification, even blasphemy. He didn't only call the sovereign Leviathan, after the biblical sea monster; he didn't only add, "or, rather, to speak more reverently . . . that *Mortal God* to which we owe . . . our peace and defence"; he also explicitly invoked the Ten Commandments to structure that reverence. For instance, subjects need to be taught "how great a fault it is, to speak evil of the Sovereign . . . or to argue and dispute his Power; or any way to use his Name irreverently. . . .

79. Arnold A. Rogow, *Thomas Hobbes: Radical in the Service of Reaction* (New York: Norton, 1986), 154.

80. *Catalogue of the Library of the Department of State of the United States: May, 1830* (n.p., n.d.), chap. 17.

81. *Catalogue of the Library of the United States* (Washington, DC, 1815).

82. On which Victoria Kahn, *The Future of an Illusion: Political Theology and Early Modern Texts* (Chicago: University of Chicago Press, 2014), is devastating. For a recent emphatic endorsement of political theology, see Wendy Brown, *Walled States, Waning Sovereignty* (New York: Zone Books, 2010), 58–61.

Which doctrine the third Commandment by resemblance pointeth to."[83]

Or, more abstract yet, you can take these images or metaphors of sovereignty as testimony to the strangely seductive power of a pyramidal picture of authority, of thinking of society (or all of existence!) as one unified hierarchy.[84] That picture doesn't even get feudal Europe right, but I leave that aside.[85] The abstraction enables people to leave open the question of just who or what—the king, the legislature, both, and so on—is the sovereign, while still insisting that whatever that entity is, it must enjoy authority endowed with the traits I've identified. And that authority must be colossal, awe-inspiring. Consider Sieyès's nicely jaundiced comment about sovereignty: "This word only looms so large in our imagination because the spirit of the French, full of royal superstitions, felt under an obligation to endow it with all the heritage of pomp and absolute power which made the usurped sovereignties shine. . . . [P]eople seem to say, with a kind of patriotic pride, that if the sovereignty of great kings is so powerful and so terrible, the sovereignty of a great people ought to surpass it."[86]

83. *Leviathan*, 87, 178.

84. Consider "Philosophy and Democracy," in John Dewey, *The Middle Works, 1899–1924*, ed. Jo Ann Boydston, 15 vols. (Carbondale: Southern Illinois University Press, 1969–83), 11:51–52.

85. Marc Bloch, *Feudal Society*, trans. L. A. Manyon (Chicago: University of Chicago Press, 1961), remains the classic demonstration of how crisscrossing oaths of fealty made a mockery of unified hierarchy. See too Georges Duby, *The Three Orders: Feudal Society Imagined*, trans. Arthur Goldhammer (Chicago: University of Chicago Press, 1980), for a wickedly amusing account of the shifting social referents that kept getting crammed into the same reassuring conceptual scheme.

86. The Opinion of 2 Thermidor, translated and quoted in Richard Tuck, *The Sleeping Sovereign: The Invention of Modern Democracy* (Cambridge: Cambridge University Press, 2016), 176–77.

It's natural to read the classic theory of sovereignty as applying to monarchs. But I'll take the theory as leaving open, as we've seen that Hobbes explicitly does, just who holds sovereignty: the king, king-in-parliament, or whatever else. I will, though, set aside popular sovereignty for now, because I think it's the answer to an altogether different question. Nor is it true that liberal democracies have converged on embracing popular sovereignty. In 2018, that distinguished British news magazine the *Economist* was relieved to report that it's "crystal clear" that sovereignty "does not lie, thank God, with that dangerous abstraction, 'the people.' It lies with Parliament, and ultimately with the House of Commons."[87] Sovereignty, as I'm treating it here, is supposed to be a feature of part or all of the government.

It takes a good deal of cultural work to puff up sovereign authority, to produce elevated dignity and suitable awe. At her 1558 coronation, Elizabeth was addressed as "O peerless sovereign queen,"[88] but the work of actually enshrining and keeping her in that exalted status sprawled through the years. Her astonishing processions through the realm didn't trigger spontaneous explosions of popular affection. They were meticulously planned. It's sobering to read the coldly bureaucratic requisitions behind the pageantries: "the bailiffs and aldermen in the receipt of her Majesty, shall ride upon comely geldings, with foot-clothes, in damask or satin cassocks or coats, or else jackets of the same, with satin sleeves in their scarlet gowns, with caps and black velvet tippets"; "her Majesty shall be gratified from the town with a cup of silver double gilt, of the value of

87. "Parliament's Silent Majority Could Thwart a Hard Brexit," *Economist* (1 March 2018).

88. John Nichols, *The Progresses and Public Processions of Queen Elizabeth I: A New Edition of the Early Modern Sources*, ed. Elizabeth Goldring et al., 5 vols. (Oxford: Oxford University Press, 2014), 1:118.

20 marks, or 10*l.* at the least, with 40 angels in the same."[89] The expenses are formidable enough even before you start thinking about providing feasts and lodgings for the queen and her retinue. And the processions were painstakingly recorded and spectacularly, impossibly luxurious. It's tempting to bask in sybaritic counterpoint to the atrocities of war I grimly slogged through before, and I bet some contemporaries succumbed to the temptation, but here's just one more glimpse: "two hundred young gentlemen, clad all in white velvet, and three hundred . . . appareled in black velvet coats . . . with fifteen hundred serving men more on Horseback" assembled to greet the queen in Suffolk.[90]

The procession rituals were often explicit about sovereignty. "Most gracious Sovereign," uttered a man playing a hermit at Theobalds Estate, "I humbly beseech you not to impute this my approaching so near to your sacred presence, so rudely at your Coming to this house, to be a Presumption of a beggar." The recorder of Warwick Castle turned to Latin to salute Elizabeth as his "chaste, holy, and most god-like sovereign." Even odder stagings emphasized sovereignty. At Kenilworth, an implausibly articulate "*Hombre Salvagio,*" savage man, talked to an echo, learned that the sovereign was a queen, and celebrated her "beautiful lineaments of countenance, the comely proportion of body, the princely grace of presence, the gracious gifts of nature with the rare and singular qualities of both body and mind in her Majesty conjoined."[91] Doubtless

89. John Nichols, *The Progresses, and Public Processions, of Queen Elizabeth*, 2 vols. (London, 1788), 2:111–12.

90. Nichols, *Progresses*, ed. Goldring, 2:719.

91. Nichols, *Progresses*, ed. Goldring, 2:31 (n. 203 for the translation); 3:735, 2:250. See more generally Sydney Anglo, *Spectacle, Pageantry, and Early Tudor Policy* (Oxford: Clarendon, 1969).

some extra work went into these rituals because Elizabeth was a woman. Maybe that's why another Elizabeth, an eight-year-old Habsburg archduchess, entered Prague in 1562 to be greeted by trumpets, kettle drums, bagpipes, fifes, fireworks, camels, four hundred splendidly attired Hungarian hussars, and posters in five languages.[92] I suppose the hope was that sovereignty could be enacted powerfully enough to overcome even misogyny. That hope was not, I think, misplaced, though there's room to argue that ardent English affection for Good Queen Bess was itself a kind of misogyny.

As Sweden's ambassador to France, Grotius himself was suitably touchy about Swedish dignity: so such trivial questions as whether England's coach should precede Sweden's and whether Grotius should be addressed as "Excellency" loomed up as formidable questions of state.[93] Or take the acidulous ripostes of readily miffed emissaries. In 1646, Anthony Fortescue, serving as the Duke of Lorraine's agent, seethed with indignation: "the Privileges belonging to my Place was strangely violated, with Two great Affronts offered, in me and my Family, to the Sovereign Dignity of his Highness my Master, by the forcible breaking open my House, and taking away my Goods with Violence."[94] In 1819, the Duke of San Fernando de Quiroga lobbed this bit of icily polite fury at John Forsyth, U.S. minister to Spain:

> I should have failed in the very high consideration I owe, to the American Government, in the due re-

92. Joseph F. Patrouch, *Queen's Apprentice: Archduchess Elizabeth, Empress María, the Habsburgs, and the Holy Roman Empire, 1554–1569* (Leiden: Brill, 2010), 151–56.

93. Henk Nellen, *Hugo Grotius: A Lifelong Struggle for Peace in Church and State, 1583–1645*, trans. J. C. Grayson (Leiden: Brill, 2014), 563–70.

94. *Journals of the House of Lords* (27 August 1646).

> spect I entertain for you, and especially in my duty as the principal secretary of His Majesty the King, my lord, by communicating to him the contents of a note which attacks the honor of His Majesty, without tending in the least to elucidate the subject in question. . . . It is, therefore, with the greatest concern that it becomes my indispensable duty to return to you such a note, with the assurance that I will, with as great pleasure, promptitude, and eagerness, submit to His Majesty such communications as you may address to me which are conceived in fit and becoming terms, as I am wholly averse to laying before him those which cannot fail to prove offensive to his exalted character and sovereign dignity.[95]

Before and after Vattel, the language and sensibilities are much the same: so Vattel is articulating and defending ongoing social practice, not designing or inventing it.

The classic theory of sovereignty resonated in popular culture, too, thanks to texts specifically designed to circulate it. Here's a sermon grimly underlining the indispensability of sovereignty: "take Sovereignty from the face of the earth, and you turn it into a Cockpit. Men would become cut-throats and Cannibals one unto another. Murder, adulteries, incests, rapes, robberies, perjuries, witchcrafts, blasphemies, all kinds of villainies, outrageous and savage cruelty, would overflow all Countries. We should have a very hell upon earth, and

95. *Congressional Record* (12 November 1819). For the text of Forsyth that so incensed the duke, see *American State Papers*, 4:668–71 (18 October 1819). (The duke's note is also in *Papers*, 4:671–72.) The context is ratifying the Adams-Onis Treaty, in which (among other issues) Spain ceded title to Florida in exchange for settling a boundary dispute in Texas.

the face of it covered with blood, as it was once with water."[96] More histrionic, hysterical, yet, but also more and more historically apt as the wars of religion drenched Europe in blood is a famous exhortation dating back to 1547, to be read out ceremoniously in church: "Take away kings, princes, rulers, magistrates, judges, and such states of God's order, no man shall ride or go by the highway unrobbed, no man shall sleep in his own house or bed unkilled, no man shall keep his wife, children, & possessions in quietness: all things shall be common, and there must needs follow all mischief and utter destruction, both of souls, bodies, goods and commonwealths." The explicit invocation of sovereignty followed immediately: "But blessed be God, that we in this realm of England feel not the horrible calamities, miseries & wretchedness, which all they undoubtedly feel & suffer, that lack this godly order. . . . God hath sent us his high gift, our most dear sovereign lord king Edward the sixth."[97] The exhortation was still trundling along over three centuries later: just swap in Victoria for Edward VI.[98] I'll offer more such glimpses later, some sustained gazes too: but I want immediately to disabuse you of the fear—

96. Robert Bolton, *Two Sermons Preached at Northampton at Two Several Assizes There* (London, 1635), 10. This sermon was delivered in 1621 (see the title page for dates of the sermons).

97. "An Exhortacion, concernyng Good Ordre and Obedience, to Rulers and Magistrates," in *Certayne Sermons, or Homelies, Appoynted by the Kynges Maiestie, to Be Declared and Redde, by All Persones, Vicars, or Curates, Every Sondaye in Their Churches* (n.p., 1547), n.p. See too *Here Begynneth a Lytell Treatyse in Englysshe, Called the Extripacion of Ignorancy* (n.p., 1536), n.p.: "Where is no soueraine / there reigneth incóuenyêce / As fraude / gyle / & extorció / with many other offêce."

98. "An Exhortation concerning Good Order, and Obedience to Rulers and Magistrates," in *Certain Sermons, or Homilies, Appointed to Be Read in Churches, in the Time of the Late Queen Elizabeth of Famous Memory* (London, 1852), 100–101.

or proud conviction—that sovereignty was the concern of rarefied theorists, that it had no uptake in daily life. (I'd like too to get you over the prejudice, or considered conviction, that it's important to draw a bright line between distinguished works of theory and the puttering and nattering on of lesser figures, but time will tell.)

So again, here's my target: the view that social and political order requires sovereign authority, and in turn unpacking the concept of sovereignty as meaning unlimited, undivided, and unaccountable authority, with exalted dignity and law as sovereign command trailing along in the wake of these constitutive commitments. Blackstone captured much of the view in crystalline purity: "How the several forms of government we now see in the world at first actually began, is matter of great uncertainty, and has occasioned infinite disputes. It is not my business or intention to enter into any of them. However they began, or by what right soever they subsist, there is and must be in all of them a supreme, irresistible, absolute, uncontrolled authority, in which the *jura summi imperii*, or the rights of sovereignty, reside."[99] Right, nothing there about divisibility. Blackstone's suggestion that the British constitution lodges sovereignty in the king and both houses of Parliament might well have struck baleful observers as decidedly unhelpful because it papers over what to do when king and Parliament are at loggerheads. But we can also see it as an effort to shore up the claim that sovereign authority is indivisible. And I want to emphasize the importance of Blackstone's "must be," Pufendorf's "necessary . . . connection," Burlamaqui's "absolutely necessary," and the like. These writers aren't offering

99. William Blackstone, *Commentaries on the Laws of England*, 4 vols. (Oxford, 1765–69), 1:48–49.

sovereignty as a model for some political regimes and leaving it open whether there are other perfectly sensible kinds of regimes. The central thrust and insistent refrain of their work is that social order must hang on sovereignty. It's that or the doom of religious civil war, of rampant disorder more generally: take your pick.

I've been a trifle diffident about the thesis that sovereignty once did deserve praise and I'll briefly say why, even though that raises issues peripheral to my agenda here. The early modern wars of religion subside—no, that's not the same as the outrageous claim that modernity is secular—but it's got to be an open question whether we owe that relief to sovereignty or to other factors, not least battle fatigue, or what the right mix is. But that's not why my applause is halfhearted. Consider some of the political problems caused by religion in England.

The medieval tradition conceiving of church and state as two swords[100] is enormously complicated. But I want to notice a stylized inversion. In 1302, Pope Boniface VIII declared that "both [swords] are in the power of the Church. . . . [O]ne sword ought to be subordinated to the other and temporal authority, subjected to spiritual power."[101] Three centuries later, an English lawyer who practiced in a church court chanted the familiar refrain. "The rights of Sovereignty or of majesty . . . are nothing else, but an absolute and perpetual power, to exercise the highest actions and affairs"; "nothing is of so high a nature in a State, as is religion: . . . therefore the

100. Luke 22:38. For a helpful introduction to these matters, see Brian Tierney, *The Crisis of Church and State, 1050–1300* (Englewood Cliffs, NJ: Prentice-Hall, 1964).

101. Unam Sanctam, at http://www.papalencyclicals.net/bon08/b8unam.htm (last visited 13 March 2018).

ordering thereof is annexed . . . to the sovereign power."[102] If the sovereign has the right to dictate his own country's religion—*cuius regio, eius religio*; or, as even a staunch critic of Hobbes put it, "there is as full and unabated Supremacy in Sovereign Powers over all manner of Ecclesiastical Authority, as if it had been entirely derived from their own special Grant"[103]—you can expect dizzying somersaults. Henry VIII turned the country Protestant. Spain's ambassador to England reported that "three Carthusians and a Bridgetine monk, all men of good character and learning," were put to death for insisting that the pope was "the true Head of the universal Church" and that Henry had invaded his sovereignty.[104] Henry's daughter Mary, a Catholic, ascended the throne in 1553 and flipped the country back to Catholic. She's infamously dubbed Bloody Mary because she burned at least 274 at the stake for refusing to convert. Many were children, not yet blessed with the world-weary cynicism that made so many adults take the somersault in stride.[105] Elizabeth ascended the throne and flipped the country back to Protestantism with the able assistance of

102. [Sir John Hayward], *A Reporte of a Discovrse concerning Supreme Power in Affaires of Religion, Manifesting That This Power Is a Right of Regalitie, Inseparably Annexed to the Soueraigntie of Euery State* (London, 1606), 6, 43 (the first bit is in Hayward's own voice, the second the pro-sovereignty speaker in his dialogue); *DNB*, s.v. "Hayward, Sir John."

103. Samuel Parker, *Religion and Loyalty: or, A Demonstration of the Power of the Christian Church within It Self; the Supremacy of Sovereign Power over It* (London, 1684), 8. For worries about toleration and disorder, [Samuel Parker], *A Discourse of Ecclesiastical Politie*, 3rd ed. (London, 1671), 160–61.

104. Chapuys to Charles V, 5 May 1535, *Letters and Papers . . . of . . . Henry VIII*, 8:250.

105. G. R. Elton, *Reform and Reformation: England, 1509–1558* (Cambridge: Cambridge University Press, 1977), 386; Susan Brigden, "Youth and the English Reformation," *Past & Present* (May 1982), 65–66.

pursuivants, "priest hunters," who tracked down priests who hid in "priest holes," culverts, wherever they could.[106] John Gerard hid in "a very cleverly built sort of cave," under a fireplace grate, "in a secret gable of the roof."[107] In Elizabeth's campaign against the Catholic danger, the government executed 161 priests.[108] Gerard, tortured in the Tower of London, decried a "deluge of persecution."[109] Sovereignty might provide an apt explanation of what's wrong with Catholic Spain sending the Armada against Protestant England, or for that matter with Pope Pius V's 1570 bull branding Queen Elizabeth a heretic and instructing English subjects and nobles alike not to obey her on pain of excommunication.[110] Both meddle in what intuitively seem like the internal affairs of other countries, and again the theory of sovereignty gives those national boundaries new significance.[111]

It's a fluke that Mary intruded on the scene after Henry's break with Rome, a fluke that Elizabeth followed in turn, or, if you like, a fluke that those in the line of royal succession

106. Jessie Childs, *God's Traitors: Terror and Faith in Elizabethan England* (London: Bodley Head, 2014), 177–96.

107. John Gerard, *The Autobiography of an Elizabethan*, trans. Philip Caraman (London: Longmans, Green, 1951), 41–42, 58–63, 151–55.

108. Diarmaid MacCulloch, *The Reformation* (New York: Viking, 2004), 392.

109. Gerard, *Autobiography*, 108–14; *The Condition of Catholics under James I: Father Gerard's Narrative of the Gunpowder Plot*, ed. John Morris (London, 1871), 20.

110. Regnans in Excelsis, at http://www.papalencyclicals.net/Pius05/p5regnans.htm (last visited 8 March 2018).

111. For a vigorous denunciation of such papal actions, see Martin Luther, *A Commentarie or Exposition uppon the Two Epistles Generall of Sainct Peter, and That of Sainct Jude*, trans. Thomas Newton (London, 1581), 144–45; and compare *A Remonstrance of the Most Gratious King James I* (Cambridge, 1616), 206–7.

would have different faiths and would take religion so seriously. (Contrast Henry IV of France, a Huguenot who famously converted to Catholicism—"Paris is worth a mass," or so he apocryphally said—in an attempt to unify the country.) But sovereign authority over religion, coupled with a pregnant thought I'm not pursuing here, that social order requires religious unity, immediately turns dissident subjects into incipient traitors. In the infamous Gunpowder Plot of 1605, Catholic conspirators planned to blow up the House of Lords while King James I was there for the state opening, and in turn to install his nine-year-old daughter Elizabeth as the new Catholic monarch of England. They got close enough that Guy Fawkes was discovered guarding thirty-six barrels of gunpowder in the building.[112] State repression redoubled resistance; resistance redoubled state repression. No wonder James brushed aside France's concern for his Catholic subjects: "If the French King in the heart of his Kingdom, should nourish and foster such a nest of stinging hornets and busy wasps, I mean such a pack of subjects, denying his absolute Sovereignty, as many Roman Catholics of my Kingdom do mine," if France's subjects were ready to "blow up [their] King with gun-powder," one might doubt that he'd urge treating them with gentle tolerance.[113]

You could then bemoan unruly subjects clinging to the wrong religion. "For a mean sequel of permitting the use of two contrary religions," warned one writer in 1587, "take the *Massacres* of *France*, look into them, weigh them," and realize that religious pluralism could bring such violence to

112. Antonia Fraser, *The Gunpowder Plot: Terror & Faith in 1605* (London: Weidenfield and Nicolson, 1996) tells the story with characteristic verve. Consider William Warmington, *A Moderate Defence of the Oath of Allegiance* (n.p., 1612), 4–5.

113. *Remonstrance of the Most Gratious King*, 247–48.

England.[114] Or you could bemoan, as one observer did a century later, "*an attempt by Gunpowder*, and *fire* from *Hell* to blow up and destroy their Sovereign."[115] You could insist, as Hobbes did, that "Factions for Government of Religion, as of Papists, Protestants, *&c*. . . . are unjust, as . . . a taking of the Sword out of the hand of the Soveraign."[116] You could, that is, take the resistance as justifying redoubled repression. Or you could learn to see an incurably perverse dynamic—and that's why my applause for sovereignty is halfhearted. Sovereignty and *cuius regio* might have solved the problem of religious war if all European countries were religiously homogeneous, or close enough. But they weren't.

Sovereignty—or at least the exercise of sovereignty to try to ensure religious uniformity—then creates the enemy within.[117] The Revolt of the Northern Earls of 1569, led by Catholic nobles hoping to topple Elizabeth from the throne and replace her with Mary, Queen of Scots (Bloody Mary's cousin), was pretty much homegrown and pretty much abortive, though Elizabeth's response was savagely repressive. The Ridolfi Plot of 1571, an attempt to assassinate Elizabeth and replace her with Mary, Queen of Scots, was partly international, but it too drew in English subjects.[118] Even English Catholics

114. Edward Hake, *An Oration Conteyning an Expostulation* (London, 1587), sig. D verso.

115. [Robert Jenkin], *The Title of an Usurper After a Thorough Settlement Examined* (London, 1690), preface, n.p.

116. *Leviathan*, 122.

117. Consider [Pierre Jurieu], *The Policy of the Clergy of France, to Destroy the Protestants of That Kingdom* (London, 1681), 199–201. For a report that in French politics, Bodin sought "unity in Religion without the noise of Arms, and the necessity of War," see [William Greaves], *Status Ecclesiae Gallicanae* (London, 1676), [pt. 2], 36.

118. Alison Weir, *Mary Queen of Scots and the Murder of Lord Darnley* (London: Jonathan Cape, 2004), 550–57.

hoping to scrape by surreptitiously, happy to count themselves loyal to Elizabeth regardless of that papal bull, found themselves caught in lethal predicaments they couldn't control. (And here you have to learn to see political contingency, not providential intervention steering God's beloved Protestants to safety.)[119] Likewise, French Huguenots continued to have a hard time after the Edict of Nantes was revoked. So in 1762 Jean Calas, a Huguenot merchant in Toulouse, was broken on the wheel and executed after his son, Marc-Antoine, was found dead. The authorities trumped up the story that Marc-Antoine had intended to convert to Catholicism, and that Jean, allegedly following Luther's teachings, had killed him in the misbegotten desire to save his soul. (The family first claimed they'd found Marc-Antoine murdered. Then they admitted he'd committed suicide, a shameful act that would consign his corpse to being tossed on the city's trash heap.) Dutifully adhering to contemporary legal procedure, the government offered to pay witnesses who'd testify that they'd heard the family threatening Marc-Antoine. Witnesses were found.[120]

The winning solution is religious toleration, or, to invoke an unhappily vague abstraction, the separation of church and state. It requires the paradoxical thought that precisely because religion has been the source of endless bloodshed and political strife, we have to treat religion as if it were private and of no political significance. We carve up authority

119. Contrast, for instance, Iohn Boys, *An Exposition of the Proper Psalmes Vsed in Ovr English Liturgie* (London, 1616), 156; G.C., *Popish Plots and Treasons* (n.p., [1676–97?]).

120. David D. Bien, *The Calas Affair: Persecution, Toleration and Heresy in Eighteenth-Century Toulouse* (Princeton: Princeton University Press, 1960). For Voltaire's scathing indictment, see his *Traité sur la tolerance*, chaps. 1–2, 25; his *Histoire d'Elizabeth Canning, et de Jean Calas* (London, 1762); and, en anglais, his *Original Pieces Relative to the Trial and Execution of Mr. John Calas* (Dublin, 1762).

and jurisdiction between church(es, and synagogues, and mosques, and . . .) and state. In Locke's famous words from 1689, "the Church itself is a thing absolutely separate and distinct from the Commonwealth. The Boundaries on both sides are fixed and immovable. He jumbles Heaven and Earth together, the things most remote and opposite, who mixes these two Societies; which are in their Original, End, Business, and in everything, perfectly distinct, and infinitely different from each other."[121] In a world of religious war, where the established church's bishops sat in the House of Lords, where Convocation brought together churchmen and statesmen to decide on political messages to be read out in sermons across the land, where poor relief was administered by parishes, this is blatantly counterfactual. It's a sweeping reform proposal, not an innocent description.[122] The basic idea was already in circulation. In 1675, William Jane sniffed at *imperium in imperio* as a "great bugbear" that "need not be so terrible as men would make it, as long as their Objects, Ends, and Offices, stand as really distinguished as their Obligations."[123] This stance also entails that it's confused to see state and church as rivals, or to think one must finally be supreme over the other. One thing to demarcate the authority and jurisdiction of the government and other institutions; another to demarcate government authority and jurisdiction internally, the very thing the classic theorists of sovereignty are appalled by. But now I'm jumping ahead of myself.

121. [John Locke], *A Letter concerning Toleration* (London, 1689), 18.

122. See my *Happy Slaves: A Critique of Consent Theory* (Chicago: University of Chicago Press, 1989), 162–71.

123. William Jane, *A Sermon Preached at the Consecration of the Honourable Dr. Henry Compton, Lord Bishop of Oxford, in Lambeth-Chappel, on Sunday, December 6 1675* (London, 1675), 31.

So my praise for sovereignty is diffident because even in its heyday, sovereignty couldn't resolve the problems of religious violence. Still, it's real praise. The idea of sovereignty wasn't dumb or pernicious on its face—not in early modern Europe. It was a weapon of state-building, and a world soaked in blood, awash in cruelty, could well long for an all-powerful central authority to staunch the wounds of rebellion and stand up to international intrigue and war. "Men have no pleasure," Hobbes warned sternly, "(but on the contrary a great deal of grief) in keeping company, where there is no power able to over-awe them all."[124]

Dueling

I want to broaden the context and the time frame a bit: even though I think pride of place—perhaps I should say shame of place—is rightly assigned to the wars of religion in grasping and appraising sovereignty, I've no interest in claiming it was the only problem early modern Europeans faced. If you're up against bellicose nobles of the sword, thugs (or fur-collar criminals, to extend a memorable coinage of Barbara Hanawalt)[125] bent on winning honor and glory by fighting with armies of private retainers or killing each other over indignities and slights, let alone stubbornly invested in their own familial politics and so sometimes caught up in international intrigue, you might well find that longing for an all-powerful central authority even more poignant. No wonder Cardinal Richelieu congratulated Louis XIII on his purging foreign influences

124. *Leviathan*, 61.

125. Barbara Hanawalt, "Fur-Collar Crime: The Pattern of Crime among the Fourteenth-Century English Nobility," *Journal of Social History* (Summer 1975).

at court ("you caused the Marshall *de Marillac*'s Head to be cut off, with so much the more reason, that being condemned with Justice, the present Constitution of the State required a great example") and on his efforts to stamp out dueling (by, for instance, executing de Bouteville and des Chapelles: "The Tears of their Wives moved me sensibly; but the Sluices of Blood of your Nobility, to which nothing could put a stop but the Effusion of theirs, encouraged me to resist my own Inclinations, and to persuade your Majesty to cause that to be put in Execution, for the good of the Kingdom")—and exhorted him to redouble his campaign.[126] No wonder Louis issued a proclamation against dueling.[127] Bouteville fought eighteen duels in thirteen years. He especially liked dueling on Sundays and holy days. As late as 1615, French nobles were mustering cannon and thousands of troops. Even when the French nobles of the sword were domesticated into nobles of the robe, easily derided as effeminate lazybones sipping on brandy and decadence, they continued to fight. Sometimes French aristocrats fought about religion. Indeed, sometimes they fought

126. *The Compleat Statesman: or, The Political Will and Testament of That Great Minister of State, Cardinal Duke de Richilieu*, trans. from the French (London, 1695), 24, 8, 114–18. On this latter famous punishment, see Richard Herr, "Honor versus Absolutism: Richelieu's Fight against Dueling," *Journal of Modern History* (September 1955), especially 284: "it is a question of cutting the throat of duels or of your majesty's edicts," said Richelieu. On the transformation of French dueling in the late sixteenth and early seventeenth centuries, see Ellery Schalk, *From Valor to Pedigree: Ideas of Nobility in France in the Sixteenth and Seventeenth Centuries* (Princeton, NJ: Princeton University Press, 1986), 160–73; or, more generally, François Billacois, *The Duel: Its Rise and Fall in Early Modern France*, ed. and trans. Trista Selous (New Haven, CT: Yale University Press, 1990).

127. *Edict dv Roy svr la prohibition & punition des querelles & duels* (Paris, 1609). French sources were translated and brought together for English readers in *The Laws of Honor: or, An Account of the Suppression of Duels in France* (London, 1685).

in church: 1536 saw a crossbow and swords drawn in church during Pentecost, with deaths and a hand hacked off; 1551 saw four men praying in church who stupidly let their target see their pistols.[128]

Aristocratic squabbling, then, could lead to dueling and worse. It's already on its face a threat to social order, if dwarfed by the scale of the wars of religion. But—here's the crux—it takes on new salience once sovereignty is on the scene. Private violence becomes intolerable when the sovereign is supposed to have exclusive power to rule. "Force is the last Appeal of Sovereign Princes, who acknowledge no Superiour upon earth," insisted one analyst. "He who takes upon him to decide his private quarrels by private Force, puts himself in the place of an independent Sovereign."[129] "The engaging in a Duel is an unsufferable Affront to the King," wrote another.[130] "A *Duel* attacks directly the Sovereign Authority, and is therefore *High-Treason*," commented a Frenchman.[131] That touchy aristocrats would brandish swords or guns to revenge insults was nothing new. The intriguing thought here is that the duel in turn insults the sovereign. It undercuts his dignity.[132]

128. Stuart Carroll, *Blood and Violence in Early Modern France* (Oxford: Oxford University Press, 2006), 170, 140, 290–96, 77, 122.

129. Richard Hey, *A Dissertation on Duelling* (Cambridge, 1784), 40.

130. T[homas] C[omber], *A Discourse of Duels, Shewing the Sinful Nature and Mischievous Effects of Them* (London, 1687), 18.

131. [Antoine de Courtin], *The Rules of Civility; or, The Maxims of Genteel Behavior . . . Containing among Other Additions, A Short Treatise of the Point of Honour* (London, 1703), 272–73. See Antoine de Courtin, *Svite de la civilité françoise, ov Traité dv point-d'honnevr* (Paris, 1680), 285: "le duel attaque directement l'autorité souveraine, & qu'il est par cette raison un crime de leze-Majesté."

132. But for dueling as a way of protecting the sovereign, see *Vincentio Saviolo His Practise* (London, 1595), sig. Z verso—sig Z2 verso. Grotius, *War and Peace*, 2:415–16 touches briefly on the narrow circumstances in which dueling is permissible.

Francis Bacon—polymath, lawyer, aristocrat, attorney general, lord chancellor—played a role in England roughly equivalent to Richelieu's in France in the campaign against dueling. Dueling, he complained, "expressly gives the Law an affront," as though the king's law had to yield to the law of reputation, laid down, he grumbled, in "some French and Italian pamphlets." Dueling was a "depraved custom" and the government had to pursue "a constant and settled resolution . . . to abolish it." Once an offended man grasped that dueling was "an insult against the King's power and authority," he would "think himself acquitted in his reputation."[133] (It took many more decades for dueling to disappear, so this last thought was too optimistic.)

No wonder we find a steady stream of royal proclamations trying to squelch the practice. Consider a few. In 1613, James I renewed the familiar claim that dueling insulted his authority, "the revenging of all private wrongs only belonging to Us," and prohibited publishing accounts of duels, lest the accounts renew quarrels or make them "immortal."[134] Another

133. *The Charge of Sir Francis Bacon Knight, His Maiesties Attourney General, Touching Duells, vpon an Information in the Star-Chamber against Priest and Wright: with the Decree of the Star-Chamber in the Same Cause* ([London], 1614), 10, 14–15. The closing language was recycled in [Thomas Frankland], *The Annals of King James and King Charles the First* (London, 1681), 5; and in William Sanderson, *A Compleat History of the Lives and Reigns of Mary Queen of Scotland, and of Her Son and Successor, James the Sixth* (London, 1696), 395. For more on the background, see the characteristically quirky and learned [John Selden], *The Dvello or Single Combat* (London, 1610). Compare "In Camera Stellata XXVII° Novembris 1616," in *The Letters and the Life of Francis Bacon*, ed. James Spedding et al., 7 vols. (London, 1862–74), 6:108: "it is a direct affront of law and tends to the dissolution of magistracy."

134. *A Proclamation Prohibiting the Publishing of Any Reports or Writings of Duels*, 15 October 1613, in *Stuart Royal Proclamations*, ed. James F. Larkin and Paul L. Hughes, 2 vols. to date (Oxford: Clarendon, 1973–), 1:295–96.

proclamation followed several months later, this one banning challenges and duels themselves.[135] In 1654, the interregnum government announced that killing in a duel would be treated as murder.[136] Biding his time during the interregnum but also pretending to rule, Charles II drafted a "Declaration against Duels."[137] Just months after being restored to the throne, he issued yet another proclamation, denouncing dueling as "the manifest violation of Our Lawes and Authority" and requiring even third parties learning of impending duels to report them to the Privy Council.[138]

Duelists, even when they ended up killing, might seem not much more than an idle curiosity. So, for instance, one 1663 pamphleteer noticed "another sad Accident": a dead gentleman with his sword, still with plenty of gold in his pockets, so obviously not a victim of robbery. The gentleman who'd killed him had been apprehended.[139] And moralists could always indict duelists' confused and pernicious attachment to honor.[140] Duelists themselves sometimes lamented it. Two friends, Colonel Richard Thornhill and Sir Cholmley Deering, were getting drunk. Thornhill casually dropped a slighting reference to a lord Deering respected. Deering threw his

135. *A Proclamation against Private Challenges and Combats*, 4 February 1614, in *Stuart Royal Proclamations*, 1:302–8.

136. *An Ordinance against Challenges, Duells, and All Provocations Thereunto* (London, 1654).

137. *His Matys Declaration against Duells*, 24 November 1658, Egerton Mss. 2542 f. 278.

138. *A Proclamation against Fighting of Duells* (London, 1660).

139. *The Bloody Whitsuntide: or The Tragicall Moneth* (London, 1663), 6–7.

140. For instance, G.F., A Defendour of Christian Valoure, *Dvell-Ease: A Worde with Valiant Spiritts Shewing the Abuse of Duells, That Valour, Refuseth Challenges and Priuate Combates* (London, 1635), 37–38; *The Rash Duellist Disected: With the Inconveniencies That Attend Him* (London, 1673).

wine in Thornhill's face and then hit him in the face with the bottle. The two had to duel even though a sober Deering was "extremely sorry." Thornhill killed Deering and then professed remorse: "I should willingly Sacrifice the very last Drop of my Blood to retrieve that which my unfortunate Hand so rashly Shedded."[141] He was convicted of manslaughter and sentenced to be burned on the hand.[142]

The affront to sovereignty explains the remarkable energy governments put into trying to stamp out dueling. Rather than stand trial for dueling in 1631, Peter Apsley fled England. Yet another royal proclamation against dueling was drafted, this one aimed "*particularly against Peter Apsley*." Apsley, it intoned, "hath secretly departed from his Lodging, and hath lurked in places unknown, to the utter contempt of Our authority."[143] The draft was apparently in the hands of the Privy Council for stylistic revision when Apsley was apprehended.[144] The Earl of Northumberland interceded to win Apsley a pardon—and later Apsley turned around and sent Northumberland "a scandalous Letter, full of provoking and disgraceful

141. *The Case of Col. Richard Thornhill, Showing the True Occasion of His Fighting Sir Cholmley Deering . . . Written with His Own Hand under Confinement* (London, 1711); *An Account of the Life of Sir Chomley Deering* (London, 1711), 4.

142. Old Bailey Proceedings Online (www.oldbaileyonline.org, last visited 22 June 2017), May 1711, trial of Richard Thornhill (t17110516–39).

143. *A Proclamation against Such as Wilfully and Presumptuously Contemne His Maiesties Royall Authority, Vsed in Preuention of the Barbarous Vse of Duels; Particularly against Peter Apsley* (London, 1631). This 9 August proclamation isn't in *Stuart Royal Proclamations.*

144. So reports Richard Cust, *Charles I and the Aristocracy, 1625–1642* (Cambridge: Cambridge University Press, 2013), 98–99 n. 205. P. H. Hardacre, "The Earl Marshall, the Heralds, and the House of Commons, 1604–1641," *International Review of Social History* (1957), 120, says that Apsley surrendered. See too *Cal. S. P., Charles I, 1633–1634*, 442 (31 January 1633/34).

Language"[145] easy enough to construe as another challenge to a duel. The Star Chamber fined him £5,000, banished him from court, barred him from office, prohibited him from wearing a sword, required him to publicly apologize to the king, and imprisoned him indefinitely.[146] Charles I's secretary of state commented, "he that takes a sword in his hand to revenge himself doth as much as in him lieth [to] depose the king, at whose dispos[al] the sword of justice is."[147] However much a scamp or scoundrel Apsley was, it's hard to see him as trying to topple Charles from the throne. But the mantra of unlimited sovereign authority makes such a specter all too real.

Postscript

I come full circle: no surprise, then, about Bacon's language when he prosecuted a member of Ireland's Parliament for saying he'd have to defer to the Catholic Church on whether the pope could absolve subjects of obedience to the king. Bacon indicted "the greatest duel which is in the Christian world, the duel and conflict between the lawful authority of sovereign kings, which is God's ordinance for the comfort of human society, and the swelling pride and usurpation of the See of Rome . . . tending altogether to anarchy and confusion."[148]

145. Star Chamber Reports, 9 Charles I, in John Rushworth, *Historical Collections: The Second Volume of the Second Part* (London, 1686), appendix, 67.

146. Hardacre, "Earl Marshall," 120. See "The Answer, by Mr. Peter Apsley," in [John Mennes], *Wit Restor'd in Several Select Poems Not Formerly Published* (London, 1658), 18–19; for context, see Timothy Raylor, *Cavaliers, Clubs, and Literary Culture: Sir John Mennes, James Smith, and the Order of the Fancy* (Newark: University of Delaware Press, 1994), 66–67.

147. Cust, *Charles*, 102.

148. "Charge against William Talbot," 31 January 1613/14, in *Letters and the Life of Bacon*, 5:5–6.

The language isn't theatrical or inflated; it's deadly serious, as serious as the wars of religion. Obstreperous aristocrats with swords were just like the Vatican, both threats to unlimited, undivided, and unaccountable sovereign authority, to the day's plausible theory for ensuring social order—both fundamental menaces that had to be met.

Sovereignty, so understood, didn't just happen to arise in early modern Europe. It was an intelligible, intelligent response to the savage strife of the wars of religion. It fueled actual programs of state-building, in ways I'm not pursuing here. And it reconfigured people's understanding of their problems and possibilities, including (not just for instance) what was at stake in dueling. It wasn't just a morsel of discourse, still less a stray bit of metaphysics or ontology merrily blundering its way across time and space, or still worse located outside them, with scant regard for the political problems of the day.

It's another question whether or to what extent it remains an incisive tool for us. I'll now turn to exploring the political conflicts that dismantled the classic theory of sovereignty. I'll take on each of what I've dubbed the constitutive criteria in turn: so, a chapter on limiting sovereignty, a chapter on dividing it, and a chapter on holding it accountable. Of course, on the ground these struggles were often tied up in each other. For instance, those who wanted to limit sovereign authority often also wanted to hold it accountable: else what good are the purported limits? Or again: often people defended dividing sovereign authority as a strategy for limiting it. I won't erase or even smudge such connections, but for expository reasons I will take the criteria one at a time, so far as I can. I'm not devoting separate chapters to the ancillary commitments that come in the wake of the classic theory, the immense dignity of sovereign authority and the command theory of law. But I'll accord them their fair share of airtime, too.

It might sound logically confounding to say that sovereignty is unlimited, undivided, and unaccountable authority, and then talk about campaigns to limit it, divide it, and hold it accountable. It would perhaps be clearer to think of sovereignty as a theory of state authority and then talk about limiting, dividing, and holding accountable state authority. But what can I do? That's overwhelmingly not the way my sources talk and I am cheerfully at their mercy.

2
Limited

The Speaker of the House was crying.

Not wistful. Not teary. Not occasionally lapsing into a blubbing sniffle or quavering jaw. I mean distraught sobbing, even hysterical bawling, in a shocking collapse of the dignities of public deportment, role, and gender: "abundance of tears" and "extremity of weeping," as the record has it.[1] Why?

Well, he was being forcibly restrained, with a bit of a melee unfolding as some members wrestled him back into his chair and others tried to free him, one member even swearing at him ("God's wounds"), threatening him, too: "he should sit still until they pleased to rise."[2] He wasn't the only one trashing parliamentary decorum. So you might surmise that his tears were a response to the helpless childishness of the position he was in. Maybe so.

But the Speaker had a much weightier reason to cry. By March 1629, King Charles I had had enough of this insubor-

1. *Commons Debates for 1629*, ed. Wallace Notestein and Frances Helen Relf (Minneapolis: University of Minnesota, 1921), 105 (2 March 1629).
2. *Commons Debates for 1629*, 104 (2 March 1629).

dinate House of Commons. He'd ordered a five days' adjournment the week before. Now he wanted it to adjourn for eight more days. So the Speaker dutifully "delivered the King's command."[3] But the House was having none of it. The members would adjourn when they were good and ready; first they had more business to do. The Speaker responded that "he had an express command from the King as soon as he had delivered his message to rise."[4] So he tried to rise, but he got wrestled back into the chair. Whatever Charles's will, there would be no adjournment yet.

The Commons had been considering different matters.[5] Baleful about religious pluralism, the Commons had decried Catholicism abroad and at home—"Ireland is now almost wholly overspread with Popery, swarming with Friars, Priests, Jesuits, and other superstitious persons of all sorts, whose practice it is daily to seduce his Majesty's subjects from their allegiance"—and had demanded "exemplary punishment to be inflicted upon teachers, publishers, and maintainers of Popish opinions, and practicing of superstitious ceremonies," stricter laws, and censoring and burning books.[6] There was a finicky question about whether seizing the goods of a member of Parliament under tonnage and poundage rules violated parliamentary privilege, and that got tangled up with the questions of whether the sheriff doing the seizing knew who he was dealing with and whether that would finally matter. (Tonnage and

3. *Commons Debates for 1629*, 103 (2 March 1629).

4. *Commons Debates for 1629*, 104 (2 March 1629).

5. For the political narrative of Parliament in 1629, compare the redoubtable Samuel Rawson Gardiner, *The Personal Government of Charles I*, 2 vols. (London, 1877), 1:46–99, with the more richly contextualized Kevin Sharpe, *The Personal Rule of Charles I* (New Haven, CT: Yale University Press, 1992), chap. 1.

6. *Commons Debates for 1629*, 96–97, 100 (23 February 1629).

poundage were customs duties stretching back to Edward II and the early 1300s. Parliament had traditionally granted them to monarchs for life, but refused to grant them to Charles. He collected them anyway.) But there was also a running thread of discussion that looks, to our eyes anyway, more constitutional: the Commons had drawn up a protestation insisting that "Whoever shall counsel or advise the taking and levying of the Subsidies of Tonnage and Poundage, not being granted by Parliament, or shall be an actor or instrument therein, shall be likewise reputed an innovator in the government, and a capital enemy to this Kingdom and Commonwealth." So too, said the next count, would anyone who voluntarily paid the duties.[7] The Commons wanted to vote on these matters.

Jammed into his chair, the Speaker balked at reading the measure, but finally yielded. Then he valiantly refused to put the question, the necessary step to launch debate and a vote. Again he appealed to the king's command; one member shot back that he had no right to refuse the House's command. That's when the Speaker started crying, and he managed to blurt out, in suitably stammering syntax, "I will not say, I will not, but I dare not." He pleaded with the other members not to "command his ruin," adding that he "would gladly sacrifice his life for the good of his country; but he durst not sin against the express command of his Sovereign." One member fumed that the Speaker "was a disgrace to his country." The substance of the protestation was read aloud and embraced "with a loud *Yea* by the House."[8]

While the spectacle unfolded, Charles wasn't idle. He sent a messenger to retrieve the royal mace from the sergeant who ceremonially carries it: the mace symbolizes the crown's

7. *Commons Debates for 1629*, 102 (2 March 1629).
8. *Commons Debates for 1629*, 105 (2 March 1629).

presence and is legally required for the validity of parliamentary proceedings. The Commons kept the mace and the sergeant, too. His messenger had failed abjectly, so next Charles sent Black Rod to dissolve the session. "Being informed that neither he nor his message would be received by the House, the King grew into much rage and passion, and sent for the Captain of the Pensioners and Guard to force the door."[9] That gesture dramatically raised the stakes, but it was finally moot: the Commons was happy to adjourn.

The next day, the king jailed nine members. The next week, he showed up at the House of Lords—some members of the Commons were present—and dissolved Parliament. Continuing his freewheeling political improvisations, the king would convene no new session for eleven years. During those years, the Venetian ambassador reported that "absolute royalty" was "definitely the goal he has set himself, because the limited sovereignty, restricted by the laws and by disorder, was plotted against by his subjects in an indiscreet and ill advised manner."[10] The next year, surveying Charles's banning popular assemblies in Scotland as high treason, the new Venetian representative agreed: "His Majesty's object at present is confined to pacifying disturbances at home and making himself sovereign, dependent on no authority but his own. If he succeeds it will be the boldest enterprise that any of his predecessors ever achieved."[11]

9. *Commons Debates for 1629*, 106 (2 March 1629).

10. "Relation of England of Anzolo Correr," 24 October 1637, *Cal S. P., Venice, 1636–1639*, 296. For a bleaker later look at Charles's aspirations, see, for instance, *The Life and Reigne of King Charls, or The Pseudo-Martyr Discovered* (London, 1651), 51.

11. Francesco Zonca, Venetian Secretary in England, to the Doge and Senate, 19 March 1638, *Cal. S. P., Venice, 1636–1639*, 387–88, italics reversed. Compare Philip Hunton, *A Treatise of Monarchie* (London, 1643), 31, 39, and the reactions in H. Fern, *A Reply unto Severall Treatises Pleading for the*

Charles took to the press to vindicate his profound dissatisfaction with this cantankerous Parliament.[12] He described himself as endlessly conciliatory, not easily roused: "We endured long with much patience . . . strange & exorbitant incroachments and usurpations, such as were never before attempted in that House." But if the Commons wanted to press claims of institutional right or to challenge his royal authority, he had no choice but to articulate the rules as he saw them. Members of Parliament wanted "to erect a universal over-

---

Armes Now Taken Up by Subjects in the Pretended Defence of Religion and Liberty (Oxford, 1643); *A Remonstrance of the Un-lawfulnesse of the Warre Undertaken by the Pretended Parliament of England, against Their Sovereign* (Paris, 1652), 133–40; Robert Sheringham, *The Kings Supremacy Asserted* (London, 1660), 87–89. For a rebuttal, [Philip Hunton], *A Vindication of the Treatise of Monarchy, Containing an Answer to Dr Fernes Reply* (London, 1644), 19, 21, 43; and see [Charles Herle], *An Answer to Mis-led Doctor Fearne* (London, [1643]), 19–20. A Lover of Truth and of His Country [James Tyrrell], *Patriarcha non Monarcha* (London, 1681), 139–43, defends Hunton against [Robert Filmer], *The Anarchy of a Limited or Mixed Monarchy* (n.p., 1648). For James III's "thirst after Absolute Sovereignty . . . as great as is the thirst of one sick of a Burning Fever," see [Giovanni Francesco Biondi], *An History of the Ciuill Warres of England betweene the Two Houses of Lancaster and Yorke*, trans. Henry Earle of Monmouth, 2 vols. (London, 1641), 2:181. For how the ambitious are seduced by visions of absolute sovereignty, Richard Braithwaite, *History Surveyed in a Brief Epitomy* (London, 1651), 247–48.

12. *By the King: A Proclamation about the Dissoluing of the Parliament* (London, 1628); *By the King: A Proclamation for Suppressing of False Rumours Touching Parliament* (London, 1628); *His Maiesties D[e]claration to All His Louing Subiects of the Causes Which Moued Him to Dissolue the Last Parliament* (London, 1628). The *Declaration* is reprinted, with minor variations, in John Rushworth, *Historical Collections*, 8 vols. (London, 1659–86), vol. 1, appendix, 1–11. Or see the largely overlapping Irish edition: *His Maiesties Declaration to All His Louing Subjects, of the Causes Which Moued Him to Dissolve the Last Parliament* (Dublin, 1629). I've followed the original London publications.

swaying power to themselves, which belongs only to Us, and not to them." This bit is crucial. Charles would have rejected the claim that no actor in contemporary government did or should enjoy unlimited power. The mistake, he thinks, is locating such power in Parliament, not in the crown. So his ensuing language, which might seem outrageous, was for him the simple truth of English government. There was "an absolute Right and power in Us, to adjourn, as well as prorogue or dissolve" Parliament.[13] He was entitled to issue an "express & peremptory command to adjourn"; he had issued just that; but that "commandment was most contemptuously disobeyed." It was "audacious insolence" to read and consider that "most seditious paper" on tonnage and poundage. The ominous kicker: Commons had tried to "give law to Sovereignty, striking at the very essence of Monarchy."[14] The appeal to sovereignty, the

13. See too *By the King: A Proclamation for Suppressing of False Rumours Touching Parliament* (London, 1629), n.p. For a later complaint that such a royal right was conjured up by papists, see *Authority Abused by the Vindication of the Last Years Transactions, and the Abuses Detected* (London, 1690), 14; for a converse complaint about the political excesses of Presbyterians, see John Hacket, *Scrinia Reservata: A Memorial Offer'd to the Great Deservings of John Williams, D.D.* (London, 1693), pt. 2, 145. *DNB* attributes *Authority Abused* (and another anonymous one, *Reflections upon the Occurrences of the Last Year* (London, 1689), presumably the *Reflections* that *Authority* refers to on its title page) to Edward Stephens, d. 1706. This Stephens says (*Authority*, 15) that he fought for Charles as a fifteen-year-old, so he is not to be confused with the Edward Stephens who represented Tewkesbury in the House of Commons (W. R. Williams, *The Parliamentary History of the County of Gloucester* (Hereford, 1898), 59), subscribed to the Solemn League and Covenant (*An Ordinance of the Lords and Commons Assembled in Parliament; with Instrvctions for the Taking of the League and Covenant* (London, 1643), 15), and was seized in Pride's Purge and then jailed ([William Prynne], *A Vindication of the Imprisoned and Secluded Members of the House of Commons* (London, 1649), 4–5, 24).

14. *D[e]claration*, 29, 34, 36–39.

language of "very essence," decisively shifts the argument's register. Charles wasn't offering some local and contingent observations about the ground rules of English politics. He was staking out a claim about the necessary conditions of governance. "Universal overswaying power" was no threat; sovereignty required it. If anything was contingent or local, it was that in England sovereignty happened to vest in him, not in Parliament, not in anyone or anything else.

Much ado about a little bit? Maybe. It's worth remembering that how one sees the stakes of these events depends on one's background beliefs and the availability of temporizing strategies. It's easier, for instance, for the Commons to claim the right to decide when to adjourn if members just happen to keep deciding to adjourn when Charles tells them to. But if you think that the sovereign's power can't be limited, lest the government collapse—and just that commitment is built into the classic theory—and you think that the king is sovereign, then it will be awfully hard to overlook even "minor" instances of defiance or attempts to impose limits.

Nor was this the first confrontation between Charles and Parliament, and I'm sure their contentious history made each side more jittery—or determined. The year before, Parliament had passed[15] a petition of right to protest what it took to be indefensibly lawless actions of Charles. Tonnage and poundage

15. 3 Cha. 1 c. 1 (1627). 1627, not 1628, because this parliamentary session convened on 17 March 1627 Old Style; leaving aside the ten-day difference with the Gregorian calendar, the new English year began on 25 March and did so until 1752. That too explains, if you were wondering, why Charles's publications defending himself for the actions of a Parliament we say met in 1629 appear in publications dated 1628. For a slight variant of the text, the one actually considered by the Commons, see *Proceedings in Parliament 1628*, ed. Robert C. Johnson et al., 6 vols. (New Haven, CT: Yale University Press, 1977–83), 3:339–41 (9 May 1628). (This edition changed title midstream; the earlier volumes' title pages say *Commons Debates 1628*.)

was already on the agenda: one member "would have us send for the customers [customs officers] and receivers, to know how they dare levy tonnage and poundage without a law."[16] The Commons had other concerns, too. Charles had billeted soldiers, that is, forced civilians to house them.[17] He had jailed men on no charges. Desperate for money, not least to do his impotent bit in the wars of religion—farcically bad in the Cádiz expedition of 1625, not much better at La Rochelle and Saint-Martin-de-Ré in 1627 and 1628—Charles had already revealed a taste for what struck legalists as dubious improvisation or worse. Loans that merchants were forced to give, "benevolences" or gifts without even the pretense that they'd be repaid: weren't these crass invasions of the liberties of the subject?[18] You can say that—some contemporaries did—without taking sides in a battle historians have had for many decades now, about whether or to what extent we should see these actors as self-consciously pursuing constitutional stakes, or instead see those stakes as the later fallout of what unfolded as largely local political struggles.[19]

16. *Proceedings*, 3:294 (6 May 1628).

17. For instance, *Proceedings*, 2:99 (25 March 1628). On this matter, see especially Paul Christianson, "Arguments on Billeting and Martial Law in the Parliament of 1628," *Historical Journal* (September 1994).

18. Richard Cust, *The Forced Loan and English Politics, 1626–1628* (Oxford: Clarendon, 1987).

19. There are multiple ironies in the historiography and its reception. I'll mention two. David Hume thought the rule of law an unintended consequence of the pursuits of the Puritans he ridiculed as religious enthusiasts, or so I've argued: see my *Without Foundations* (Ithaca, NY: Cornell University Press, 1985), 193–99. So a view awfully like what we now call revisionism, or a critique of "Whig history," comes centuries earlier than it's commonly supposed to. And despite the book's reputation as the high-water mark of that critique, Conrad S. R. Russell, *Parliaments and English Politics, 1621–1629* (Oxford: Clarendon, 1979), 343–89, argues that the Parliament of 1628 was self-consciously pursuing the rule of law against sovereign incursions.

Charles sent the Commons reassuring messages.[20] But the members disagreed about whether his word was enough to secure those precious liberties of the subject. "The King's word is greater security to us than any law we can make," declared one.[21] "We have nothing thereby but shells and shadows," scoffed another. "If we come to one that owes us 100 *l*.," he added, "and he say, 'I owe you nothing, but I pray you trust me,' will this be good satisfaction?"[22] Sir Edward Coke, the distinguished and agile lawyer, effortlessly shifted gears. "He is God's lieutenant," conceded Coke. "Trust him we must." Still, general assurances couldn't suffice. Parliament had to pass a petition of right, "because we cannot take his trust but in a parliamentary way," with the proper legal forms observed, not just back-channel communications.[23] Legal language might be just as invidiously general as the king's assurances, and surely Coke knew that. His rhetoric politely rejected his opponents' deference.

At first, Charles spurned the Petition of Right, even parts of it you might imagine had to be unexceptionable. The bit about not committing a man to prison without identifying the charges he faced? Charles was willing again to pledge that he wouldn't abuse this power; he wouldn't, for instance, throw men in jail for "not lending of money unto us." But it had to be up to him: "without overthrow of sovereignty we cannot suffer this power to be impeached."[24] Charles's earlier reassurances

20. *Proceedings*, 2:275–76 (3 April 1628), 2:297 (4 April 1628), 3:125 (28 April 1628).

21. *Proceedings*, 3:285 (6 May 1628).

22. *Proceedings*, 3:270 (6 May 1628).

23. *Proceedings*, 3:272 (6 May 1628). See too *Proceedings*, 4:54 n. 22, 4:55 (2 June 1628).

24. *Proceedings*, 3:372 (and see 5:715) (12 May 1628).

had the same structure: he'd make sensible choices, but Parliament couldn't try to bind him. His discretion, his authority, had to be unlimited. The same impulse had led Charles to growl that he would "sweep all their benches" when judges in 1626 refused to sign off on the legality of his forced loans.[25] The law had to be what he said it was, not what others claimed.

Lords and Commons continued tense negotiations over the wording of the petition, with the Lords wanting to soften the language to comport with Charles's strictures.[26] For instance, the Lords wanted to describe Charles's forced loans not as "unlawful," as the Commons had put it, but as "not warrantable by the laws." One member of the Commons—the Privy Council had already thrown him in prison for refusing one of Charles's forced loans—rejected that mollifying gesture: "*quaere* whether there is not a tacit concession that such a thing may be put upon us by some means above the law."[27] Another sticking point was whether the text should assure the king Parliament was not challenging or limiting his sovereign power. The Commons refused to include the language.[28] Eventually, Charles folded, more or less, with legally significant wording that Coke swooned over: "I am half dead for joy."[29] "With what joy this was heard," echoed Francis Nethersole, a member of

25. Cust, *Forced Loan*, 54–55. Note Francis [Bacon], *The Essayes or Counsels, Civill and Morall* (London, 1625), 324: "Let *Judges* also remember, that *Solomon's Throne* was supported by Lions, on both Sides; Let them be Lions, but yet Lions under the Throne; Being circumspect, that they do not check, or oppose any Points of *Sovereignty*."

26. *Proceedings*, 5:405 (10 May 1628), 410, 3:382 (12 May 1628).

27. *DNB*, s.v. "Constable, Sir William (baronet), 1590–1655"; *Proceedings*, 3:500 (20 May 1628).

28. *Proceedings*, 5:475–76, 483 (20 May 1628); 515–16 (23 May 1628); 528 (24 May 1628).

29. *Proceedings*, 4:185 (7 June 1628).

Parliament and diplomat, who added there were "bonfires at every door" in London.[30] (Nethersole's diplomatic career came crashing to an end five years later, when an importunate note he wrote offended Charles, who had him arrested and tossed into the Tower.)[31]

The struggles between Charles and this Parliament lay bare two features of sovereignty that I want to pursue in this chapter. First is one of the constitutive criteria of the classic concept: that sovereign authority must be unlimited. Second is one of the two commitments that routinely follow in the wake of the classic theory: that law is the command of the sovereign. The commitment dovetails nicely with the criterion: both turn into arguments that it is incoherent and pernicious to try to limit sovereign authority. Both are in play with the deployment of the odd but everyday spatial metaphor casting the sovereign as "above the law." Here I will introduce a little parade of political actors working hard to limit sovereignty. I'll trace pointed debates about whether they were idiotic anarchists or valiant tinkerers trying to rework not just the theory of sovereignty, but also actual political and legal institutions and practices, to better secure good governance.

Charles wasn't the first English king to grapple with an obstreperous Parliament worried about overweening claims of regal authority. When Charles's father, James I, was on the throne, John Cowell wrote in *The Interpreter* that the king "is above the Law by his absolute power."[32] Parliament exploded

30. Francis Nethersole to Queen Elizabeth of Bohemia, 7 June 1628, *Proceedings*, 6:195.

31. *DNB*, s.v. "Nethersole, Sir Francis."

32. John Cowell, *The Interpreter* (Cambridge, 1607), s.v. "king." Compare *Interpreter*, s.v. "parlament": "either the king is above the Parliament, that is, the positive laws of his kingdom, or else . . . he is not an absolute king";

over this and other putatively extravagant claims.[33] As the episode unfolded, James assured Parliament he wanted Cowell's book suppressed and explicitly disavowed one of its positions: "that the king may take subsidies without the consent of his people, he condemns the doctrine[]as absurd."[34] And James duly issued a royal proclamation demanding that anyone holding a copy of Cowell's book turn it in to be suppressed. (Plenty of copies survived.) James bemoaned the "unsatiable curiosity in many men's spirits, and such an itching in the tongues and pens of most men" that led them to "freely wade by their writings in the deepest mysteries of Monarchy."[35] But James himself—not, let's say, famous for his modesty about his authority—already had announced that he had "proved, that the King is above the law, as both the author and the giver of strength thereto."[36] (He first offered this delicious nugget as king of Scotland, five years before ascending the English

---

Robert Monro, *Monro His Expedition with the VVorthy Scots Regiment (Called Mac-Keyes Regiment) Levied in August 1626* (London, 1637), 87, also in [Robert] Monro, *The Scotch Military Discipline Learned from the Valiant Swede, and Collected for the Use of All Worthy Commanders* (London, 1644), pt. 1, 87.

33. *Parliamentary Debates* (2–11 March 1610); *DNB*, s.v. "Cowell, John." For a review of the episode, see J. P. Sommerville, *Politics and Ideology in England, 1603–1640* (London: Longman, 1986), 121–27.

34. *Proceedings in Parliament, 1610*, ed. Elizabeth Read Foster, 2 vols. (New Haven, CT: Yale University Press, 1966), 2:50 (8 March 1610) (and compare 1:29, 31).

35. "A Proclamation Touching D. Cowels Booke Called the Interpreter," 25 March 1610, in *Stuart Royal Proclamations*, ed. James F. Larkin and Paul L. Hughes, 2 vols. to date (Oxford: Clarendon, 1973–), 1:243–45.

36. *The Trve Lawe of Free Monarchies* (Edinburgh, 1598), sig. D recto f., reprinted, for instance, in *The VVorkes of the Most High and Mightie Prince, Iames* (London, 1616), 203. For comments, see *The Secret History of the Court and Reign of Charles the Second*, 2 vols. (London, 1792), 1:xx; [John Forbes], *Duplyes of the Ministers & Professors of Aberdene* (Aberdeen, 1638), 22–23.

throne. I doubt that made skeptics in Parliament any happier about it, not least because the work was reprinted when he was king of England, but it was surely easier to go after Cowell than go after the king.)

Cowell wasn't unique; there is indeed an itch here that gets scratched repeatedly, if not quite the one James had in mind, of writers outdoing themselves in the shrill and buzzing defense of the crown and Parliament swatting them down. One of Charles's sycophants, Roger Maynwaring, penned sermons gushing in awe. "Lawful Sovereigns are no less than *Fathers*, *Lords*, *Kings*, and *Gods* on earth," insisted the bishop and king's chaplain. "No *Power* . . . can lay restraint upon these *supremes*." Even if the sovereign's commands departed from the law, "no Subject may, without hazard of his own Damnation, in rebelling against God, *Question*, or *disobey* the will and pleasure of his *Sovereign*." Maynwaring was defending Charles's right to raise money without Parliament's consent—that was the immediate topical stake behind his rhapsodies about "sublime and independent *Sovereignty*" and "unresistable *Authority*"—and Parliament was not even grimly amused.[37] Members decided he should be imprisoned at their pleasure, that he pay a whopping fine of £1,000 to the king, that he no longer be able to preach at court or hold "any ecclesiastical dignity," and that his book be burned. They required too that he show up and acknowledge his offenses, which of course Maynwaring did,

37. Roger Maynwaring, *Religion and Alegiance: In Two Sermons Preached before the Kings Maiestie* (London, 1627), 4, 8–9, 19 (and see 27), 12. For more gushing that produced more conniptions, see Robert Sybthorpe, *Apostolike Obedience: Shewing the Duty of Subiects to Pay Tribute and Taxes to Their Princes* (London, 1627). For some of the fallout, Dr. Robert Sibthorpe to [Sir John Lamb], 18 November 1641, *Cal. S. P., Charles I, 1641–43*, 169–70; Sibthorpe to [Lamb], 27 November 1641, *Cal. S. P., Charles I, 1641–43*, 182–83.

though you can decide how sincere he was in professing "all sorrow of heart and true repentance"—and why Parliament might sensibly insist on such a command performance without beginning to believe the churchman was genuinely apologetic.[38] I don't know whether Charles had assured Maynwaring that he was about to pardon him and install him as a rector, as the ever-gracious king did a couple of weeks later.[39]

Later I'll pick up the thread—cable—of commotions in English politics and law and how they bear on sovereignty. For now, one last story from the closing months of the reign of James II, whose abdication-cum-deposition (for reasons both partisan and constitutional, Whigs and Tories hotly disputed how to characterize it, as well as just what abdication might or might not mean)[40] in December 1688 after a few fractious years on the throne put an end to the Stuart line of kings. James II, ruling as a Catholic over an officially Protestant realm, raised eyebrows and resistance in building up a standing army and using his dispensing power to enable Catholics to take on important military roles without their taking the religious oaths required by the Test Act. He also invited the papal nuncio to

38. *Proceedings*, 4:309–10 (14 June 1628), 403 (21 June 1628). Glenn Burgess, "The Divine Right of Kings Reconsidered," *English Historical Review* (October 1992), emphasizes the difference between divinely imposed obligation and the king's absolute sovereignty. There's something there, but not everything Maynwaring and Sibthorpe say fits his analysis. So too for plenty of other commentators, for instance, *A Looking-Glasse for Rebells: or The True Grounds of Soveraignty, Proving the Kings Authority to Be from GOD Only* (Oxford, 1643). For a more focused account of the religious dimensions of this clash, see Hillel Schwartz, "Arminianism and the English Parliament, 1624–1629," *Journal of British Studies* (May 1973).

39. *Cal S. P., Charles I, 1628–1629*, 196, 198, 217.

40. J. P. Kenyon, *Revolution Principles: The Politics of Party, 1689–1720* (Cambridge: Cambridge University Press, 1977), remains incisive.

a formal reception at court, for the first time since the reign of Bloody Mary; and it's an apparently minor incident in that episode I want to introduce.

The problem? "All commerce with the See of Rome" counted as high treason at law. The Duke of Somerset, whose official role as lord of the bedchamber would require his ceremonial participation, consulted with his lawyers. "They told him, he could not safely do the part that was expected of him in the audience." So the duke told the king he wouldn't participate. "The King asked him, if he did not know that he was above the law. The other answered, that, whatever the King might be, he himself was not above the law." Annoyed, the king stripped the duke of "all employments" at court. The king's language and actions met a frosty reception during his own processions through the countryside.[41]

You might think the royal dispensing power looks illegal or extralegal: it gives the monarch the power to wave a magic wand and waive the applicability of a law. Better, though, to see the dispensing power as itself a creature of the law. The distinction would be moot if the law gave the crown sweeping authority to dispense with any and every law in any and every case. But it didn't. At least on the ordinary view, it applied to statutes, not common law; it didn't apply to crimes of "malum in se," those where the act would count as wrongful even without a statute; and so on. Courts regularly heard and decided challenges to exercises of the royal dispensing power.[42] Anx-

41. *Bishop Burnet's History of His Own Time*, 3rd ed., 4 vols. (London, 1766), 2:427–28; and see Roger Acherley, *The Britannic Constitution: or, The Fundamental Form of Government in Britain* (London, 1727), 638. For James's friction with the pope, see John Miller, *James II: A Study in Kingship* (Hove, UK: Wayland, 1977), 152–54.

42. I've relied on the work of Carolyn A. Edie: "Tactics and Strategies: Parliament's Attack upon the Royal Dispensing Power 1597–1689," *Ameri-*

ious critics charged that James II had treated the power as the all-purpose magic wand it was decidedly not. "And for Officers to be employed not taking the Tests, it is dispensing all the Laws at once," worried one member of Parliament about James installing Catholics in government posts: "For we must remember, it is Treason for any man to be reconciled to the Church of *Rome*; for the Pope, by Law, is declared an enemy to this Kingdom."[43] That inflammatory inference betrays the ongoing deep commitment to a confessional state—and how such a state effortlessly generates disloyal subjects in its midst—at least as much as it reveals any commitment to the rule of law.

But worries about the dispensing power went well beyond anxieties about James's Catholicism. In the parliamentary debates over the settlement of the Glorious Revolution, with worries about James safely in the past, Henry Capel assaulted a "universal Dispensing Power." The use of the word *universal* might sound like a reminder that however robust the dispensing power was, it had its legal limits. But Capel was onto something deeper. "We are slaves if it be so, and no freer than in Turkey. We know the king has prerogatives, but to say, 'he has a Dispensing Power,' is to say, 'there is no law.'"[44] You

---

can Journal of Legal History (July 1985), and "Revolution and the Rule of Law: The End of the Dispensing Power, 1689," *Eighteenth-Century Studies* (Summer 1977). On the meaning and later reception of one important case, see Dennis Dixon, "*Godden v Hales* Revisited—James II and the Dispensing Power," *Journal of Legal History* (August 2006).

43. *Debates in the House of Commons* (12 November 1685). Lois G. Schwoerer, *Gun Culture in Early Modern England* (Charlottesville: University of Virginia Press, 2016), 157, led me to this passage.

44. *Parliamentary History* (16 May 1689). Compare [John Floyd], *God and the King: or, A Dialogue, Wherein Is Treated of Allegiance Due to Our Most Gracious Lord, King Iames, within His Dominion* (Cullen, 1620), 19–20; J[ohn] M[ilton], *Eikonoklastes in Answer to a Book Intitl'd Eikon Basilike*

can write a law giving the king—or any other state actor—such power. You can follow all the mandated procedures for passing it. But, Capel would insist, it flouts the very idea of law. Even John Locke would agree on the importance of a prerogative power, in his most extreme formulation a "power to act according to discretion, for the public good, without the prescription of the law, and sometimes even against it." That raises difficulties, too. But they fall short of those summoned up by the dispensing power. The law, as Locke noticed in this same discussion, "makes no distinction of Persons."[45] But the dispensing power made nonsense of this commitment to equality under the law. It permitted the crown to suspend laws because of the particular actors they would apply to, but leave those laws in place for others similarly situated.

Theory Talk

Let's turn to the register of political theory and examine what theorists of sovereignty have to say about legally imposed limits. Bodin is crystal clear in linking law as sovereign command to the thought that the sovereign can't be bound: "If then the sovereign prince be exempted from the laws of his predecessors, much less should he be bound unto the laws and ordinances he maketh himself: for a man may well receive a law

---

(London, 1650), 104. For allegiance as itself legally qualified, see Nath[aniel] Bacon, *The Continuation of an Historicall Discourse, of the Government of England* (London, 1651), 89. For prerogative as "not a Crumb *Arbitrary*, because sweeten'd with the Cadences of Justice [and] in all things directed by *Clarified Reason*, Law," see *Defensio Legis: or, The Whole State of England Inquisited and Defended for General Satisfaction* (London, 1674), 137–38.

45. [John Locke], *Two Treatises of Government* (London, 1690), 383 (*Second Treatise*, § 160).

from another man, but impossible it is in nature for to give a law unto himself. . . . There can be no obligation, which taketh state from the mere will of him that promiseth the same: which is a necessary reason to prove evidently that a king or sovereign prince cannot be subject to his own laws."[46] If you can bind yourself, you're always free to unbind yourself. No wonder Robert Filmer, the great English defender of the king's unlimited authority, saluted "the great modern politician *Bodin*" and agreed that sovereignty was "*an absolute power not subject to any Law*."[47] "When as they shall limit and restrain the Sovereign Power of a *Monarch*," he warned elsewhere, "to subject him to the general Estates, or to Council"—read Parliament—"the Sovereignty hath no firm Foundation, but they frame a popular confusion, or a miserable *Anarchy*."[48] Filmer's language bitterly rejects Parliament's struggles to tie Charles down, but it is, as theory is wont to be, more sweeping. More emphatically, Filmer declared, "There can be no laws without a Supreme Power to command or make them." No matter whether sovereignty inhered in a king or the nobility or even the people; it had to be above the law. It followed that "in

46. Jean Bodin, *The Six Bookes of a Commonweale: A Facsimile Reprint of the English Translation of 1606 Corrected and Supplemented*, ed. Kenneth Douglas McRae (Cambridge, MA: Harvard University Press, 1962), 91–92. Note Peter Charro, *Of Wisdome: Three Bookes*, trans. Samson Lennard (London, 1608), 489.

47. [Filmer], *Anarchy*, 30, also in Robert Filmer, *The Free-holders Grand Inquest* (London, 1679), 299.

48. [Robert Filmer], *The Necessity of the Absolute Power of All Kings: and in Particular, of the King of England* (London, 1648), 12; with incidental variations in Robert Filmer, *The Power of Kings: and in Particular, of the King of England* (London, 1680), 12. Contrast Samuel Rutherford, *A Treatise of Civil Policy* (London, 1656), 421.

a Monarchy the King must of necessity be above the Laws."[49] Here again we've moved away from the twists and turns of English politics to claims about the necessary structure of political authority. So too with Thomas Hobbes, razor-sharp in the pursuit of coruscating wisdom and ludicrous folly alike. "Law in general," he declared, "is not Counsel, but Command." "The Legislator in all Common-wealths, is only the Sovereign." "The Sovereign of a Common-wealth . . . is not Subject to the Civil Laws. For having power to make, and repeal Laws, he may when he pleaseth, free himself from that subjection, by repealing those Laws that trouble him, and making of new."[50] Filmer and Hobbes aren't defending the royal dispensing power, defined and limited as it is by law. They are insisting on something more freewheeling.

Jump forward a century and once again, Blackstone offered formulations that in their crystalline simplicity turned out to matter in these debates. The "royal dignity" ascribed to the king "certain qualities, as inherent in his royal capacity, distinct from and superior to those of any other individual in the nation . . . attributes of a great and transcendent nature; by which the people are led to consider him in the light of a superior being, and to pay him that awful respect, which may enable him with greater ease to carry on the business of government." Blackstone reached back to that "ancient and fundamental maxim" of English law, "the king can do no wrong," which he glossed

49. Robert Filmer, *Patriarcha: or The Natural Power of Kings* (London, 1680), 99–100. See too R[obert] Filmer, *Observations concerning the Original and Various Forms of Government* (London, 1696), 299–300.

50. Thomas Hobbes, *Leviathan* (London, 1651), 137–38. For a response to this sort of thing, Edward [Hyde], Earl of Clarendon, *A Brief View and Survey of the Dangerous and Pernicious Errors to Church and State, in Mr. Hobbes's Book, Entitled Leviathan* (Oxford, 1676), 125–26.

this way: "Besides the attribute of sovereignty, the law also ascribes to the king, in his political capacity, *absolute perfection*." "The king, moreover, is not incapable of *doing* wrong, but even of *thinking* wrong: he can never mean to do an improper thing: in him is no folly or weakness."[51] Blackstone knew full well that the kings of England were not, shall we say, all that saintly or brainy. But—as so often, or always? with sovereignty talk—there is an as-if game being played. Kings and queens are, well, men and women. Each one might as well be some unassuming fellow from Kansas stranded when his balloon went kaput. But subjects and others must not peek behind the curtain. Instead they must be dazzled by the image on the screen.

Centuries before Oz, commentators saw what was going on. In 1648, one ridiculed the sweeping claims made for "the rights of Sovereignty" allegedly held by the king. "Preach these doctrines to the simple country men of *Wales*," he guffawed, "whose ears are astonished with Majestic language . . . and whose eyes are dazzled with the glorious Robes, glittering Crown, and golden Scepter of the *King*."[52] Whatever you make of the swipe at country bumpkins (local yokels, rednecks, hillbillies, white trash, etc. ad nauseam), it's a vintage bit of the rhetoric of demystification. To describe it that way is of course to take a political stand. As I say, then, it's a vintage bit of the rhetoric of demystification.

51. William Blackstone, *Commentaries on the Laws of England*, 4 vols. (Oxford, 1765–69), 1:238–39. See too John Reeves, *Thoughts on the English Government, Addressed to the Quiet Good Sense of the People of England . . . Letter the First* (London, 1795), 10.

52. *Salus Populi Salus Rex: The Peoples Safety Is the Sole Soveraignty, or The Royalist Out-reasoned* (n.p., 1648), 21, and see 12–13. Compare the mockery in Henry Carey, *A Learned Dissertation on Dumpling*, 6th ed. (London, 1754), 14; "Manor of St. George," *The Spirit of the Public Journals*, 21 vols. (London, 1797–1825), 2:367–70.

That ancient maxim "The king can do no wrong" has different strands. You might think of one as a political norm about the symbolic head of state: it's rude to criticize the king, better to assail an evil or misguided minister. But another goes to the absurdity of trying to enforce legal limits against the king. "No suit or action can be brought against the king," averred Blackstone, "even in civil matters, because no court can have jurisdiction over him. For all jurisdiction implies superiority of power: authority to try would be vain and idle, without an authority to redress; and the sentence of a court would be contemptible, unless that court had power to command the execution of it: but who . . . shall command the king?" The king could never be tried and punished, "even though the measures pursued in his reign be completely tyrannical and arbitrary."[53] So you can also gloss the maxim this way: of course the king can do bad things, can inflict grievous harm on others; but none of that will count as an injury at law, so none of it is a wrong, strictly speaking. There's a profound link here between sovereign dignity and the king's being above the law. Blackstone wasn't alone. Here's the Scottish Enlightenment figure Adam Ferguson: "The sovereign, being accustomed to will, or to command, cannot submit merely to interpret, or to follow a rule." "The sovereign, having no superior, may follow prejudice or passion at discretion."[54] As late as 1885, an English legal academic and judge was devoutly preaching the old-time religion: "to speak of the authority of the sovereign body being limited, or of its acts being illegal, is a confusion of terms."[55]

53. Blackstone, *Commentaries*, 1:234, 238, 239, 235. See too [Marchamont Nedham], *A Plea for the King, and Kingdome* (n.p., 1648), n.p.

54. Adam Ferguson, *Institutes of Moral Philosophy* (Edinburgh, [1775]), 304.

55. William Markby, *Elements of Law Considered with Reference to Principles of General Jurisprudence*, 3rd ed. (Oxford, 1885), 18. De Maistre, the great

Again, Blackstone wrote over a century after Charles's wrestling with his Parliaments, but nothing in the great lawyer's language would have struck Charles's contemporaries as unintelligible or startling. Some of Charles's opponents accepted this basic account of sovereignty. They argued only that Parliament, not Charles, was sovereign. So, for instance, William Prynne in 1643 bubbled over with approving references to Bodin—elsewhere he'd style him "that most famous Grand Lawyer and Statesman *John Bodin*"[56]—and Grotius. Parliament, he urged, "is the most high and absolute power . . . it is above the Law itself." The king, though, was "not above, but subordinate to the Laws of the Realm."[57] Parliament, he

---

reactionary opponent of the French Revolution, was even blunter about the stakes. "Every species of sovereignty is absolute of its nature," indeed, "an absolute power which is able to commit evil with impunity, which is thus . . . *despotic* in the full force of the term and against which there is no defense other than rebellion." De Maistre had learned the lessons of the classic theory's great copy-books. "The sovereign cannot therefore be judged: if he could be, the power possessing this right would be sovereign and there would be two sovereigns, which implies contradiction. The sovereign can no more modify than alienate itself: to *limit* is to *destroy* it" (*Study on Sovereignty* [1794], in *The Works of Joseph de Maistre*, trans. Jack Lively (New York: Macmillan, 1965), 112–13). For a latter-day fan, embracing de Maistre's "metaphysical conservatism" and mocking an allegedly misguided quest for "constitutional limits on sovereignty," see T. John Jamieson, "De Maistre as Conservative Thinker," *Salisbury Review* (July 1985).

56. William Prynne, *The Second Tome of an Exact Chronological Vindication and Historical Demonstration of Our British, Roman, Saxon, Danish, Norman, English Kings Supream Ecclesiastical Jurisdiction* (London, 1665), 320.

57. William Prynne, *The Soveraigne Power of Parliaments and Kingdomes* (London, 1643), 46, italics removed; also in [William Prynne], *The Treachery and Disloyalty of Papists to Their Soveraignes* ([n.p., 1643]), 23. Prynne defended his reading of Bodin in *The Falsities and Forgeries of the Anonymous Author of a Late Pamphlet . . . Intituled The Fallacies of Mr. William Prynne, Discovered and Confuted* (London, 1644). See *The Fallacies of Mr. VVilliam Prynne, Discovered and Confuted* (Oxford, 1644), esp. 13.

stressed in another book, "is the absolute Sovereign power within the Realm, not subject" to the law, but "having an absolute Sovereignty over the Laws themselves," even Magna Carta.[58] Irate over Cromwell's dissolution of the House of Lords, Prynne would return to the fray to denounce the "gross Ignorance" of those who thought the Commons alone could claim sovereignty.[59]

So the classic theory insisted that the sovereign had to be above the law. But that theory faced trenchant critics. In 1642, Henry Parker complained, "if Nations by common consent, can neither set limits, or judge of limits set to sovereignty, but must look upon it as a thing merely divine, and above all human consent or comprehension, then all nations are equally slaves, and we in *England* are born to no more by the Laws of *England* then the Asinine Peasants of *France*."[60] Denouncing Hobbes, the Earl of Clarendon appealed to Roman history to urge "that the Sovereign power may admit limitations without any danger."[61] James Tyrrell staged a dialogue in which Mr. Mean-

58. William Prynne, *The Fourth Part of The Soveraigne Power of Parliaments and Kingdomes* (London, 1643), 15. See too [Thomas Rymer], *A General Draught and Prospect of Government in Europe, and Civil Policy* (London, 1681), 48–49, repeated with incidental variations in *Of the Use and Abuse of Parliaments; in Two Historical Discourses*, 2 vols. (London, 1744), 1:43; [Henry Parker], *A Discourse concerning Puritans*, 2nd ed. corr. (London, 1641), 52. For the argument that the king must be sovereign because Parliament isn't always in session, Thomas Goddard, *Plato's Demon: or, The State-Physician Unmaskt* (London, 1684), 282.

59. William Prynne, *The First Part of an Historical Collection of the Ancient Parliaments of England* (London, 1649), 3.

60. [Henry Parker], *Some Few Observations upon His Majesties Late Answer to the Declaration* ([London, 1642]), 15. But for divine limits, see Edward Gee, *The Divine Right and Original of the Civill Magistrate from God* (London, 1658), 292–93.

61. Clarendon, *Brief View*, 51.

well, a civil lawyer, trotted out the classic theory. It was a "*Solecism* in Politics to affirm, that a *Monarch* . . . could be thus *limited* by *Laws*, or *Fundamental Constitutions*." But Mr. Freeman—no points for guessing whose side Tyrrell was on—dismissed Meanwell's arguments as "more subtile than true."[62] Algernon Sidney took on Filmer. "It cannot be for the Good of the People that the Magistrate have a power above the Law." Reviling the likes of Nimrod and Nebuchadnezzar, embracing Deuteronomy's strictures on how kings should rule, turning to history, Sidney discarded "unlimited power" as pernicious, not "essential to kings."[63] The historical record suggested more possibilities than the theory of sovereignty allowed. And the turn to scripture was a nice touch: it made Filmer out to be a blasphemer. Much later, Jeremy Bentham would take the same line in shredding Blackstone's announcement that there "must be in all [governments] a supreme, irresistible, absolute, uncontrolled authority." "To say," responded Bentham dryly, "that not even by convention can any limitation be made to the power of that body in a state which in other respects is supreme, would be saying, I take it, rather too much: it would be saying that there is no such thing as government in the German Empire; nor in the Dutch Provinces; nor in the Swiss Cantons; nor was of old in the Achaean league."[64] But here Bentham's friend and often acolyte, John Austin, hewed to the party line: "the power

62. [James Tyrrell], *Bibliotheca Politica* (London, 1694), 338, 339; and for more of Meanwell on this matter, 648–49. For the identification of the speakers, who appear by the first letters of their last names, see *Bibliotheca*, 1.

63. Algernon Sidney, *Discourses concerning Government* (London, 1698), 348, 352.

64. Jeremy Bentham, *A Comment on the Commentaries and A Fragment on Government*, ed. J. H. Burns and H. L. A. Hart (London: Athlone, 1977), 488–89.

of a sovereign is incapable of legal limitation," he opined; that thesis "follows inevitably from the nature of sovereign power," and in denying it, "the error is remarkable."[65]

Some of those critics were explicit about the importance of constitutional limits. Take Puritan divine Richard Baxter. It would be unlawful, he insisted, for the people "to limit or restrain the sovereign Power from disposing so far of the estates of all, as is necessary to the safety of all." "But yet it is just and wisdom for the people in the constitution to limit the Ruler by convenient cautions that he may not under pretence of Preserving them have advantage to oppress them."[66] (Yes, a lot hangs on how those convenient cautions work. And yes, there has always been plausible skepticism about quite what Baxter and others had in mind by "constitution," since notoriously England didn't have a written constitution.)

After the Glorious Revolution of 1688, it was easier to sound serene about these matters—for Whigs, anyway. "Our Constitution is a limited mix'd Monarchy," suggested John Trenchard; "our Government may truly be called an Empire of Laws, and not of Men."[67] This suggestion denies that the sovereign has to be above the law, but unless Trenchard was assuming the king was sovereign, it says nothing explicit about limiting sovereignty. But some understood that they were re-

65. John Austin, *The Province of Jurisprudence Determined* (London, 1832), 294–95. For a wrinkle on international relations, *Province*, 388–90.

66. Richard Baxter, *A Holy Commonwealth, or Political Aphorisms Opening the True Principles of Government* (London, 1659), 114–15, and see 117–18; but consider too 337–38.

67. [John Trenchard], *An Argument, Shewing, That a Standing Army Is Inconsistent with a Free Government* (London, 1697), 2. See too A Minister of the Church of England, *A Friendly Debate between Dr. Kingsman, A Dissatisfied Clergy-man, and Gratianus Trimmer, a Neighbor Minister* (London, 1689), 15.

jecting the classic theory's insistence that sovereignty had to be unlimited. One contemporary historian thought that, surveying the careers of his ancestors, Charles II should have figured out "that those that grasp'd at *Immoderate Power* . . . were always Unfortunate, and their Reigns inglorious." Indeed, Charles I's "*Immoderate Desire of Power,* beyond what the Constitution did allow of, was the Rock he split upon." And James I received, and acted on, the vicious advice that he had a dispensing power, necessarily attached to monarchy—"all other Sovereign Princes" had it, too—leaving "*our* Laws *and* Constitution *to be trampled upon colour of Law*."[68] So much the worse for the classic theory's insistence that only unlimited sovereignty could endure. That theory got things backwards; limits were a source of strength, not fragility. So too for Daniel Defoe's endorsing "a Monarchy . . . limited by Parliament, and *dependent upon Law*" as "the best Government in the World."[69] One sermon easily summoned up a consensus. "'Tis sufficiently known the Monarchy of this Nation is limited, and what the Sovereign has, he has by Law."[70]

Again, some of these critics might be pressing a local point about English monarchy; they might even agree with Prynne in adopting the classic theory of sovereignty even while insisting the king wasn't sovereign. But not all of them:

68. James Welwood, *Memoirs of the Most Material Transactions in England, for the Last Hundred Years*, 3rd ed. corr. (London, 1700), 156, 87, 194–95; the first and third excerpts, with typographical variation, are also in [John Banks], *The History of the Life and Reign of William III* (London, 1794), 134, 148.

69. [Daniel Defoe], *Jure Divino: A Satyr* (London, 1706), iv. See too [Charles Lucas], *A Tenth Address to the Free Citizens, and Free-holders, of the City of Dublin* (Dublin, 1748), 5.

70. Thomas Sawbridge, *A Sermon Preached at the Assizes in St. Maries Church in Leicester* (London, 1689), 13.

some are quite obviously critics of sovereignty. Those writers are wonderfully calm about the very prospect that gave Bodin, Hobbes, and the rest nightmares. Lend a fresh eye to the settlement of 1688 or other historical cases, including our own institutions today, and you can see that the classic theory of sovereignty fails ignobly as a general theory of political authority. Limits needn't be crippling. They don't inexorably send the people ostensibly suffering under them down a lethal and slippery slope to anarchy. In some contexts, they might, and it's plausible that early modern Europe was one such context. (I say plausible, not true, because I happen to think it's false.) But not everywhere, not all the time, not no matter what.

Or try it this way: if you stop thinking of sovereignty as a timeless or necessary conceptual prop in appraising politics, if you wrest free of the mysterious allure exerted by those who would conjure up metaphysics and ontology, if you learn instead to see sovereignty as a tool or weapon designed to fight against early modernity's wars of religion and the like, to see the theory as a contingent blueprint for state-building, a contingent scheme to deal with contingent problems, you can then see how it might become a problem in turn, how an almighty state might leave its subjects defenseless. John Locke nailed the point. Mocking champions of absolute monarchy, he reported laconically, "if it be asked, what Security, what Fence is there, in such a State, against the Violence and Oppression of this Absolute Ruler? The very Question can scarce be borne." Subjects, his opponents thought, could demand legal protection from fellow subjects, but never from their own government. Locke was right: the mere prospect made his opponents frantic, because their theory told them such demands were a recipe for civil war and anarchy. But the theory was hopelessly misguided in missing how dangerous an all-powerful state could be, in denying that anything could or should be done about it. "This is to think that Men are so foolish, that they take care to avoid what Mischiefs may be done them by *Pole-Cats*, or *Foxes*, but are content, nay, think it Safety, to be devoured by *Lions*."[71]

If unlimited sovereignty once looked plausible, even inviting, as a strategy for securing social order, the antics of the Stuart monarchs and their ilk made it look repellent. Strictly speaking, no European state ever attained full sovereignty as described by the classic theories. But efforts by some state actors to pursue such sovereignty inspired their opponents not just to rethink the theory, though they sure did, but also to engineer actual limits on political authority.

American Innovations

So let's zip ahead to 1775, to the outbreak of war between the American colonies and Britain. Entering the lists against the Americans, Samuel Johnson thundered, "In sovereignty there are no gradations. There may be limited royalty, there may be limited consulship; but there can be no limited government. There must in every society be some power or other from which there is no appeal, which admits no restrictions."[72] Johnson was infuriated by various pronouncements of the Second Continental Congress, which he saw as lighting the fuse of explosive war. The only way to achieve peace was for the colonists to submit to parliamentary sovereignty.

71. *Treatises*, 312–13 (*Second Treatise*, § 93). Consider [Thomas Richard Bentley], *Considerations upon the State of Public Affairs* (London, 1798), 39.

72. [Samuel Johnson], *Taxation No Tyranny* (London, 1775), 24.

But, or so it seemed to many Americans, sovereignty wasn't a beneficent salve to bloody conflict. It precipitated such conflict. Some of the Second Continental Congress's language was unhappily prolix, but its members clearly grasped the case against unlimited sovereignty.

> If it was possible for men who exercise their reason to believe, that the divine author of our existence intended a part of the human race to hold an absolute property in, and an unbounded power over others, marked out by his infinite goodness and wisdom as the objects of a legal domination, never rightfully resistible, however severe and oppressive, the inhabitants of these colonies might at least require from the parliament of Great Britain some evidence, that this dreadful authority over them has been granted to that body. But a reverence for our great Creator, principles of humanity, and the dictates of common sense, must convince all those who reflect upon the subject, that government was instituted to promote the welfare of mankind, and ought to be administered for the attainment of that end.

Britain's Parliament, they complained, was "blinded . . . by their intemperate rage for unlimited domination."[73]

Back in London, James Macpherson—once the progenitor of the Ossianic literary hoax, now serving the government

73. *A Declaration by the Representatives of the United Colonies of North America, Now Met in General Congress in Philadelphia, Setting Forth the Cause and Necessity of Their Taking Up Arms* ([Philadelphia?, 1775]), 2.

as a hired gun[74]—sneered at Congress's style and substance alike: "The declaration of the Congress begins with an involved period, which either contains no meaning, or a meaning not founded on the principles of reason. They seem to insinuate, that no body of men, in any Empire, can exercise an 'unbounded authority over others'; an opinion contrary to fact under every form of Government. No maxim in policy is more universally admitted, than that a supreme and uncontrollable power must exist somewhere in every state." The language might as well have been lifted from Blackstone. Maybe it was. Macpherson was happy to concede that such power would be "justly dreaded and reprobated" in a king: the Stuart monarchs would have been appalled, but the point is a useful reminder that the classic theory of sovereignty leaves open whether sovereignty lies in a monarch, a parliament, both jointly, or whatever other government actors one could invoke. Negotiations would be impossible, declared Macpherson, as long as the colonies pretended to sovereignty themselves. "Nations, as well as individuals, have a character, a certain dignity, which they must preserve at the risk of their existence."[75] Sovereign dignity isn't only a matter of courtiers fawning and scraping, of ambassadors huffing and puffing, of Queen Elizabeth's aggrandizing and feasting. It would be degrading for Parliament to stoop to negotiate with the unruly colonists. Better to kill them.

Not that everyone in Britain saw it that way. Hugh Baillie pounced on Macpherson's concession that it would be disastrous to vest sovereignty in one man and insisted that it would

74. *DNB*, s.v. "Macpherson, James (1736–1796)."

75. [James Macpherson], *The Rights of Great Britain Asserted against the Claims of America: Being an Answer to the Declaration of the General Congress* (London, 1776), 14, 87.

be as disastrous to vest it anywhere else. "Placing unbounded, or arbitrary power above the law, in any number of men, is equally bad and destructive of property, as placing that power in one man."[76] Nor did everyone in America rally to the Continental Congress. But John Adams saw the same menacing implications of sovereignty as did Baillie. "The fundamental article of my political creed," he wrote to Jefferson, "is, that despotism, or unlimited sovereignty, or absolute power, is the same in a majority of a popular assembly, an aristocratical council, an oligarchical junto, and a single emperor. Equally arbitrary, cruel, bloody, and in every respect diabolical."[77] If you were taken aback by the stunts of the Stuarts, you had to realize that the problem wasn't monarchy and the solution wasn't transferring sovereignty to Parliament or whoever or wherever or whatever else. The problem was sovereignty.

Like the Continental Congress, Tom Paine clearly grasped the stakes; unlike that body, he could turn a phrase. In *Common Sense*, that runaway bestseller of 1776, Paine exulted, "in America the law is king. For as in absolute governments the King is law, so in free countries the law *ought* to be King, and there ought to be no other."[78] Or, as he put it on another occasion, "I am a Citizen of a country which knows no

76. [Hugh Baillie], *Some Observations on a Pamphlet Lately Published, Entitled The Rights of Great-Britain Asserted against the Claims of America, Being an Answer to the Declaration of the General Congress* (London, 1776), 1. See too M[anasseh] Dawes, *The Nature and Extent of Supreme Power* (London, 1783), 23; *The Means of Effectually Preventing Theft and Robbery* (London, 1783), 104.

77. John Adams to Thomas Jefferson, 13 November 1815, in *The Works of John Adams*, ed. Charles Francis Adams, 10 vols. (Boston, 1850–56), 10:174. See too John Adams, *A Defence of the Constitutions of Government of the United States of America*, 3 vols. (London, 1787–88), 3:304–5.

78. An Englishman, *Common Sense* (Philadelphia, 1776), 32.

other Majesty than that of the People—no other Government than that of the Representative body—no other Sovereignty than that of the Laws."[79] This is more than a republican rejection of monarchy. It's an emphatic rejection of the command theory of law. Twenty years after *Common Sense*, a letter in a newspaper fastened on the essential contrast: "In Monarchical governments the King is law—In Representative governments the law is King."[80] In 1812, a Maryland legislative committee reporting on Baltimore riots appealed to "the sovereignty of the law."[81]

Triumphant in their revolution, having learned a bitter lesson on the joys of untrammeled political authority, the colonists turned to sculpting a new federal constitution with limits built into it, some, canonically, by the enumeration of congressional powers in Article I, some by the constitutional amendments demanded in one state ratifying convention after another and adopted soon after.[82] In other ways, too, the new federal government was sclerotic by design, with Congress's

79. Thomas Paine, *Thoughts on the Peace, and the Probable Advantages Thereof to the United States of America*, new ed. (London, 1791), 23. See too "Democracy," *Boston Quarterly Review* (January 1838), in *The Early Works of Orestes A. Brownson*, ed. Patrick W. Carey, 7 vols. (Milwaukee: Marquette University Press, 2000–2007), 3:277–78.

80. Philo Virtutus, "Monarchical and Representative Government Contrasted," *Otsego Herald* (21 April 1796).

81. *The War of 1812: Writings from America's Second War of Independence*, ed. Donald R. Hickey (New York: Library of America, 2013), 55, 68. For explicit rejections of "law is king" in the name of popular sovereignty, see "The People Are King," *Kansas Agitator* (26 January 1893); "Jo McDill's Musings," *Kansas Agitator* (13 February 1903).

82. For an illuminating history of the shifting referents of what we now think of as the Bill of Rights, see Gerard N. Magliocca, *The Heart of the Constitution: How the Bill of Rights Became the Bill of Rights* (New York: Oxford University Press, 2018). Thanks to Richard Primus for the reference.

two houses responsive to different constituencies, serving with different staggered terms, open to presidential veto of the measures they manage to agree on, and so on. Many colonists understood the stakes. In print, James Wilson already had thumbed his nose at Blackstone's insistence on sovereignty.[83] In person, he thumbed his nose at Blackstone's thought that Parliament's power was "absolute without control. The idea of a constitution, limiting and superintending the operations of legislative authority, seems not to have been accurately understood in Britain. There are, at least, no traces of practice, conformable to such a principle. The British constitution is just what the British parliament pleases. . . . To control the power and conduct of the legislature by an over-ruling constitution, was an improvement in the science and practice of government, reserved to the American states."[84] Tenacious as a terrier with a squirming rodent in his jaws, Wilson returned to savaging Blackstone in lectures he gave as a law professor and Supreme Court justice. With its background insistence on sovereign power, Blackstone's view of law, he declared, was "dangerous and unsound"; indeed, it held the "seeds of despotism." It didn't even make sense of English government.[85]

So too St. George Tucker, the law professor and judge who prepared America's 1803 edition of Blackstone's *Commentaries*, calmly took issue with Blackstone's celebrated view of sovereignty. "That supreme, irresistible, absolute, uncontrolled

83. [James Wilson], *Considerations on the Nature and Extent of the Legislative Authority of the British Parliament* (Philadelphia, 1774), 2–3.

84. *Debates of the Convention, of the State of Pennsylvania, on the Constitution Proposed for the Government of the United States* (Philadelphia, 1788), 38 (26 November 1787).

85. *Lectures on Law*, chap. 5, in *The Works of the Honorable James Wilson, L.L.D.*, 3 vols. (Philadelphia, 1804), 1:179–85. See too Representative Daniel Buck (F-VT), *History of Congress* (7 March 1796); A Southern Inquirer, *"Popular Sovereignty": The Reviewer Reviewed* ([Washington, DC, 1859?]), 19.

authority, of which the commentator makes mention . . . doth not reside in the legislature, nor in any other of the branches of the Government, nor in the whole of them united. For if it did reside in them, or either of them, then there would be no limits, such as may be found in all the American Constitutions, to the powers of Government."[86] Americans who imbibed their Blackstone from this edition were assured right away that the master had made a mistake—or, if you like, were inoculated against the virus of sovereignty.

The colonists didn't just draft and ratify the new federal Constitution. They were already hurling themselves into the task of forging and renewing state constitutions, too.[87] Scant months after the Declaration of Independence, Pennsylvania adopted a new constitution. Denouncing the "most cruel and unjust war" George III was waging against the colonies "for the avowed purpose of reducing them to a total and abject submission to the despotic domination of the British parliament"—or, as English loyalists would have had it, to sovereignty—the constitution opened with a generous dollop of individual rights against the state.[88] So did Maryland's and North Carolina's constitutions, later that same year.[89] One provision of New Jersey's constitution of 3 July 1776 is telling: "That all criminals shall be admitted to the same privileges of witnesses and counsel, as their prosecutors are or shall be entitled to."[90] Contrast Charles insisting he had to have the right to throw

86. *Blackstone's Commentaries*, 5 vols. (Philadelphia, 1803), 1:49 n.; and see 1:228.

87. The texts of all state constitutions over time are available at http://www.stateconstitutions.umd.edu/index.aspx (last visited 27 August 2018).

88. Constitution of Pennsylvania, 28 September 1776.

89. Constitution of Maryland, 10 November 1776; Constitution of North Carolina, 18 December 1776.

90. Constitution of New Jersey, 3 July 1776, Art. IX.

men in jail without even charging them. Whether you're inclined to celebrate such protections for criminal suspects is irrelevant for my purposes. What matters instead is seeing a limit to sovereign authority. Squint as hard as I can, I just can't get myself even to glimpse a political solecism, an incoherent and lethal defiance of the necessary logic of political authority. All I can see is a homespun but important reminder of how salutary limits on state authority can be. The usual story is that American state governments enjoy indefinite police powers. But state constitutions impose limits, too. As one 1832 observer put it, "It will be observed on consulting some of the state constitutions, that they contain words expressive of a grant of powers, which though limited, are sovereign within the limits."[91]

By the 1830s, John Quincy Adams sounded serene in rubbishing the insistence that sovereignty had to be unlimited. Airily dismissing Hobbes's *Leviathan* in his diary, Adams wrote, "there is nothing in the book worth retaining." Filmer's account, he added days later, was "utterly absurd."[92] Nor did Adams keep his sentiments secret. Addressing the citizens of Quincy at their 1831 celebration of the Fourth of July, he branded Blackstone's bits on sovereignty "a false definition of the term *sovereignty*; an erroneous estimate of the extent of *sovereign* power!" Blackstone had it backwards. "Unlimited power belongs not to the nature of man; and rotten will be the foundation of every government leaning upon such a maxim for its support." In the clutches of Blackstone's invidious fantasy, Parliament had misunderstood the colonies from

91. Benjamin L. Oliver, *The Rights of an American Citizen* (Boston, 1832), 136.

92. John Quincy Adams, *Diaries*, ed. David Waldstreicher, 2 vols. (New York: Library of America, 2017), 2:353 (26 March 1835), 355 (31 March 1835).

the start. "There was no such thing in [state] constitutions as an absolute, irresistible, despotic power, lurking *somewhere* under the cabalistic denomination of *sovereignty*."[93] In 1833, Daniel Webster remarked, "The sovereignty of government is an idea belonging to the other side of the Atlantic. No such thing is known in North America. Our governments are all limited . . . all being restrained by written constitutions."[94]

Then again, the apparent serenity had to be laced with jittery tension. The stakes by the 1830s were more fraught than they might have looked immediately after the revolution. Adams and Webster were also fencing with South Carolina's insistence on the right of sovereign states to nullify federal laws, with what they took to be the baleful genius of John Calhoun threatening the fundamentals of American government. No wonder that one exasperated critic charged that "the Nullifiers draw all their arguments from England and other monarchies, among whom, of course Sovereignty and Allegiance are absolute terms. This is the very point in which our system is so peculiar. There is nothing very extraordinary in

93. John Quincy Adams, *An Oration Addressed to the Citizens of the Town of Quincy, on the Fourth of July, 1831* (Boston, 1831), 12–13, 21–22. For an approving review, see "Mr. Adams's Oration," *American Traveller* (26 July 1831). For partial agreement with Adams, see G.S., "Sovereignty," *Examiner, and Journal of Political Economy: Devoted to the Advancement of the Cause of State Rights and Free Trade* (5 March and 16 April 1834). See too Adams, *An Oration Delivered before the Inhabitants of the Town of Newburyport, at Their Request, on the Sixty-First Anniversary of the Declaration of Independence* (Newburyport, 1837), 9, 25–26. Decades later, one of Adams's grandsons would sketch a history with the same lesson: Henry Brooks Adams, "The Session," *North American Review* (July 1870). And see the remarks of Senator William B. Bate (D-TN), *Congressional Record* (20 December 1892).

94. "The Constitution Not a Compact between Sovereign States," in *The Works of Daniel Webster*, 6 vols. (Boston, 1851), 3:469; or in *Gales & Seaton's Register* (16 February 1833).

the Constitution of the United States, except this very thing, a Government at once Sovereign and limited."[95] No wonder that a savvy writer at the *Charleston Courier*—we'll see more of his remarkable work—joined the squadron taking deadly aim at Blackstone in 1834: "the doctrine of Blackstone . . . is fatal to the idea, as familiar in *practice* as it is in the theory, of *limited* sovereignty, and makes sovereignty synonymous with despotism and arbitrary rule."[96] No wonder that in his 1859 address at the opening of the University of Chicago's law school, David Dudley Field returned with a vengeance, without an acknowledgment, to Paine's formulation. "The law is our only sovereign. We have enthroned it."[97] The view resounded in the far reaches of the frontier: "Laws are the sovereigns of sovereigns," declared one Montana newspaper in 1878; "constitutions and laws are above sovereigns," agreed another in 1902.[98] If you're

95. *An Answer to Tract No. 16, of the Free Trade Association* (Charleston, 1834), 6. This pamphlet is responding to G.S., "For the Examiner: Sovereignty—No. 1," *Examiner, and Journal of Political Economy: Devoted to the Advancement of the Cause of State Rights and Free Trade* (5 March 1834), agreeing that Vattel's and Grotius's "definitions of sovereignty are objectionable," Blackstone's "still more objectionable," but still rejecting John Quincy Adams's Quincy oration of 4 July 1831, quoted and cited above. See too G.S., "Sovereignty—No. 2," *Examiner, and Journal of Political Economy* (16 April 1834).

96. "Sovereignty," *Charleston Courier* (7 May 1834); and see "Mr. Smith's Speech," *Charleston Courier* (8 May 1834); "The Compromise," *Charleston Courier* (16 January 1835); "Conventions, and the South Carolina State Convention," *Charleston Courier* (9 September 1862). I wonder whether the *Answer* of the preceding note is the work of the same writer.

97. David Dudley Field, *The Magnitude and Importance of Legal Science* (n.p., n.d.), 16. Some of the address is reported in "Address of Hon. David Dudley Field on the Opening of the Law School of the University of Chicago, Sept. 21, 1859," *Press and Tribune* (22 September 1859). There are contradictory accounts of the history of that law school. See James E. Babb, "Union College of Law, Chicago," *Green Bag* (August 1889).

98. "Golden Sheaves," *Rocky Mountain Husbandman* (9 May 1878); "Timely Topics," *Western News* (9 July 1902), also in *Lewiston Teller* (3 July

Bodin or Hobbes or Blackstone or . . . , that's puerile nonsense. If you're an American with your wits about you, it names a live and valuable possibility. Genuine serenity came easier to Woodrow Wilson, lecturing on sovereignty to Princeton's faculty club decades after the nullification controversy and the Civil War alike: "We have been mistaken in looking for any unlimited power."[99] True, you can trace a line of later American political scientists who seem not to have heard the news. The founder of Johns Hopkins's political science department was still at it in 1924, with a boldface typographical flourish you'll forgive me for dropping: "Sovereignty Cannot Be Limited."[100]

1902). For doggerel, see "Law Is King," *Record-Union* (11 August 1894), also in Osman Castle Hooper, *The Shepherd Wind and Other Verses* (Columbus, OH, 1916), 11. Paine's sentiment made it back across the Atlantic: John Barnard Byles, *A Discourse on the Present State of the Law of England* (London, 1829), 16–17.

99. "Lecture on Sovereignty" (9 November 1891), in *The Papers of Woodrow Wilson*, ed. Arthur S. Link et al., 69 vols. (Princeton, NJ: Princeton University Press, 1966–94), 7:333.

100. Westel W. Willoughby, *The Fundamental Concepts of Public Law* (New York: Macmillan, 1924), 76. With the dubious trademark insistence on a "logical deduction" of what "must necessarily be" true, see too Westel Woodbury Willoughby, *An Examination of the Nature of the State: A Study in Political Philosophy* (New York, 1896), 181–82. One wishes Willoughby had read, or taken to heart, George H. Smith, *A Critical History of Modern English Jurisprudence* (San Francisco, 1893), 12: "the term *sovereignty* has come to be, what is called, a question-begging term. For, as commonly used, it assumes the theory connoted by it; and argument in support of it becomes superfluous, and against it impossible"; or that he had read, or taken to heart, the more sweeping attack in Philemon Bliss, *Of Sovereignty* (Boston, 1885), for instance, 71: "The fetich of sovereignty—the exacting, imposing something—has so commanded our worship as to blind us to the fact that it is but a gilded, dumb image." For more insistence that sovereignty cannot be limited, see Frederic A. Ogg and P. Orman Ray, *Introduction to American Government* (New York: Century, 1922), 10–13; Hans J. Morgenthau, "The Problem of Sovereignty Reconsidered," *Columbia Law Review* (April 1948), 360–61. More recently—eyebrows up, please—Rod Hague and Martin

It's best, I think, to see this chorus as defiantly—or unknowingly—clinging to a now obsolete and pernicious view.

Today we take constitutional restraints on government power for granted. For instance, today's state constitutions, routinely more detailed than the federal Constitution, rattle off one restriction on taxation after another. Let a bit of New York's constitution stand in for a zillion more examples: "Intangible personal property shall not be taxed ad valorem nor shall any excise tax be levied solely because of the ownership or possession thereof, except that the income therefrom may be taken into consideration in computing any excise tax measured by income generally. Undistributed profits shall not be taxed."[101] The mind-numbing detail might obscure the stakes: should the legislature pass any rule running afoul of the provision, it would be legally void. Any New York taxpayer allegedly owing tax under such a rule would have standing to challenge it in court. Were New York stupid—and resourceful—enough to hire lawyers hypnotized by Blackstone's incantation, those lawyers might appeal to the *Commentaries*: Parliament "hath sovereign and uncontrollable authority in the making, confirming, enlarging, restraining, abrogating, repealing, reviving, and expounding of laws, concerning matters of all possible denominations, ecclesiastical or temporal, civil, military, maritime, or criminal: this being the place where that absolute despotic power, which must in all governments reside somewhere, is intrusted by the constitution of these kingdoms."[102] And they might insist—you can imagine, or lampoon, a certain kind of originalist thinking this way—that New York's legislature inherited whatever powers Parliament had. But no

---

Harrop, *Comparative Government and Politics: An Introduction*, 7th ed. (New York: Palgrave Macmillan, 2007), 17.

101. Art. XVI, § 3.

102. Blackstone, *Commentaries*, 1:156.

real lawyer would press such a ludicrous argument. No real New York court would be even vaguely tempted by it. Whatever British lawyers still say about parliamentary omnicompetence, American legislatures are different. We can limit the state's taxing authority, just as we can limit any and every exercise of state authority.

Well over a century before these rhapsodies to constitutionalism, Hobbes had rolled his eyes at the rule of law: "What man, that has his natural Senses, though he can neither write nor read, does not find himself governed by them he fears, and believes can kill or hurt him when he obeyeth not? or that believes the Law can hurt him; that is, Words, and Paper, without the Hands, and Swords of men?"[103] Within several years, James Harrington had ridiculed Hobbes's gibe: as if, he quipped, an army facing a gunner with a cannon weren't afraid of the weapon, "which without a hand to give fire unto it, is but cold Iron," but afraid only of the gunner.[104]

To say the screamingly obvious, there are tricky issues attempting to institutionalize the rule of law. Madison was right to caution that "parchment barriers" won't do the trick, that it takes more than writing down rules.[105] News flash from the Department of Banal Truths: the Soviet constitution, a masterpiece of human rights, didn't stop the gulag. So arises the crucial appeal to checks and balances, the uneasy jostling created by the separation of powers: "Ambition must be made to counteract ambition. The interest of the man must be connected with the constitutional rights of the place."[106] So too for

103. *Leviathan*, 377–78.

104. [James Harrington], *The Common-wealth of Oceana* (London, 1656), 2.

105. *Federalist* no. 48.

106. *Federalist* no. 51. See too Alexander Addison, *Observations on the Speech of Albert Gallatin* (Washington, [PA], 1798), 15.

ongoing rivalry between state and federal governments. Addressing New York's ratifying convention, Hamilton underlined the point. "This balance between the National and State governments ought to be dwelt on with peculiar attention, as it is of the utmost importance. It forms a double security to the people. If one encroaches on their rights they will find a powerful protection in the other. Indeed, they will both be prevented from overpassing their constitutional limits by a certain rivalship, which will ever subsist between them."[107] Once again, the classic theory of sovereignty has things all wrong. Insisting on constitutional limits doesn't threaten political collapse and anarchy. Nor does fracturing government authority to secure those limits. The classic theory of sovereignty doesn't lay out some timeless truths of politics. It doesn't identify some metaphysical or ontological necessity, whatever that might mean. It's a contingent bid to deal with the problems of early modern Europe, especially religious civil war.

So it's also a mistake, or so I'll argue later, to imagine that the project of making good on the rule of law is necessarily quixotic, that somehow a moment of pre-legal will or command must always emerge, as if say Hobbes were onto

107. *The Works of Alexander Hamilton*, ed. Henry Cabot Lodge, 12 vols. (New York: G. P. Putnam's Sons, 1904), 2:28 (21 June 1788). See too George Ramsay, *A Disquisition on Government* (Edinburgh, 1837), 60, 106. On separation of powers and state/federal relations, see too John Taylor, *Construction Construed, and Constitutions Vindicated* (Richmond, 1820), 52–53, and the blurb on it Jefferson "cooked up," in his words: Jefferson to Judge Spencer Roane, 27 June 1821, in *The Writings of Thomas Jefferson*, ed. Paul Leicester Ford, 10 vols. (New York, 1899), 10:189–90 n.; but note too Jefferson to Thomas Ritchie, 25 December 1820, in *Writings*, 10:169–71. Finally, see John Quincy Adams's inaugural address of 1825: *A Compilation of the Messages and Papers of the Presidents*, ed. James D. Richardson, 11 vols. (n.p.: Bureau of National Literature and Art, 1910), 2:862.

something, when in fact he was just mocking a reification that no one has ever been clueless enough to fall for. I confess too that I've delicately sidestepped some appeals to popular sovereignty in the sources I've introduced, most notably perhaps from St. George Tucker and James Wilson. I don't think they matter. Later I'll explain why.

I'll close this chapter with an excerpt from a 1916 account of Americanism: "What constitutional government intended to do was to end forever the idea that there is any rightful depository of unlimited power; in brief, to destroy the error that anyone's will is law, and to establish the principle that law is not a product of will, but a system of rules for the regulation of will, derived from the authority of reason."[108] You might well think that last line an obscure bit of jurisprudence. But I want to insist on how utterly banal—for us, here, now, where it happens that "us" is hundreds of millions of people, and "here" is not just the United States, and "now" has been for quite some time—this bid to constrain unlimited power is, how odd it makes the command theory of law look, and then how weirdly counterintuitive the classic theory of sovereignty must now seem, with its insistence that sovereign authority must be unlimited. The shift here is not one of "discourse," a mere *façon de parler*. It depends on actual changes in governing arrangements, on successful struggles in one country after another to constrain political authority. And again I see no reason to construe these changes in some detached or value-neutral or relativist way, as if we happen to have different commitments these days. I think it painfully obvious we should embrace limits on political authority as beneficial, even crucial.

108. David Jayne Hill, *Americanism: What It Is* (New York: D. Appleton, 1916), 103.

Standing alone, constitutional limits don't gut the concept of sovereignty. Recall that the classic theory defines sovereignty with three criteria: it's a locus of political authority that's unlimited, undivided, and unaccountable. So far all I've done is rehearse some of the battles surrounding limits. So there's room yet for the sort of view the attorney general of Massachusetts articulated in 1791: "Sovereignty must, in its nature, be absolute and uncontrollable by any civil authority, with respect to the objects to which it extends. A subordinate sovereignty is nonsense: a subordinate, uncontrollable power is a contradiction in terms: But there may be a political sovereignty, limited as to the objects of its extension: It may extend to some things, and not to others, or be vested for some purposes, and not for others."[109] There's room, that is, to surrender on limits but think that we still need sovereign authority, so modified: undivided and unaccountable authority.

Quite so. But the classic theory would suffer other crippling, even mortal, blows. Time to chart a new set of catastrophic injuries.

109. James Sullivan, *Observations upon the Government of the United States of America* (Boston, 1791), 22. Sullivan is identified on the title page; later he became the state's governor. See too William Tooker, *Of the Fabrique of the Church and Church-mens Liuings* (London, 1604), 99–100; Philip Warwick, *A Discourse of Government* (London, 1694), 19–20; "Federal Relations," *Richmond Enquirer* (24 March 1833); George Ramsay, *A Disquisition on Government* (Edinburgh, 1837), 60, 106; Joseph Story, *Commentaries on the Law of Bills of Exchange*, 2nd ed. (Boston, 1847), 31; "Political Truths—Right of Self-Government—Popular Sovereignty," *National Era* (31 December 1857); *Secession: Letters of Amos Kendall* (Washington, [DC], 1861), 16; *Daily Courant* (28 May 1863); Alpheus Todd, *On Parliamentary Government in England*, 2 vols. (London, 1867–69), 1:168 (but compare 1:246).

3
Divided

In the parliamentary debates of 1628, John Eliot spoke eloquently on behalf of the Petition of Right—and he took pains to urge that the Commons "not circumscribe the power of his Majesty." "All that I spoke," he emphasized, "was in all duty and loyalty to the king."[1] Don't chortle at what might seem Eliot's disingenuous pose. Eliot thought Charles needed to be alerted that the realm was in profound trouble, with military ventures a shambles, irreligion mounting, the government's coffers empty. Offering such advice was a time-honored parliamentary task. And in an episode I'm not exploring, Eliot was sure the Duke of Buckingham was a stereotypically evil minister who needed to be impeached. None of this necessarily indicated the slightest desire to pull down monarchy, even if Charles would jail Eliot in the Tower for his troubles.

1. *Proceedings in Parliament, 1628*, ed. Robert C. Johnson et al., 6 vols. (New Haven, CT: Yale University Press, 1977–83), 4:70, 67 (3 June 1628). See generally 4:59–79 for Eliot's prominent role on that day.

Whiling away his time there—he had plenty on his hands until he died, still a prisoner, a few years later[2]—Eliot would write *De Jure Maiestatis*, a little treatise every bit as enthusiastic about sovereignty as Bodin's or Hobbes's work. "Sovereignty in name without supreme power, is but an idle trifle," he declared. "The chief respect of order in a state consists in governing, & ruling. And ergo that is to be esteemed chief which itself rules all & is governed of none." And from supremacy follows indivisibility: "Summum (the chief) being quiddam indivisible it cannot possibly be distributed to two or more, but that in both or all the nature of chief must be diminished, if not destroyed."[3]

It isn't trivial to sort out just how this vigorous defense of an abstract conception of sovereignty does and doesn't connect up with the unfolding of Parliament's digging in against Charles. It isn't trivial to figure out just what Eliot intended in arguing for the Petition, in denying any attempt to limit Charles's power, in penning his prison treatise: nor in sorting out what contemporaries could and did make of his efforts. But I don't want to figure out those things here, though I do want to emphasize that Eliot's life and work offer a helpful reminder that there's often no tight deduction leading from abstract views of sovereignty to policy implications.

Instead I want now to explore the next criterion of the classic concept of sovereignty—that sovereign authority is "quiddam," something, indivisible. I'll conduct a tour of one political conflict after another in which partisans adamantly deny that you can divide political authority, or, as we might

2. *DNB*, s.v. "Eliot, Sir John (1592–1632)."

3. *De Jure Maiestatis . . . (1628–30) and The Letter-Book of Sir John Eliot*, ed. Alexander B. Grosart, 2 vols. ([London]: privately printed, 1882), 1:3, 9.

put it now, give one government actor jurisdiction over one set of issues, another over another. (Here I reluctantly leave aside concurrent jurisdiction, an arrangement not without theoretical or practical interest. I also leave aside the European Court of Human Rights's margin of appreciation, allowing guaranteed rights to bend in response to different nations' laws.) So it's a tour of episodes where the theory of sovereignty occluded many people's view of valuable political options; and where it also served not as any kind of peace treaty, but actually caused conflict, even war. I shouldn't have to hasten to add this, but I will. To say the theory caused conflict is not to say it was the only cause. I find that sort of idealism no more tempting than I find its classic rival, some kind of materialism on which say economic interests drive social and political change. The only thing either view has going for it is the manifest inadequacy of the other, and we'd be better off if we didn't imagine the ideal/material distinction was deep or important, some profound bit of social theory, when in fact it's just another of a zillion distinctions that might or might not be worth drawing for particular reasons in particular settings. The perennial spectacle of political actors embracing defunct or pernicious ideas might seem a familiar bit of stupidity, ironically amusing at worst: but don't dismiss the body count. Remember that political stupidity can be lethal.

We've already seen bids to divide sovereign authority, especially in the Founders' embracing the separation of powers and ongoing rivalry between state and federal governments. Dividing political authority is in fact a classic strategy for limiting it. "Opponents of unlimited sovereignty" seek "to bestow a little sovereignty here and a little there and absolute sovereignty nowhere," in Irving Babbitt's insouciant phrase, and "then . . . set up a judiciary sufficiently strong to put a veto on any of these partial sovereignties that tend to overstep their prescribed limits."[4] There's no analytic necessity here. One can imagine in principle splitting up authority between two government actors, such that whatever one can't do, the other can do: then you'd have division but no limits overall. In the real world, though, that grubby locale theorists might profitably deign to visit now and again, division and limits often come together. Regardless, if only for artificial expository purposes, here I'm focusing on dividing authority among governments and setting aside whether there are things *no* government may do. Remember that the classic theory dictates that there be a single, undivided locus of political authority.[5] Seeing how that view comes undone is on our itinerary here.

Our primary destinations are the run-up to the American Revolution; ratifying the American Constitution; nullification and the Civil War; and struggles over the League of Nations, the United Nations, and Brexit. Along the way we'll touch down briefly at other dreary vacation spots.

The Colonies Come Unglued

If you had to choose a single slogan to capture the American Revolution, the canonical choice would be "No taxation without representation!" One thing to respond to colonists'

4. Irving Babbitt, "The Political Influence of Rousseau," *Nation* (18 January 1917). See too *The Anas*, in *The Works of Thomas Jefferson*, ed. Paul Leicester Ford, 12 vols. (New York: G. P. Putnam's Sons, 1904), 1:285; Alexander Addison, *Observations on the Speech of Albert Gallatin* (Washington, [PA], 1798), 15.

5. That's why W[illiam] A[twood], *The Fundamental Constitution of the English Government* (London, 1690), repeatedly takes up Filmer, Hobbes, Grotius, Pufendorf, and Bodin.

complaints by pointing out that because of the crazed mix of unrepresented cities and rotten boroughs, the result of not reapportioning representation for endless decades, plenty of English subjects couldn't vote for parliamentary representatives either. Still, went the theory, they were virtually represented: people like them voted, and so representatives tended to their interests. After all, residents of Birmingham were governed by the same laws as residents of Old Sarum. It was another and intractably harder thing, though, to meet the colonists' riposte that English law could and did treat the colonies differently, so the theory failed. But there was also a dispute about sovereignty. And *that* dispute explains why taxation was such a big deal.[6]

Disputes between colonies and mother countries are nothing new. In the case of the American colonies, they go back over a century before the run-up to the revolution. So, for instance, Virginia's assembly, the House of Burgesses, remonstrated against the Puritans' assertion of authority in the interregnum. Like some in England, members insisted that they'd sworn oaths of allegiance and supremacy, so "no power on earth can absolve or manumit us from our obedience to our Prince, and his lawful successors." The arrival of Cromwell's gunboats shed caustically illuminating light on the matter, but the colony's articles of surrender included the sort of gesture

6. Compare John Quincy Adams, *An Oration Delivered before the Inhabitants of the Town of Newburyport, at Their Request, on the Sixty-First Anniversary of the Declaration of Independence* (Newburyport, 1837), 9; and H. T. Dickinson, "Britain's Imperial Sovereignty: The Ideological Case against the American Colonists," in *Britain and the American Revolution* (London: Longman, 1998), 81. Compare too, for instance, [Israel Mauduit], *Considerations on the American War* (London, 1776), esp. 43–44, with *Plan of Re-union between Great Britain and Her Colonies* (London, 1778), vii.

that would resonate later: "That *Virginia* shall be free from all taxes, customs, and impositions whatsoever, and none to be imposed on them without consent of the Grand Assembly, And so that neither forts nor castles be erected or garrisons maintained without their consent."[7] No one in these scanty sources explicitly invokes sovereignty.

Then too, in 1651 Maine pushed back against a parliamentary measure to regulate the colonies' trading partners. Sir Ferdinando Gorges, who'd been assigned the province, had died; so had his son. In legal limbo, the men of Maine's legislature petitioned for authority to govern and for affirmation of their "Immunities and Privileges as freeborn Englishmen." This petition was rejected, again with no one, as far as I can tell with this scanty evidence, explicitly invoking sovereignty.[8]

Not so in 1678, when the Massachusetts legislature implored Charles II "that your Majesty, according to your innate wisdom and goodness, will receive no impressions from any that, for their own evil ends, shall endeavour (by false or mistaken reports) to represent us as affecting and aspiring to a

7. Declaration of the Assembly, March 1650/51, in *Journals of the House of Burgesses of Virginia, 1619–1658/59*, ed. H. R. McIlwaine (Richmond: n.p., 1915), 77, 79. For context, Warren M. Billings et al., *Colonial Virginia: A History* (White Plains, NY: kto, 1986), 50–51. Ex-president Tyler adduced the episode: "Celebration at Jamestown: Report of the Proceedings of the Celebration of the Two Hundred and Fiftieth Anniversary of the English Settlement at Jamestown," *Southern Literary Messenger* (June 1857), 446. See Novanglus no. 7 in John Adams, *Revolutionary Writings, 1755–1775*, ed. Gordon S. Wood (New York: Library of America, 2011), 519–20 (6 March 1775).

8. *Documentary History of the State of Maine . . . Containing the Farnham Papers, 1603–1688*, comp. Mary Frances Farnham (Portland: Maine Historical Society, 1901), 268 (15 December 1651). For the Act for Prohibiting Trade with the Barbadoes, Virginia, Bermuda, and Antego, see *Acts and Ordinances of the Interregnum, 1642–1660*, ed. C. H. Firth and R. S. Rait, 3 vols. (London: His Majesty's Stationery Office, 1911), 2:425–29 (3 October 1650).

greatness independent on your Majesty's sovereignty over us."[9] Summoning Massachusetts's agents, Whitehall demanded an explanation of why individuals were buying land from the Sachem Indians without complying with the legal requirement that they get the magistrates' permission. Dissatisfied with the response,

> His Majesty ordered that letters be sent to Massachusetts and all the Colonies in New England, requiring them to leave all things relating to the King's Province in the same posture it now is as to the possession and government, and to give them to understand that the absolute sovereignty and particular propriety of all that country is vested in His Majesty by the surrender of the Sachems, and that no further settlement be there made upon any title whatsoever until those who pretend any claim have made out their title, and that they send over persons duly instructed to make the same appear, or in default His Majesty will give order for the government and settlement of said Province.[10]

It would be wrong to infer that sometime between 1651 and 1678, the concept of sovereignty abruptly took over. But it would also be wrong to assume that those earlier exchanges must have depended implicitly on the concept of sovereignty. That would beg the question. I don't doubt that sovereignty is one conceptual frame for apprehending—and swatting

9. "Copy of a *Petition and Address of the General Court of Massachusetts to the King*," in *Hutchinson Papers*, 2 vols. (Albany, 1865), 2:255 (10 October 1678).

10. *Cal. S. P. Col., 1677–1680*, 309 (13 December 1678).

away—a putative jurisdictional division of labor. But I deny that it's the only available frame, let alone a necessary one. Put it this way: if you think it obvious that the earlier exchanges are already about sovereignty, maybe you're not discerning something deep but unstated. Maybe you're imposing a structure that isn't there.

Now compare 1749, when the House of Commons was considering petitions from the agents for Connecticut, Pennsylvania, and Rhode Island. Connecticut's agent was worried about the Bill to Regulate and Restrain Paper Bills of Credit. He urged that the charter from Charles II entitled Connecticut to have a governor, a deputy governor, and twelve elected assistants, all "impowered . . . to make, ordain, and establish, all manner of wholesome and reasonable laws." On behalf of Rhode Island, Richard Partridge invoked a similar royal charter. One could see these assertions of legal independence as grounded in the concept of sovereignty—if one thinks the king's issuing royal charters was an exercise of sovereignty. No wonder that Partridge reminded Parliament that "when any expeditions have been on foot, against the common enemy, by wars commenced in Europe," the colony's inhabitants "have always most readily joined their assistance, when required from their sovereign."[11] So here sovereignty doesn't drive a wedge between the colonies and Britain; it explains how they can continue to get along. The bill died in committee.

Notoriously, by the 1760s, these waters were less easily calmed. In March 1764, Lord Grenville insisted that Britain could, should, must collect more than customs duties. "Some-

11. *Proceedings and Debates of the British Parliaments respecting North America,* ed. Leo Francis Stock, 5 vols. (Washington, DC: Carnegie Institution of Washington, 1924–41), 5:304–8 (15 March 1749); for the introduction of the bill, 5:298; for its death, 5:298 n. 14.

thing farther must be thought of. A stamp duty in America; 'twas easily collected, without a large body of officers. Britain has an inherent right to lay inland duties there. The very sovereignty of this kingdom depends on it."[12] "A power to lay on taxes," fumed a bellicose Pacificus, "is inseparable from the rights of Sovereignty. Who ever heard of a Sovereign who could not tax his subjects? . . . An American only could have thought of so impotent a Sovereignty, a Sovereignty which would be such only in name; but, like the Log in the fable, might be insulted at pleasure by American frogs."[13]

These appeals to sovereignty could turn into pure symbolic politics. Take, for instance, the January 1766 joint meeting of the Houses, when some members denounced the government for being too complaisant. Defending the Stamp Act, Hans Stanley announced, "The tax was not a twentieth part of what they could afford to pay; but that was not the point: he had rather have a peppercorn to acknowledge our sovereignty, than millions paid into the Treasury without it." I suspect sovereignty was in the margins, too, when Lord Clare held "that the honour and dignity of the kingdom obliged us to compel the execution of the stamp act, except where the right was acknowledged, and the repeal solicited as a favour."[14] (A decade later, such bids to maintain dignity inspired an incredulous response: "I am well aware that it is said we must maintain the dignity of Parliament. Let me ask, what dignity is that which

12. *Proceedings and Debates of the British Parliament respecting North America, 1754–1783*, ed. R. C. Simmons and P. D. G. Thomas, 6 vols. (Millwood and White Plains, NY: Kraus International, 1982–87), 1:492 (9 March 1764).

13. Pacificus, "To the Printer," *Gazetteer and New Daily Advertiser* (26 October 1765).

14. *Proceedings and Debates, 1754–1783*, 2:81, 84 (14 January 1766).

will not descend to make millions happy . . . ? What dignity is that which, to enforce a disputed mode of obtaining revenue, will destroy commerce, spread poverty and desolation, and dry up every channel, every source from which revenue or any real substantial benefit can be expected?")[15] The same symbolic politics motivated Lord North to dig in on a financially insignificant tax on tea: "the duty on tea must be maintained, as a mark of the supremacy of Parliament, and an efficient declaration of their right to govern the colonies."[16] No surprise: North already had insisted that "whatever prudence or policy might hereafter induce," he wouldn't back down on the Paper and Glass Act "*till we saw America prostrate at our feet*."[17] The language of peppercorns and prostration elicited jeers, but a supercilious North didn't back down.[18] "They deny our legislative authority," he snarled. "If they deny authority in one instance it goes to all. We must control them or submit

15. *Proceedings and Debates, 1754–1783*, 6:400 (Mr. Cruger, 20 February 1776).

16. *Proceedings and Debates, 1754–1783*, 3:239 (5 March 1770).

17. *Proceedings and Debates, 1754–1783*, 3:13 (8 November 1768). See too Manlius Torquatus, "Written on the Repeal of the Excise on Cyder," in *A New and Impartial Collection of Interesting Letters, from the Public Papers*, 2 vols. (London, 1767), 2:149, complaining that "The Americans seek a total exemption from taxes laid on by the supreme legislature" and that "ministers, actuated by factious views, patronize demands which their duty to the nation commands them to crush."

18. *Proceedings and Debates, 1754–1783*, 3:304–5 (Burke, 9 May 1770); 4:38 (William Dowdeswell, 7 March 1774); 4:373 (North, 2 May 1774). Protests continued: *Proceedings and Debates, 1754–1783*, 4:434 (Marquess of Rockingham, 18 May 1774); 5:542 (Lord Camden, 16 March 1775); 6:117 (Burke, 26 October 1775), leading to North's protest that his words had been misconstrued and misreported, 6:118 (26 October 1775). That reference to peppercorns was scornfully hurled back in the wonderfully intemperate "The London Cit," *Gazette of the United States* (13 May 1789).

to them."[19] Earl Talbot glared at the colonies' dismal record: "they have been obstinate, undutiful and ungovernable from the beginning." So Parliament would have to teach the same old lesson, "that the supreme power retains the sovereignty over its several subordinate members, and of course" that includes "the right of taxation."[20] Before we saw James I assuring Parliament in 1610 "that the king may take subsidies without the consent of his people, he condemns the doctrine[] as absurd": that concession had been forgotten. So had Clarendon's realization that governments could readily forswear the right to tax without consent: "As there is no Sovereign in *Europe* who pretends to this right of Sovereignty, so there was never any Kingdom, or considerable Country lost by want of it, or preserv'd by the actual exercise of it."[21]

I'm generally reluctant to draw tight links between texts in political theory and what political actors are up to—the "transmission" lines are tangled, the "messages" routinely garbled, the political actors transfixed by exigencies not incandescent in theory's firmament—but in February 1766 Lord Chancellor Northington offered a striking rendition of the classic account of sovereignty, and it wouldn't surprise me if Northington, himself a lawyer, had read Blackstone's account, published the previous year. "Every government can arbitrarily impose laws on all its subjects," said Northington; "there must be a supreme dominion in every state; whether monarchical, aristocratical, democratical, or mixed. And all the subjects of

19. *Proceedings and Debates, 1754–1783*, 4:76 (14 March 1774).

20. *Proceedings and Debates, 1754–1783*, 6:441 (5 March 1776).

21. Edward [Hyde], Earl of Clarendon, *A Brief View and Survey of the Dangerous and Pernicious Errors to Church and State, in Mr. Hobbes's Book, Entitled Leviathan* (Oxford, 1676), 176.

each state are bound by the laws made by government."[22] The next month, the Declaratory Act unceremoniously—or, perhaps, quite ceremoniously—shoved aside any and all claims to autonomy the colonies offered: "all resolutions, votes, orders, and proceedings, in any of the said colonies or plantations, whereby the power and authority of the Parliament of *Great Britain* to make laws and statutes as aforesaid is denied, or drawn into question, are, and are hereby declared to be, utterly null and void to all intents and purposes whatsoever."[23] Thomas Pownall urged the Commons to rivet its attention on "the sovereignty and supremacy of Parliaments. That is a line from which you ought never to deviate, which ought never to be out of sight. The Parliament hath and must have . . . has had, and ever will have, a sovereign supreme power and jurisdiction over every part of the dominions of the state, to make laws in all cases whatsoever; this is a proposition which exists of absolute necessity." Parliament's Declaratory Act was "a visible sign and symbol of its sovereignty . . . and if ever anyone . . . should attempt to erase, or to remove it, the whole edifice would fall to pieces."[24] A 1768 pamphleteer insisted too on "supreme and absolute sovereignty." "Without a right to tax," he asserted, "there can be no sovereignty."[25] In 1769, Allan Ramsay sneered at the "vulgar misapprehension" that taxation would be illegitimate without popular consent. In the colonies, in England, in Turkey, anywhere and everywhere, sovereignty was good enough. "*Sovereignty* admits of no degrees, it is always

22. *Proceedings and Debates, 1754–1783*, 2:129 (3 February 1766); *DNB*, s.v. "Henley, Robert, first Earl of Northington (c. 1708–1772)."

23. 6 Geo. III c. 11 (18 March 1766).

24. *Proceedings and Debates, 1754–1783*, 3:154–55 (19 April 1769).

25. *The Constitutional Right of the Legislature of Great Britain, to Tax the British Colonies in America, Impartially Stated* (London, 1768), 41, 5.

supreme, and to level it, is, in effect, to destroy it."[26] Thomas Hutchinson, royalist governor of Massachusetts, saluted Ramsay's text as "the best thing I have ever seen on the subject."[27]

Various actors repurposed *imperium in imperio* to drive home the alleged fallacies of the colonists' appeal for some kind of jurisdictional autonomy. "Two supreme independent authorities cannot exist in the same state," Massachusettensis instructed his readers. "It would be what is called *imperium in imperio*, the height of political absurdity."[28] The king, insisted Joseph Galloway, "cannot constitute inferior communities with rights, powers, and privileges independent of the State; because this would be either to dismember them from it, or to establish an *imperium in imperio*, a State within a State, the greatest of all political MONSTERS!"[29] (That last came with an explicit nod to Pufendorf's warning that a supreme governor who tried to establish an unaccountable body would be setting up "a State within a State," "admitting two Heads in the

26. [Allan Ramsay], *Thoughts on the Origin and Nature of Government* (London, 1769), 53. See too *The Late Occurrences in North America, and Policy of Great Britain, Considered* (London, 1766), 3; John Wesley, *A Calm Address to Our American Colonies* ([London?], [1775?]), n.p. (broadside), or Wesley, *A Calm Address to Our American Colonies*, new ed., corr. and enlarged (London, [1775]), 20. For scoffing at Wesley's view, see *Political Empiricism: A Letter to the Rev. John Wesley* (London, 1776), 27.

27. Bernard Bailyn, *The Ordeal of Thomas Hutchinson* (Cambridge, MA: Belknap Press, Harvard University Press, 1974), 77.

28. Massachusettensis, "To the Inhabitants of the Province of Massachusetts-Bay," *New-Hampshire Gazette, and Historical Chronicle* (24 March 1775).

29. An American [Joseph Galloway], *Political Reflections on the Royal, Proprietary, and Charter Governments of the American Colonies* (London, 1782), 30–31. See too [Joseph Galloway], *A Candid Examination of the Mutual Claims of Great-Britain, and the Colonies* (New York, 1775), 5–6. "To the Author of a Pamphlet, Entitled, 'A Candid Examination . . . ,'" *Pennsylvania Journal, and The Weekly Advertiser* (8 March 1775), seized on the apparently contradictory concession Galloway offered at 43.

Constitution" and making it "irregular and monstrous; which no one in his Wits will do, unless upon extreme Necessity.")[30] Then again, Massachusetts's House of Representatives flipped the script, urging that "to suppose a Parliamentary Authority over the Colonies under such Charters, would necessarily induce that Solecism in Politics, *Imperium in Imperio*."[31]

In the 1760s and '70s, many other colonists also put the classic theory of sovereignty front and center in their work. James Wilson conceded that many defenders of Parliament appealed to Blackstone. But, he continued, it didn't make sense to insist on parliamentary sovereignty if it would undo "the ultimate end of all government."[32] (Jefferson dutifully copied the passage into his commonplace book.)[33] James Otis and Stephen Hopkins flatly denied that Britain could exercise sovereignty over Americans.[34] Why the commotion about a penny tax on tea? What grownup gets frantically exercised over such

30. Samuel Pufendorf, *The Law of Nature and Nations*, trans. Mr. Carew, 5th ed. (London, 1749), 648–49.

31. *The Speeches of His Excellency Governor Hutchinson, to the General Assembly . . . with The Answers of His Majesty's Council and the House of Representatives* (Boston, 1773), 39. So too [Moses Mather], *America's Appeal to the Impartial World* (Hartford, 1775), 44.

32. [James Wilson], *Considerations on the Nature and Extent of the Legislative Authority of the British Parliament* (Philadelphia, 1774), 2–3. Contrast [Francis] Bernard, *Select Letters on the Trade and Government of America; and The Principles of Law and Polity, Applied to the American Colonies* (London, 1774), 71–85, echoing and extending Blackstone. For a characteristically amusing rendition of Wilson's maneuvers, see Carl Becker, *The Declaration of Independence: A Study in the History of Political Ideas* (New York: Harcourt, Brace, 1922), 105–13.

33. *The Commonplace Book of Thomas Jefferson: A Repertory of His Ideas on Government*, ed. Gilbert Chinard (Baltimore: Johns Hopkins University Press, 1926), 316–17.

34. James Otis, *The Rights of the British Colonies Asserted and Proved* (Boston, 1764); [Stephen Hopkins], *The Rights of Colonies Examined* (Providence, 1765).

a pittance? Writing as A Son of Liberty, Silas Downer averred, "if they can take away one penny from us against our wills, they can take all. If they have such power over our properties they must have a proportionable power over our persons; and from hence it will follow, that they can demand and take away our lives, whensoever it shall be agreeable to their sovereign wills and pleasure."[35] This isn't any old slippery-slope argument. Downer is nauseated by the same symbolic stakes that so enchanted Stanley and Lord North. If Parliament could tax tea, it would be sovereign, and if it were sovereign, there could be no limits on its authority. So the tea had to be doused in the harbor.

You can see the cosmic stakes in the alarmed October 1773 missive of Massachusetts's Committee of Correspondence. Parliament and the king were refusing to give ground on the Revenue Acts, warned the committee. "Such is the Disposition of the parliament . . . to consider themselves as *the Sovereign* of America. Is it not of the utmost importance that our Vigilance should increase?"[36] You can see the cosmic stakes too in John Adams's reflections the day after the Boston Tea Party. Letting the tea land, he recorded in his diary, would be "subjecting our Posterity forever to Egyptian Taskmasters—to Burdens, Indignities; to Ignominy, Reproach and Contempt, to Desolation and Oppression, to Poverty and Servitude."[37] You can see the cosmic stakes yet again in John Hancock's perturbed speech in

35. A Son of Liberty [Silas Downer], *A Discourse, Delivered in Providence, in the Colony of Rhode-Island . . . at the Dedication of the Tree of Liberty* (Providence, 1768), 10–11.

36. The Committee of Correspondence of Massachusetts to Other Committees of Correspondence, 21 October 1773, in *The Writings of Samuel Adams*, ed. Harry Alonzo Cushing, 4 vols. (New York: G. P. Putnam's Sons, 1904–8), 3:64.

37. Diary, 17 December 1773, in Adams, *Revolutionary Writings, 1755–1775*, 287.

Boston a few months later. The British, he announced, "have declared that they have, ever had, and of right ought ever to have, full power to make laws of sufficient validity to bind the colonies in all cases whatever." Those "mad pretensions" explained their "pretended right" to tax without American consent, and those pretensions were why the colonists' persons and property alike were insecure.[38] You can see the cosmic stakes finally in George Washington's grim acknowledgment the summer after the tea party: "I shall not undertake to say where the Line between Great Britain and the Colonies should be drawn. . . . But the Crisis is arrived when we must assert our Rights, or Submit to every Imposition that can be heap'd upon us, till custom and use, will make us as tame, & abject Slaves, as the Blacks we Rule over with such arbitrary Sway."[39] Edmund Burke famously warned that the colonists "augur misgovernment at a distance; and snuff the approach of tyranny in every tainted breeze." That's no lazy appeal to political culture. It immediately follows his announcements that the colonists read Blackstone and that General Gage thought those he was supposed to govern were "lawyers, or smatterers in law."[40] I think Burke was warning that the classic theory of sovereignty has lethal uptake.

38. John Hancock, *An Oration; Delivered March 5, 1774, at the Request of the Inhabitants of the Town of Boston*, 2nd ed. (Boston, 1774), 7. I doubt the account of Parliament's reaction offered by Lord Duncannon, *Parliamentary Debates* (12 June 1781).

39. Washington to Bryan Fairfax, 24 August 1774, in George Washington, *Writings*, ed. John Rhodehamel (New York: Library of America, 1997), 158.

40. *Speech of Edmund Burke, Esq. on Moving His Resolutions for Conciliation with the Colonies, March 22, 1775*, 3rd ed. (London, 1775), 35, 34. Contrast John Phillip Reid, *Constitutional History of the American Revolution*, 4 vols. (Madison: University of Wisconsin Press, 1986–93), 2:41–42; Paul A. Rahe, *Republics Ancient and Modern: Classical Republicanism and the American Revolution* (Chapel Hill: University of North Carolina Press, 1992), 551–55.

Whatever I think about the likes of Blackstone on sovereignty—I'll be decorous, prim, tight-lipped, and say, not much—I don't think it quite right to cast this sorry episode as British rigidity finally driving sensible Americans to rebel. Some British actors were enchanted by sovereignty, some not; some American actors were enchanted by sovereignty, some not. Whatever his parliamentary language about sovereignty and the Declaratory Act, there was also room for Pownall to sound rueful: "Those in America who have held the language and the doctrines, that there is no line between sovereign power (absolute in all cases whatsoever) and no power at all . . . have driven a people, already half mad, to utter desperation." Here Pownall was willing to carve up jurisdiction, to allow the colonial legislatures jurisdiction over "internal" affairs, making them "as such, and so far forth, absolute and sovereign."[41]

But again, there weren't enough takers for such gambits to succeed, and the theory of sovereignty is one reason why. Sovereignty polarized the debate between Britain and the colonies. No hopes for temporizing, for changing the subject and refusing to say anything about sovereignty, about "all that nonsense," as Captain Phipps jeered in vain.[42] I'm not indulging in

41. Thomas Pownall, *The Administration of the British Colonies*, 5th ed., 2 vols. (London, 1774), 2:ix, 36. See too Libermoriturus in *Boston Evening-Post* (9 November 1767). So Story is wrong in summoning up a consensus among English politicians on the Declaratory Act and Parliament's sovereignty: Joseph Story, *Commentaries on the Constitution of the United States*, 3 vols. (Boston, 1833), 1:153. Consider too Bernard Bailyn, *The Ideological Origins of the American Revolution*, enlarged ed. (Cambridge, MA: Belknap Press, Harvard University Press, 1992), 202–3. And John Quincy Adams, *An Address, Delivered . . . at the City of Washington on the Fourth of July 1821*, 2nd ed. (Cambridge, MA, 1821), 9–10, is wrong in summoning up "throughout the colonies, one general burst of indignant resistance" at Britain's "unblushing allegation of absolute and uncontrollable power [to tax] without representation and without consent."

42. *Proceedings and Debates, 1754–1783*, 4:69 (14 March 1774).

anachronism, not pretending to some superior vantage point, in suggesting that sovereignty made people stupid. Plenty of contemporaries saw it the same way. "The spirit of blindness and infatuation is gone forth," lamented Whig churchman Jonathan Shipley. "We are hurrying wildly on without any fixed design, without any important object. We pursue a vain phantom of unlimited sovereignty, which was not made for man; and reject the solid advantages of a moderate, useful and intelligible authority."[43] No hopes for deflecting sovereignty and thinking instead about prudent ways of raising money: so Burke's cry—"I am not here going into the distinctions of rights, nor attempting to mark their boundaries. I do not enter into these metaphysical distinctions; I hate the very sound of them"—fell on deaf ears.[44] Lord Camden wanted nothing to do with "the abstruse and metaphysical distinctions necessary to the investigation of the omnipotence of parliament."[45] The Earl of Chatham rose and "entirely acquiesced": "the present was not a subject proper for nice, metaphysical discussion."[46] Yet today we have political theorists keen on pursuing sovereignty as a

43. [Jonathan Shipley], *A Speech Intended to Have Been Spoken on the Bill, for Altering the Charters of the Colony of Massachusetts* (London, [1774]), 11–12.

44. *Speech of E. Burke, Esq; on American Taxation, April 19, 1774*, 3rd ed. (London, 1775), 69 (and compare 71–73). For more explicit skepticism from Burke, see *Proceedings and Debates, 1754–1783*, 6:265 (16 November 1775): "sovereignty was not in its nature an idea of abstract unity, but was capable of great complexity and infinite modification." For incisive observations about what Parliament permitted Ireland, see *An Argument in Defence of the Exclusive Right Claimed by the Colonies to Tax Themselves* (London, 1774), 112.

45. *Proceedings and Debates, 1754–1783*, 5:273 (20 January 1775). Camden would return to denouncing "the high sounding, unintelligible phrases of legislative supremacy": *Proceedings and Debates, 1754–1783*, 5:389 (7 February 1775).

46. *Proceedings and Debates, 1754–1783*, 5:273 (20 January 1775).

metaphysical topic, suitably mesmerized by the pursuit, imagining themselves as deeply perspicuous in so doing. Go figure.[47]

In the garish, blinding light of sovereignty, there were no hopes for a distinction between internal and external taxation. That distinction, like plenty of others, is rough or blurry, but still perfectly serviceable. Ben Franklin testified in Parliament that it was the key to understanding where the Americans would yield.[48] In November 1775, the colonial governor of New York thought that carving up tax jurisdiction that way might stop the combat—"could it be compatible with the dignity . . . of the British Sovereignty."[49] The distinction was found wanting not because it was blurry, but because sovereignty is indivisible: so any proposed incursion on it was an insult. That's why Joseph Galloway contemptuously branded it a distinction "which never existed, nor can exist, in reason or common sense": "there must be in every state a supreme legislative authority, universal in its extent, over every member."[50]

47. If or insofar as *metaphysics* is a term of abuse, it's available to both sides of this debate. Consider Charles Francis Adams, "The Pitfall of a Divided Sovereignty," May 1914 lecture at Johns Hopkins University, Charles Francis Adams Papers, box 38, folder 3, Massachusetts Historical Society, repeatedly sneering at "the metaphysical abstraction of a divided sovereignty" (typescript, 21; and see 11, 17). See too "Law Reports: U.S. Circuit Court: The Trial of the Savannah Pirates," *Commercial Advertiser* (28 October 1861): "counsel said he never could understand the metaphysical doctrine of a divided sovereignty." For the opinion in the case, *United States v. Baker*, 24 F. Cas. 962 (S.D.N.Y. 1861).

48. *Proceedings and Debates, 1754–1783*, 2:227–51 (13 February 1766).

49. Governor William Tyron to the Earl of Dartmouth, 11 November 1775, in *Documents Relative to the Colonial History of the State of New-York*, ed. E. B. O'Callaghan and B. Fernow, 15 vols. (Albany, 1856–57), 8:643.

50. [Joseph Galloway], *A Candid Examination of the Mutual Claims of Great-Britain, and the Colonies: with a Plan of Accommodation, on Constitutional Principles* (New York, 1775), 2, 4.

That's why William Knox furiously rejected the distinction, along with others like it. "All distinctions destroy this union; and if it can be shewn in any particular to be dissolved, it must be so in all instances whatever. There is no alternative: either the Colonies are a part of the community of Great Britain, or they are in a state of nature with respect to her, and in no case can be subject to the jurisdiction of that legislative power which represents her community, which is the British parliament."[51] That's why Hutchinson instructed his refractory assembly, "I know of no line which can be drawn between the supreme Authority of Parliament and the total Independence of the Colonies: It is impossible there should be two independent Legislatures in one and the same State."[52] (Imagine holding that view staunchly enough to say, "there is no slavery you can entail upon your children equal to that which follows from a disputed supreme authority in Government."[53] Imagine saying that with a straight face in a society where chattel slavery flourishes. It's slavery, avers Washington that same month, with unflinching recognition of blacks' "abject" plight, to live under a sovereign; it's slavery, asserts Hutchinson, not to. Want to take sides? Yes, you could cavil at this description of the alternatives. Still, if you had to choose?) That's why a member of Parliament declared "taxation and supreme au-

51. [William Knox], *The Controversy between Great Britain and Her Colonies Reviewed* (London, 1769), 50–51.

52. *Speeches of His Excellency Governor Hutchinson,* 11. See too Thomas Hutchinson, "A Dialogue between an American and a European Englishman [1768]," ed. Bernard Bailyn, *Perspectives in American History* (1975), 391, 405–6.

53. Hutchinson to ——, 8 August 1774, in *The Diary and Letters of His Excellency Thomas Hutchinson*, comp. Peter Orlando Hutchinson, 2 vols. (Boston, 1884), 1:214.

thority inseparable."[54] That's why Jonas Hanway's dialogue offered a speaker insisting, "Unless *Britain* has the *supreme legislative power*, she is not the sovereign. She cannot defend her *American Dominions*; and let who will be master of them, there must be a supreme legislative power, or the government cannot exist."[55] If you subscribe to the theory of sovereignty, so much is just common sense—no wonder Hanway chose that for his title, just as Paine chose it for his.[56] If you slip free of sovereignty's domineering clutches, this calm inference suddenly looks exactly like the bit of frantic hand-waving that it is.

Again, my claim is not that the concept of sovereignty explains the American Revolution. But I do think sovereignty enthusiasts on both sides of the Atlantic helped polarize the debate. They made the conciliatory measures offered by those who hoped to muddle through seem unacceptable, even incomprehensible. And all because of the conviction that sovereignty must be indivisible. In October 1775, scurrilous radical John Wilkes rose in the House of Commons and denounced appeals to "unmeaning phrases. . . . The *supremacy* of the legislative authority of Great Britain! This I call unintelligible jargon; instead of running the different privileges belonging to the various parts of the empire into one common mass of power, gentlemen should consider that the very first principles of good government in this wide-extended dominion, consist in sub-dividing the empire into many parts and giving to each individual an immediate interest, that the community

54. *Proceedings and Debates, 1754–1783*, 4:182 (Mr. Rice, 19 March 1774).

55. [Jonas Hanway], *Common Sense: In Nine Conferences, between a British Merchant and a Candid Merchant of America* (London, 1775), 52.

56. Sophia Rosenfeld, *Common Sense: A Political History* (Cambridge, MA: Harvard University Press, 2011), is wonderful.

to which he belongs should be well regulated."[57] But war had broken out months before. This bid to think prosaically about jurisdiction got nowhere.

So 1779 found John Adams instructing John Jay, "there is at this Hour no Medium between unlimited submission to Parliament, and entire Sovereignty."[58] So 1797 found Adams delivering his first inaugural address, recalling as if it were from days long gone, which in a way it was, "when it was first perceived, in early times, that no middle course for America remained between unlimited submission to a foreign legislature and a total independence of its claims."[59] So 1831 found John Quincy Adams ruefully confiding in his diary. "In truth the question of right as between Parliament and the Colonies, was one of those upon which it is much easier to say who was wrong, than who was right—The pretension that they had the right to bind the Colonies, in all cases whatever, and that which denied them the right to bind in any case whatever, were the two extremes, equally unfounded—and yet it is extremely difficult to draw the line where the authority of Parliament commenced, and where it closed."[60] I don't want to pretend that debates about jurisdiction are easy once you discard the con-

57. *Proceedings and Debates, 1754–1783*, 6:106 (26 October 1775).

58. John Adams to John Jay, 27 February 1779, in Adams, *Revolutionary Writings, 1775–1783*, ed. Gordon S. Wood (New York: Library of America, 2011), 206.

59. John Adams, *Writings from the New Nation, 1784–1826*, ed. Gordon S. Wood (New York: Library of America, 2016), 329.

60. John Quincy Adams, *Diaries*, ed. David Waldstreicher, 2 vols. (New York: Library of America, 2017), 2:246–47 (17 January 1831). For a more indignant retrospective look at these alleged alternatives, consider Levi I. Palmer's address in the *Independent American* (4 July 1809). And compare John Quincy Adams, *An Oration, Pronounced July 4th, 1793, at the Request of the Inhabitants of the Town of Boston* (Boston, 1793), 17.

cept of sovereignty. But I do want to insist that the difficulties driving England and the colonies to these two extremes were the fallout of that concept.

Ratifying the Constitution

Fast-forward just a bit and consider the debate over ratifying the new Constitution. You know the tale: under the Articles of Confederation, the national government's authority was more notional than real, its inability to raise troops or taxes a perpetual embarrassment, its requisitions no better than meek requests. John Adams suggested that under the Articles, "congress is not a legislative assembly, nor a representative assembly, but only a diplomatic assembly": as if it were a conference of foreign states.[61] That sounds quirky, but Adams was onto something. When Jefferson complained about this statement, Adams demurred that he'd framed it "as a Problem, rather for Consideration, than as an opinion. . . . It is a most difficult Topic."[62] Some of those difficulties surfaced again during the ratification debates.

Supporters of the Constitution rallied to George Washington's threat-cum-prediction "that unless the States will suffer Congress to exercise those prerogatives, they are undoubtedly invested with by the Constitution, every thing must very

61. John Adams, *A Defence of the Constitutions of Government of the United States of America*, 3 vols. (London, 1787–88), 1:362–63.

62. Jefferson to Adams, 23 February 1787, in *The Adams-Jefferson Letters: The Complete Correspondence between Thomas Jefferson and Abigail and John Adams*, ed. Lester Cappon, 2 vols. (Chapel Hill: University of North Carolina Press, 1959), 1:174; Adams to Jefferson, 1 March 1787, in *Adams-Jefferson Letters*, 1:176–77. The relevant volume of Adams's book appeared, and this exchange occurred, before the constitutional convention convened (25 May 1787), so the two must be referring to the Articles.

rapidly tend to Anarchy and confusion, That it is indispensable to the happiness of the individual States, that there should be lodged somewhere, a Supreme Power to regulate and govern the general concerns of the Confederated Republic, without which the Union cannot be of long duration."[63] They relished Hamilton's applause for energy and vigor in *The Federalist*. (No, not just for the executive branch. Take *Federalist* no. 1's embrace of "an enlightened zeal for the energy and efficiency of government.") Some even insisted that the new national government would and should enjoy undivided sovereignty.[64] Popular sovereignty and state sovereignty, maintained Benjamin Rush, were "errors or prejudices . . . which lead to the most dangerous consequences." Congress would be "the only *sovereign* power in the united states."[65] "The idea which has

63. *A Circular Letter from His Excellency George Washington* (Philadelphia, [1783]), 19–20. Note too Washington's Letter to Congress, 15 September 1787, in *The Constitution or Frame of Government, for the United States of America* (Boston, 1787), 27; Washington to Benjamin Harrison, 18 January 1784, in Washington, *Writings*, 552; Washington to James McHenry, 22 August 1785, in *Writings*, 588; Washington to James Warren, 17 October 1785, in *Writings*, 591; and Washington's dourer prediction about the consequences of "the darling Sovereignties of the States individually" in Washington to Henry Knox, 3 February 1787, in *Writings*, 634–36. On that last, contrast Fabius, "Observations on the Constitution Proposed by the Federal Convention," *Pennsylvania Mercury and Universal Advertiser* (17 April 1788), growling that "the trustees or servants of the several states will not dare, if they retain their senses, so to violate the *independent sovereignty* of their respective states, that justly darling object of *American* affections." But Fabius agreed with Washington, give or take an adverb, on the merits: "the government of each State is, and is to be, *sovereign* and *supreme* in *all* matters that *relate* to each state *only*. It is to be *subordinate* barely in those matters that *relate* to *the whole*."

64. For instance, *Observations on the Articles of Confederation of the Thirteen United States of America* (New York, [1787]), 5–6.

65. Benjamin Rush, "Address to the People of the United States," *American Museum* (January 1787). See too Rush in the *Pennsylvania Packet, and*

been so long and falsely entertained of each being a sovereign State, must be given up," announced Charles Pinckney; "for it is absurd to suppose there can be more than one sovereignty within a Government."[66]

But opponents' arguments were ready to hand: the new national government would be sovereign, so the states would be contemptible weaklings. Under the new Constitution, warned Rawlins Lowndes, "a state individually must dwindle into a shadow."[67] Ponder that *must* and what it relies on. Think too about what the last couple of centuries suggests about the cogency of that claim. (If you think we're on a slippery slope, or that the Supreme Court greased the skids,[68] well, we're slipping awfully slowly, no?) All the opponents had to do—and a startling amount of what they did do—was recycle the colonists' arguments against Britain from the immediately preceding decades. Why, even convening a state convention to consider the framers' proposal was absurd: the new Constitution was "a manifest insult . . . to the Sovereignties of the States."[69] The category *insult* isn't accidental: it underlines the outrageous affront to dignity. The recycling extended even or es-

---

Daily Advertizer (5 December 1787); Remarker to the Citizens of Massachusetts, *Independent Chronicle and the Universal Advertiser* (17 January 1788).

66. Charles Pinckney, *Observations on the Plan of Government Submitted to the Federal Convention, in Philadelphia, on the 28th of May, 1787* (New York, 1787), 12. See too An Old Citizen of New York, *The Verdict of Condemnation* (New York, 1829), 11–12.

67. *The Documentary History of the Ratification of the Constitution*, ed. John P. Kaminski et al., 27 vols. to date (Madison: Wisconsin Historical Society Press, 1976–), 27:125 (Lowndes in the South Carolina House of Representatives, 17 January 1788). See too "An Officer of the Late Continental Army," *Independent Gazetteer* (6 November 1787).

68. For instance, in *Wickard v. Filburn*, 317 U.S. 111 (1942).

69. A Countryman no. 3, *New-York Journal and Daily Patriotic Register* (3 December 1787). Note too, after ratification, Greenwichiensis in *Newport Herald* (25 February 1790).

pecially to worries about the new central government's power to tax: "If the States give up to Congress the power of raising money from them & of disposing of that money, their particular sovereignties will, in fact, be all absorbed in one mighty Sovereignty—Against the abuses of which they will retain only the power of complaining & receiving for answer that they can have no remedy. . . . The pretensions of the particular States to Sovereignty after they have parted with the control of their purses will be no less ridiculous than the claim of the man in the Fable to enjoy the Shadow after he had sold his Ass, alleging that although he had parted with his Ass, he had not parted with the Shadow."[70] "The whole power and sovereignty of our state governments," warned A Real Federalist, "are swallowed up by the general government."[71] A worried participant in North Carolina's ratifying convention echoed the point, indicting the Constitution's supremacy clause, so dreaded by its opponents. "It appears to me to sweep off all the constitutions of the states. . . . It will produce an abolition of the state

70. David Howell to William Greene, 5 February 1784, in *Letters of Delegates to Congress, 1774–1789*, ed. Paul H. Smith et al., 26 vols. (Washington, DC: Library of Congress, 1976–2000), 21:341. See too William Findley in the Pennsylvania ratifying convention, 1 December 1787, in *Pennsylvania and the Federal Constitution, 1787–1788* (Lancaster, PA, 1888), 770–71; and the justly famous parade of horribles offered by Brutus, *New York Journal* (27 December 1787). Consider the rebuttal of Aristides [Alexander Contee Hanson], *Remarks on the Proposed Plan of a Federal Government* (Annapolis, [1788]), 38.

71. *Albany Register* (5 February 1789), from the remarks of Thomas Tredwell at New York's ratifying convention, 2 July 1788, in *The Debates in the Several State Conventions on the Adoption of the Federal Constitution*, collected by Jonathan Elliot, 2nd ed., 4 vols. (Washington, [DC], 1854), 2:403. See too, for instance, "Centinel No. III," *Independent Gazetteer* (8 November 1787); Vox Populi, "To the People of Massachusetts," *Massachusetts Gazette* (23 November 1787).

governments. Its sovereignty absolutely annihilates them."[72] "I stumble at the Threshold," Sam Adams famously fretted. "I meet with a National Government, instead of a Federal Union of Sovereign States." Adams's distinction might have depended on his ensuing worry that congressional power "shall extend to every Subject of Legislation, and its Laws be supreme & control the whole."[73] The traditional response would be that Article I's enumeration of Congress's powers quite obviously does not "extend to every subject of legislation." Adams, no slouch, misses the response, I conjecture, precisely because of the immense gravitational force of the view that sovereignty can't be divided. So too, I conjecture, for the dissenters in Pennsylvania's ratifying convention, who slid briskly from reciting "two co-ordinate sovereignties would be a solecism in politics" to announcing "there is no line of distinction drawn between the general, and state governments."[74] So too for James Winthrop's dread of being "subject to all the horrors of a divided sovereignty, not knowing whether to obey the Congress or the state."[75]

Opponents balked at reminders of powers the states would retain. Yes, their legislatures would choose senators. But "the exercise of sovereignty does not consist in choosing masters, such as the senators would be, who, when chosen, would be beyond control, but in the power of dismissing, impeaching,

72. Thomas Bloodworth, *Debates*, collected by Elliot, 2:179 (29 July 1788).

73. Samuel Adams to Richard Henry Lee, 3 December 1787, in *Writings of Samuel Adams*, 4:324.

74. *The Address and Reasons of Dissent of the Minority of the Convention of the State of Pennsylvania, to Their Constituents* (Philadelphia, 1787), 2.

75. Agrippa [James Winthrop], "To the People," *Massachusetts Gazette* (11 December 1787). For the attribution to Winthrop, see *The Debate on the Constitution*, ed. Bernard Bailyn, 2 vols. (New York: Library of America, 1993), 1:474.

or the like, those to whom authority is delegated."[76] The additional power of nominating members of the electoral college wouldn't help. The new federal government would grab other decisive powers from the states, "and yet you are clear the sovereignty remains. Did you think, Sir, that you was speaking to men or to children, when you hazarded such futile observations?"[77] The indignant scorn depends on the thought that the theory of sovereignty is so bone-shatteringly obvious that only a child could get it wrong.

No wonder Alexander Hamilton urged that the Articles of Confederation already had given Congress "the exclusive right of war and peace," "the sole power of making treaties." No wonder he demanded, "Are not these among the first rights of sovereignty, and does not the delegation of them to the general confederacy, so far abridge the sovereignty of each particular state? Would not a different doctrine involve the contradiction of *imperium in imperio*?"[78] If under the Articles, Congress already had exercised sovereignty, what was all the fuss about? But—the appeal to *imperium in imperio* gives away the game—for some time, Hamilton too was a foe of divided sovereignty. At the constitutional convention, he urged that sovereignty had to be assigned to the national government. "The general power whatever be its form if it preserves itself, must swallow

76. "The Fallacies of the Freeman Detected by a Farmer," *Independent Gazetteer* (22 April 1788).

77. Cincinnatus, "To James Wilson, *Esq.*," *New-York Journal, and Weekly Register* (29 November 1787). Compare Rufus King's remarks in *The Records of the Federal Convention of 1787*, ed. Max Farrand, 4 vols. (New Haven, CT: Yale University Press, 1937), 1:323–24, 328 (19 June 1787).

78. *A Letter from Phocion to the Considerate Citizens of New-York, on the Politics of the Day* (New York, 1784), 11; reprinted in Alexander Hamilton, *Writings*, ed. Joanne B. Freeman (New York: Library of America, 2001), 132. See the much-reprinted "Circular Letter from Congress to State Governors," 25 April 1787, for instance, in the *Massachusetts Gazette* (4 May 1787).

up the State powers. [O]therwise it will be swallowed up by them. . . . Two Sovereignties can not co-exist within the same limits."[79] "No amendment of the confederation can answer the purpose of a good government," he insisted, "so long as state sovereignties do, in any shape, exist."[80]

So Hamilton and Antifederalists shared the view that sovereignty is indivisible, just as Lord North and American revolutionaries shared it. John Adams found the constitutional scheme so baffling that he ventured blatantly contradictory observations. "Who can tell where the Sovereignty of this Country is!" he exclaimed in consternation. First he thought the Constitution placed it in the national government, but that this wasn't well understood—or enforceable. So he suggested sovereignty would eventually vest wherever "the greatest & best Men" were.[81] Scant weeks later, though, he agreed that the Constitution was "an avowed Attempt to make the national Government Sovereign in Some Cases and the State Government in others," but he doubted that this division could be sustained. "It is too clear that in a course of Time, the little fishes will eat up the Great one unless the great one Should devour all the little ones."[82] Yet again, I bet that that putative clarity depends on the theory that sovereignty is indivisible.

That of course wasn't Madison's view. Writing as Publius, Madison had a field day undoing worries about the allegedly crucial distinction between a national consolidation of

79. Farrand, *Records*, 1:287 (18 June 1787).

80. Farrand, *Records*, 1:294 (19 June 1787). See too the barbed language of Roderick Razor, *Daily Advertiser* (11 December 1787); Joseph Hall, *An Oration, Pronounced July 4, 1800* (Boston, [1800]), 23, but contrast 14–15.

81. Adams to Nathaniel Peaslee Sargeant, 22 May 1789, in Adams, *Writings from the New Nation*, 205–6.

82. Adams to William Tudor, Sr., 28 June 1789, in *Writings from the New Nation*, 223.

sovereignty and a confederacy of sovereign states.[83] No wonder Publius canvassed ancient and modern confederacies to show that sovereignty not only could be divided, but had been, over and over again.[84] "Let it be the patriotic study of all," urged Madison, "to maintain the various authorities established by our complicated system, each in its respective constitutional sphere."[85] I wonder—it is not a trivial question—just how and why this understanding didn't stick in the 1760s. (And I report that in an undergraduate lecture around 1980, Bernard Bailyn lamented that the American Revolution was a terrible misunderstanding. I wondered then, and wonder now, if this is what he meant.)

Madison's view, or something awfully close to it, is now the standard or official account of American constitutionalism. We teach it in political science departments and law schools; it makes unremarkable appearances in court opin-

83. *Federalist* nos. 39, 45, 62. See too Farrand, *Records*, 1:263–64 (Rufus King's notes, 16 June 1787); 1:471 (Madison, 29 June 1787); Madison to Jefferson, 24 October 1787, in *The Republic of Letters: The Correspondence between Thomas Jefferson and James Madison, 1776–1826*, ed. James Morton Smith, 3 vols. (New York: Norton, 1995), 1:498–500; and Madison at Virginia's ratifying convention, 6 June 1788, in *Debates and Other Proceedings of the Convention of Virginia*, taken in shorthand by David Robertson, 2nd ed. (Richmond, 1805), 76. In *Federalist* no. 9, Hamilton seems closer to Madison's view. And Hamilton's advice to President Washington insists on divided sovereignty: "Opinion on the Constitutionality of a National Bank," 3 February 1791, in Hamilton, *Writings*, 614. For the bank itself as an *imperium in imperio*, F. L. Waddell, "A Card," *Evening Post* [NY] (7 April 1834); also *Courier and Enquirer* [NY] (5 February 1831), quoted in A Journalist, *Memoirs of James Gordon Bennett* (New York, 1855), 127; "Letter of Mr. Rush," *Albany Argus* (30 September 1834).

84. *Federalist* nos. 18–20.

85. "Public Opinion," *National Gazette* (19 December 1791), in James Madison, *Writings*, ed. Jack N. Rakove (New York: Library of America, 1999), 500.

ions ("the Framers split the atom of sovereignty,"[86] declares Justice Kennedy) and legislative debates. We appeal to Madison himself: "Other Governments present an individual & indivisible sovereignty. The Constitution of the U.S. divides the sovereignty. . . . If sovereignty cannot be thus divided, the Political System of the United States is a chimaera, mocking the vain pretensions of human wisdom."[87] We summon other early canonical authors and texts: so, for instance, Chief Justice Marshall declared, "In America, the powers of sovereignty are divided between the government of the Union, and those of the States."[88] We conscript President Monroe's widely circulated ruminations on the power of the federal government to pursue internal improvements: "There were two separate and independent governments established over our Union, one for local purposes over each State by the people of the State, the other for national purposes over all the States by the people of the United States." Each, he continued, was a "complete sovereignty"—as far as its power went.[89] Like Madison, like

86. United States Term Limits v. Thornton, 514 U.S. 779, 838 (1995) (Kennedy, J., concurring).

87. Madison to Nicholas P. Trist, 15 February 1830, in *The Writings of James Madison*, ed. Gaillard Hunt, 9 vols. (New York: G. P. Putnam's Sons, 1900–10), 9:354. See too Madison to Robert Young Hayne, 3 April 1830, in *Writings of Madison*, 9:390; Madison to George Washington, 16 April 1787, in Madison, *Writings*, ed. Rakove, 80.

88. McCulloch v. Maryland, 17 U.S. 316, 410 (1819). See too Marshall writing for the Court in *Cohens v. Virginia*, 19 U.S. 264, 434 (1821); and Samuel Holden Parsons to William Cushing, 11 January 1788, in *Debate on the Constitution*, 1:753.

89. "Views on the Subject of Internal Improvements," 1822, in *The Writings of James Monroe*, ed. Stanislaus Murray Hamilton, 7 vols. (New York: G. P. Putnam's Sons, 1902), 6:223. See too Senator Daniel Webster (National Republican–MA), *Gales & Seaton's Register* (27 January 1830); George McDuffie, *Defence of a Liberal Construction of the Powers of Congress, as*

Marshall, like Monroe, we say that we've divided sovereignty. The federal government enjoys enumerated powers; the states enjoy police powers; there is a jurisdictional division of labor. That's why we don't quiver in fear, as the Antifederalists did, over the necessary-and-proper and supremacy clauses. Each of us is both a citizen of a state and a citizen of the United States. That last has seemed familiar, pedestrian, for a long time: it was, for instance, advanced as innocent fact in an 1899 textbook.[90] And—this is crucial—when we say these things, when we effortlessly adopt this view as our own, we are junking one of the defining criteria of the classic concept of sovereignty. Recall where my argument is headed: sure, you can junk one of the criteria. But junk all three—unlimited, undivided, and unaccountable—and you won't have anything left.

Anyway, Madison found no consensus for dividing sovereignty, even if his view wasn't as relentlessly ignored as his (too?) ingenious theory about expanding the sphere of the republic to rescue self-government from its characteristic ills.[91] Nor, as we'll see next, did it quickly become a consensus view. I doubt there's really a consensus today. Many seem never to

---

Regards Internal Improvement (Philadelphia, 1831), 10–12; Jefferson, "Communication: Mr. McDuffie and Disunion," *National Journal* (4 June 1831); and "The Governor at Carthage," *Kansas City Times* (30 September 1894).

90. A. Norton Fitch, *The Civil Government of the United States*, rev. A. H. Campbell (Rochester, NY, 1899), 266–78. See too John Quincy Adams to H. C. Wright, *Liberator* (18 October 1839), suggesting that dual citizenship was introduced by the Declaration of Independence; John L. Gow, "Introductory Lecture on Municipal Law, Addressed to the Students of Washington College," *Washington Reporter* (21 February 1849). See too Richard H. Leach, *American Federalism* (New York: Norton, 1970), 1: "The people in federal systems are held to possess what amounts to dual citizenship. Sovereignty, in the classic sense, has no meaning; divided as power is, the element of absoluteness which is essential to the concept of sovereignty is not present."

91. On that last, Larry D. Kramer, "Madison's Audience," *Harvard Law Review* (January 1999) is irresistible.

have gotten Madison's memo. Many others seem to have gotten it but recoiled in disgust. Here's just one for now: in 1841, a newspaper writer dubbing himself Jefferson acknowledged Madison's view—and promptly rejected it: "sovereignty, from its very nature, must of necessity be indivisible."[92] (*From its very nature* and *of necessity*: there's the telltale confusion, as if the logic of a concept revealed something about the actual possibilities of the world.) So the ratification of the Constitution is by no means the end of my tale.

Nullification and the War between the States

Jump forward a bit in time. The detested "tariff of abominations" seemed to many Southerners to serve Northern interests at the expense of the South. In 1828, John C. Calhoun penned South Carolina's proposed response, an *Exposition and Protest*. It's both searing and pedantic, a curious combination very much Calhoun's trademark. (In 1841, Clay would lampoon Calhoun to his face on the Senate floor, calling him "tall, care-worn, with furrowed brow, looking as if he were dissecting the last and newest abstraction which sprung from metaphysician's brain." The record reports "loud laughter.")[93]

92. Jefferson, "To the Ohio Statesman," *Ohio Statesman* (16 March 1841). See too John William Burgess, *Political Science and Comparative Constitutional Law*, 2 vols. (Boston, 1891), 1:56: "Really, the state cannot be conceived without sovereignty; *i.e.* without unlimited power over its subjects. That is its very essence." And see *United States v. Curtiss-Wright Export Co.*, 299 US. 304, 316–17 (1936): "Rulers come and go; governments end and forms of government change; but sovereignty survives. A political society cannot endure without a supreme will somewhere. Sovereignty is never held in suspense."

93. Senator Henry Clay (Whig-KY), *Congressional Globe*, appendix (2 September 1841). I owe the reference to Richard Hofstadter, *The American Political Tradition: And the Men Who Made It* (New York: Knopf, 1948), 73.

Calhoun discerned "two distinct and independent sovereignties," the state and federal governments. But the states had to have the right to decide when the federal government had overstepped the rightful boundaries of its jurisdiction. "The right of judging, in such cases, is an essential attribute of sovereignty of which the states cannot be divested, without losing their sovereignty itself."[94]

In 1832, to put it with shamelessly indefensible teleology, South Carolina ran a conceptual dress rehearsal for the civil war. The state legislature convened a special convention that claimed in the name of state sovereignty the right to nullify the despised tariff, whose passage by Congress was a "GROSS & PALPABLE . . . VIOLATION of the CONSTITUTION." (You learn something about constitutional law if you reconstruct why the legislators didn't see it as a humdrum use of Congress's Article I, section 8 power "to regulate commerce with foreign nations, and among the several states, and with the Indian tribes.") They claimed too the right to secede from the union. "The redeeming spirit of our system," they announced, "is STATE SOVEREIGNTY." "South Carolina claims to be a sovereign State. She recognizes no tribunal upon earth as above her authority." Ratifying the Constitution had changed nothing. True, "a foreign or inattentive reader" might think the states had "divested themselves of their Sovereignty." "But this is an error. The States are as Sovereign now, as they were prior to their entering into the compact. . . . Sovereignty is a unit. It is

---

See too John Quincy Adams, *Diaries*, 2:304 (12 April 1833): Calhoun's "learning is shallow—His mind, argumentative, and his assumption of principle, destitute of discernment. His insanity begins with his principles; from which his deductions are ingeniously drawn."

94. *Exposition and Protest, Reported by the Special Committee of the House of Representatives, on the Tariff* (Columbia, SC, 1829), 26, 30.

'one, indivisible, and unalienable.' It is therefore an absurdity to imagine, that the Sovereignty of the States, is surrendered in *part*, and retained in *part*."[95] The absurdity, I suppose, is one of logic: the classic theory of sovereignty requires indivisibility. The question is precisely the cogency of that theory. An amiably baleful reminder: saying your position is true by definition isn't an especially impressive way of securing it. It's a way of making it empty. The convention's vehement small capital letters are typographical evidence of hypnotic bluster standing in the way of actual argument.

A bit of shrapnel from the state's explosive gambit is instructive. The convention imposed a loyalty oath to the state for all state officials—but conspicuously dropped any loyalty oath to the federal government.[96] One Edward M'Cready, sympathetic to the union, showed up for his new commission as lieutenant in Charleston's military corps, refused this new oath, and took the old one instead. Colonel Hunt, commanding officer of that regiment, balked at commissioning

95. *The Report, Ordinance, and Addresses of the Convention of the People of South Carolina* (Columbia, 1832), 14, 21, 22; *Address*, separately paginated, at 4. For the threat of secession, *Report*, 27. For a counter insisting on the undivided sovereignty of the federal government, see "Tariff Meetings," *Albany Argus* (22 February 1833). For a Mississippi newspaper insisting on a strict reading of Congress's enumerated powers, lest the states become "mere ciphers," only zeroes, see "Nullification," *Liberty Advocate* (24 January 1837). In the debate on admitting Maine and Missouri, Senator William Pinkney (Democratic-Republican–MD) launched a bitterly amusing tirade against the thought that Congress had the power to do anything about slavery: "if you have this power, you may squeeze down a new-born sovereign State to the size of a pygmy, and then taking it between finger and thumb, stick it into some niche of the Union, and still continue, by way of mockery, to call it a State in the sense of the Constitution" (*History of Congress* (15 February 1820)).

96. *Report*, 26.

M'Cready, who sued to force Hunt to do it. M'Cready's lawyer archly scorned the convention's language: "I will be told, that sovereignty is a unit; and that allegiance is indivisible—and that allegiance is only due to sovereign power; and that the United States have no sovereignty—and consequently, no allegiance. And if I would consent to follow, I might be led through a labyrinth of metaphysical reasoning and disputation . . . worthy the casuistry of the best days of the Jesuits. But splitting hairs is a business that won't pay, and I am unwilling to embark on it." He blithely held it was "certain and notorious" that the United States was sovereign, just like the state: that meant that sovereignty was divided. And he mockingly reminded the court that Calhoun had admitted as much, no, proclaimed as much, in the *Exposition*, "the book of the gospel of nullification," which "recognizes in the highest terms the sovereignty of the Union, and the divisibility of sovereignty." More prescient than you might think, he added, "This was the beginning of our metaphysical political philosophy—and I fear too much learning has made us mad."[97]

Opponents of nullification outside the courtroom cheerfully joined in. Parrying South Carolina's nullification gambit in a widely reprinted December 1832 proclamation, President Andrew Jackson said easily, "The States severally have not retained their entire sovereignty." And he played a trump card: one could commit treason against the United States, but not

97. W. R. Hill, *Reports of Cases at Law, Argued and Determined in the Court of Appeals, of South Carolina*, 3 vols. in 2 (Charleston, 1857), vol. 2, pt. 1, 408–9. The lengthy opinions in the case, cited also as South Carolina ex rel. M'Cready v. Hunt, 20 S.C.L. 230 (S.C. Ct. App. 1834) but not on Lexis, are in that same volume. Or see generally *The Book of Allegiance: or A Report of the Arguments of Counsel, and Opinions of the Court of Appeals of South Carolina, on the Oath of Allegiance* (Columbia, SC, 1834).

against an individual state. "Treason is an offence against *sovereignty*, and sovereignty must reside with the power to punish it."[98] Yes, this way of putting it teeters into making the federal government the undivided sovereign. And whatever the intuitive appeal of Jackson's suggestion, many states had treason statutes—and still do.[99] One senator calmly assured the chamber that "there was really no physical or metaphysical impossibility" in divided sovereignty.[100] An elderly Madison drew up notes emphatically renewing the case for divided sovereignty against Calhoun—and sharply distinguishing the resolutions

98. "Proclamation," 10 December 1832, in *Annual Messages, Veto Messages, Protest, &c. of Andrew Jackson, President of the United States*, 2nd ed. (Baltimore, 1835), 114. For a reprint conscripting Madison to back up Jackson, see Cato, "The President's Proclamation," *Richmond Enquirer* (31 January 1833). On the argument about treason, see too "May Order Acquittal in Mine Treason Trial," *Miami Herald* (18 May 1922): William Blizzard's lawyer argues "That treason against a state which had only limited sovereignty, was impossible." But contrast Madison's notes from the constitutional convention, *Writings of Madison*, 4:248 (18 August 1787); Farrand, *Records*, 2:437 (20 August 1787); Jefferson to Madison, 1 October 1792, in *Republic of Letters*, 2:740; Senator Robert Rhett (D-SC), *Congressional Globe* (27 February 1852); *The Statutes of the State of Connecticut* (New Haven, 1854), Title VI, chap. 1, p. 305; Edward D. Mansfield, *The Political Manual: Being a Complete View of the Theory and Practice of the General and State Governments of the United States* (New York, 1868), 186; "Our Curiosity Shop," *Inter Ocean* (9 June 1877), reprinted in *The Inter Ocean Curiosity Shop*, comp. George E. Plumbe (Chicago, 1878), 115; *The Code of Virginia* (Richmond, 1887), Title 52, chap. 179, sec. 3658, p. 877. In general, contrast Jackson's view with Polk's: "Message from the President," *Journal of the Senate* (5 December 1848).

99. For instance, Ala. Code § 13A-11-2; Cal. Penal Code § 37; Ga. Code Ann. § 16-11-1; Mass. Ann. Laws ch. 264, § 1; § 576.070 R.S.Mo.; Vt. Stat. Ann. tit. 13, § 340; Va. Code Ann. § 18.2-481. Thanks to Barry Cushman for the heads-up.

100. Senator Felix Grundy (D-TN), *Gales & Seaton's Register* (20 February 1833). For a mischievous ad hominem suggestion about defenders of state sovereignty, see "Nullification," *American Quarterly* (March 1833), 242–43.

of Kentucky and Virginia from Virginia's response to the Alien and Sedition Acts.[101] Here's a tantalizing glimpse of how ordinary citizens could reflect on the constitutional and policy questions. In April 1835, a Virginia man was "somewhat surprised" that his brother had supported the Whigs, opponents of President Jackson. "I consider our government twenty-four independent sovereign states connected together by the federal compact which they have signed for their mutual benefit and safety." It was the president's job "to superintend to the affairs of their Confederate government"—Jackson's reframing the presidency had paid off—and most citizens "approve of those measures for which he has been so much censured, therefore he was right to carry them into effect."[102] The political possibilities were kaleidoscopic, the room for quarrel capacious: *Niles' Weekly Register* cobbled together dozens and dozens of pages of texts from the ratification of the Constitution with sharply different views on state sovereignty.[103] I'll note just one difficulty. Defenders of the federal government's sovereignty often emphasize that the Constitution was ratified by special popular conventions, not state legislatures: that ratification is an act of the people, not the states. The obvious rejoinder is that the people acted state by state, not as a nation. The facts of ratification underdetermine the normative point about sovereign authority.[104]

101. "Notes on Nullification," 1835, in *Writings of Madison*, 9:573–607. The notes are assigned to December 1834 at http://founders.archives.gov/documents/Madison/99-02-02-3065 (last visited 28 August 2018).

102. Reuben G. Meredith to Thomas G. Meredith, 20 April 1835, in William Meredith, Letters, 1830–1837, Accession 308718, Personal Papers Collection, The Library of Virginia, Richmond.

103. *Niles' Weekly Register*, supplement to vol. 43 (September 1832–March 1833).

104. At the Virginia ratifying convention, Madison repelled the claim that the national government would have "consolidated" authority by not-

Mad or not, metaphysical or not, by 1851 Calhoun was no longer sanguine about divided sovereignty. Now he urged that "of course . . . the States have retained their separate existence, as independent and sovereign communities." He managed to adduce evidence from the constitutional convention to insist that "the United States" continued to mean just what it had meant under the Articles of Confederation. Otherwise, he insisted, we'd face the "perplexing question" of how sovereignty could be divided, a view indeed "impossible to conceive. Sovereignty is an entire thing;—to divide, is—to destroy it."[105] No

---

ing that the ratifiers would be "the people—but not the people as composing one great body—but the people as composing thirteen sovereignties." Fair enough. But he went on to say, "no State is bound by it, as it is, without its own consent," and that's tendentious: Art. VII stipulates that the approval of nine of thirteen states would suffice to bind those nine, and that would leave the other four in a desperately precarious position, more or less forcing them to join whether they liked it or not. See *Debates and Other Proceedings of the Convention of Virginia*, 76 (6 June 1788). For the worry Madison was responding to, see Patrick Henry: "That this is a consolidated Government is demonstrably clear, and the danger of such a Government, is, to my mind, very striking. . . . Who authorized them to speak the language of, *We, the People*, instead of *We, the States*?" *Debates and Other Proceedings*, 36 (4 June 1788). But see too Madison to Spencer Roane, 29 June 1821, in Madison, *Writings*, ed. Rakove, 778: "Our Governmental System is established by a compact . . . between the States, as sovereign communities."

105. John C. Calhoun, *A Disquisition on Government and A Discourse on the Constitution and Government of the United States*, ed. Richard K. Cralle (Charleston, 1851), 117–18, 146. He earlier announced this sort of view in the Senate (*Congressional Globe*, appendix (27 June 1848)) and was still insisting on it within weeks of his death (*Congressional Globe* (4 March 1850)). Somewhat surprisingly, compare "Sub-Treasury Bill," *Boston Quarterly Review* (July 1838), in *The Early Works of Orestes A. Brownson*, ed. Patrick W. Carey, 7 vols. (Milwaukee: Marquette University Press, 2000–2007), 3:418. For Brownson's view, see especially O[restes] A. Brownson, *The American Republic: Its Constitution, Tendencies, and Destiny* (New York, 1866), 322–23. See too E[lisha] Mulford, *The Nation: The Foundations of Civil Order and Political Life in the United States* (New York, 1871), 334–35.

longer sanguine, with sanguinary consequences to be realized soon enough.

The clichéd cauldron of sectional conflict bubbled merrily, maliciously away, with the intoxicating fumes of Calhoun's commitments wafting their toxic way south. Calhoun's thesis was rubbished on the floor of Congress in 1857 by Texas representative L. D. Evans, weirdly erudite enough to appeal to Spinoza and even to a footnote in Hobbes's *De Cive*. "Every beardless undergraduate from the University of Virginia," said Evans derisively, thought sovereignty was indivisible, but that was just confused "dogma."[106] And views like Calhoun's were sharply challenged in the antebellum South. A noteworthy case is the pugnacious *Charleston Courier*. Again in 1852, another South Carolina convention had resolved "that the frequent violations of the Constitution of the United States by the Federal Government, and its encroachments upon the reserved rights of the sovereign States of this Union," justified secession, even if the convention wasn't yet ready to take that step.[107] The *Courier* refused to be "muzzled" by the resolution. "We believe in a divided sovereignty, granted sovereignty in the Union to the full extent of its constitutional authority, and residuary sovereignty in the State to the full extent of the reserved rights, and within the limits of the State Constitution. We recognize despotic or illimitable authority nowhere,

106. *Congressional Globe*, appendix (4 February 1857). Evans had been a lawyer: *Biographical Directory of the United States Congress*, s.v. "Evans, Lemuel Dale (1810–1877)."

107. *Journal of the State Convention of South Carolina; Together with the Resolution and Ordinance* (Columbia, 1852), 18. And from a decade before, see "South Carolina: Report of the Committee on Federal Relations, on So Much of the Governor's Message as Relates to the Tariff, December, 1842," *Niles' National Register* (28 January 1843).

under our republican system, neither in State Legislatures or State Conventions, nor in National Legislatures or National Conventions, but believe that all sovereignty, in this country, whether State or Federal, is *limited sovereignty, defined by written constitutions*."[108] The *Courier* sneered at "the old politico-metaphysico theory" that insisted sovereignty was indivisible as flying in the face of the facts.[109]

But it's worth remembering—we've seen this motif before—that some Northerners embraced Calhoun's view that sovereignty was indivisible. They chose instead to assign it to the federal government. A Northern representative pronounced on the floor of the House in 1862, "we will wage this war while there is a patriot to strike, or a foe to fall. We will, at every sacrifice, maintain our national unity, territorial integrity, and undivided sovereignty."[110] After the war, too, some Northerners sang from the same hymnbook. "The whole case must be settled now," pleaded Charles Sumner in a November

108. "The Evening News and the Right of Secession," *Charleston Courier* (3 April 1857). The paper's sentiments stretched back to "The Sovereign People," *Charleston Courier* (13 February 1834). On the *Courier*, see Carl R. Osthaus, *Partisans of the Southern Press: Editorial Spokesmen of the Nineteenth Century* (Lexington: University Press of Kentucky, 1994), 69–76.

109. "The Evening News and the Right of Secession," *Charleston Courier* (8 April 1857). See too "The Right of Secession," *Charleston Courier* (15 April 1857); "The Errors of the News," *Charleston Courier* (17 April 1857); "Where Does Sovereignty Reside?" *Charleston Courier* (21 January 1862); "Conventions and the State Convention of South Carolina," *Charleston Courier* (11 September 1862). And see "Federal Union," *Vermont Phoenix* (10 January 1861); Mr. Negley in *The Debates of the Constitutional Convention of the State of Maryland, Assembled at the City of Annapolis, Wednesday, April 27, 1864*, reported by Wm. Blair Lord and Henry M. Parkhurst, 3 vols. (Annapolis, 1864), 1:343–44.

110. Representative Edward McPherson (R-PA), *Congressional Globe* (14 February 1862).

1867 lecture. "The National Unity must be assured,—in the only way which is practical and honest,—through the principles declared by our Fathers and inwoven into the national life." Nope, not divided sovereignty and dual citizenship. "As in the Nation there can be but one Sovereignty, so there can be but one citizenship."[111]

Lincoln tried in vain to sidestep the debate, as had Burke and others in the 1760s. "Much is said about the 'sovereignty' of the States," he told Congress in July 1861; "but the word, even, is not in the national Constitution; nor, as is believed, in any of the State constitutions." If sovereignty meant "a political community, without a political superior," only Texas had ever had it—and Texas surrendered it in joining the Union.[112] That last thought sounds more like a pitch for national sovereignty than a plea that Americans stop talking and thinking about sovereignty. But I think the right category is in fact *sidestep*. Lincoln went on to propose a deliberately humdrum account of jurisdictional competence: "Whatever concerns the whole should be confided to the whole—to the General Government; while whatever concerns *only* the State should be left exclu-

111. Charles Sumner, *Are We a Nation?* (New York, 1867), 3, 34. Compare B. G. Wright to Joseph A. Howland, "Dissolution of the Union," *Liberator* (11 September 1857); Jefferson to Garrison, "The Dissolution of the Union," *Liberator* (23 April 1858); and Governor Oliver Morton of Indiana in "Governor's Message," *Marshall County Republican* (23 November 1865), also in *Documents of the General Assembly at the Forty-Third Regular Session, Begun on the Fifth of January, A.D. 1865* (Indianapolis, 1866), pt. 1, p. 25.

112. Compare "Address to the People of Texas" by a committee convened by citizens of Galveston, *Niles' National Register* (26 April 1845). For quizzical amusement at the extensive role played by appeals to "Vattel and Grotius, Pufendorf and Burlamaqui, Blackstone" and more during the congressional debates on admitting Texas, see Senator Daniel Dickinson (D-NY), *Congressional Globe*, appendix (22 February 1845).

sively to the State. This is all there is of original principle about it."[113] That last shrug would have surprised Madison every bit as much as it would have Hamilton.

Jefferson Davis never faltered in his ardent devotion to state sovereignty. He recalled that as a young man serving in the House of Representatives, he'd already staked out his position: "the basis of my Political Creed was the Sovereignty of the States; and the Strict Construction of the grants made by them to the Federal Government." He displayed these views in an 1846 debate on the Harbor and Rivers Bill. He paraded them when he made it to the Senate in an 1848 debate on the Oregon Bill. Defeated in a run for Mississippi governor, he unfurled them in an 1852 speech at Jackson, another that year in Oxford, one the next in Philadelphia (Mississippi). Back in the Senate, with sectional strife ever more frenzied, Davis pointedly suggested—shades of John Adams, as if nothing here had changed in swapping the Articles of Confederation for the Constitution, which indeed was precisely Davis's view—that members of the chamber met "as ambassadors of sovereign States." He proudly announced the same views in

113. "Message of the President," *Congressional Globe*, appendix (4 July 1861). I am setting aside Lincoln's passing appeal to popular sovereignty; but see "Speech at Columbus, Ohio," 16 September 1859, in Abraham Lincoln, *Speeches and Writings, 1859–1865*, ed. Don E. Fehrenbacher (New York: Library of America, 1989), 35–36; echoed in substance the next day in "Speech at Cincinnati, Ohio," in *Speeches, 1859*, 82. See too Francis Lieber, *Lincoln or McLellan: Appeal to the Germans in America*, trans. T.C. (New York, [1864]), 2–4. Contrast "Mr. John M. Botts' Fourth of July Speech in Baltimore," *Daily News and Herald* (13 July 1866), pressing the same point about Texas but inferring that the federal government was "a consolidated Government for the exercise of every sovereign power for all national and foreign purposes; there was not and could not be a divided sovereignty." Botts was a Unionist from Virginia: *Dictionary of Virginia Biography*, ed. John T. Kneebone et al., 3 vols. to date (Richmond: Library of Virginia, 1998–), 2:114–17.

Portland in 1858. Citizens of Maine were free, they had to be free, to decide the slavery question for themselves. "Should any attempt be made . . . to disturb their sovereign right, he would pledge himself in advance, as a States-rights man, with his head, his heart and his hand, if need be, to aid them in the defense of this right of community independence, which the Union was formed to protect, and which it was the duty of every American citizen to preserve and to guard as the peculiar and prominent feature of our government." Leaving the Senate in January 1861, he declared that of course Massachusetts could leave the Union if it wished. In 1864, now president of the Confederacy, Davis was happy to prostrate himself: "I am among the disciples of him from whom I learned my lessons of State Rights—the great, the immortal John C. Calhoun."[114] You can dismiss his stance on states' rights as pretextual shadowboxing on behalf of slavery, his promise to fight for Maine as disingenuous. I don't doubt for an instant that Davis and others enlisted state sovereignty to defend slavery. I do deny that we should therefore brush it aside.

Devious or deluded, one Confederate general instructed people in the Northwest that "their own state governments, in the exercise of their sovereignty," could negotiate a separate peace if the Union remained stubborn.[115] This jurisdictional

114. *The Papers of Jefferson Davis*, ed. Haskell M. Monroe, Jr., et al., 14 vols. (Baton Rouge: Louisiana State University Press, 1971–2015), 2:698, 501 (if the federal government could develop the harbors, it would have "the powers of absolute sovereignty itself"); 3:332–73; 4:268–69, 281–83; 5:29–34; 6:375, 215; 7:20–21; 11:86. On Massachusetts, compare Calhoun presenting a legislative committee report from South Carolina, *Journal of the Senate* (7 February 1842).

115. Braxton Bragg to the People of the Northwest, 26 September 1862, in *The Civil War*, ed. Brooks D. Simpson et al., 4 vols. (New York: Library of America, 2011–14), 2:552.

version of "divide and conquer" of course went nowhere. Worse, state sovereignty left Davis and his generals in a bind. What could the new Confederate government do to muster troops from its sovereign states? Weren't they facing the same difficulties as Congress did under the Articles of Confederation? (But then consider a not particularly surprising fact about partisans and constitutional interpretation: during the War of 1812, Madison's opponents generated doubts about the federal government's mustering troops.)[116] However perversely, didn't they want to be, need to be, embracing those difficulties as the very point of their commitment to state sovereignty, what they were officially fighting for? Early in the war, mass support eased this predicament. A whopping 89 percent of Virginia's white men aged fifteen to fifty, in areas of the state not occupied by Union forces, served between 1861 and 1865.[117] Already in November 1861, though, there was a draft riot in Nashville.[118] And as the tide turned in favor of the Union, Confederate soldiers deserted and the generals pleaded for more manpower. In April 1862, the Confederacy passed a law for conscripting troops.[119] Enforcement was swift, even peremptory. In August 1863, one North Carolina man jotted down some lines to let his wife "no whair I am and what I am doing me and John Revis and Jonas pace and fransus farmer started

116. Representative Richard Stockton (F-NJ) and Representative Daniel Sheffey (F-VA), *History of Congress* (10 December 1814); A New-England Farmer [John Lowell], *Perpetual War, the Policy of Mr. Madison* (Boston, 1813), 48.

117. Aaron Sheehan-Dean, "Everyman's War: Confederate Enlistment in Civil War Virginia," *Civil War History* (March 2004), 9.

118. *The Rebellion Record*, ed. Frank Moore, 11 vols. (New York, 1861–68), 4:25.

119. *A Digest of the Military and Naval Laws of the Confederate States*, comp. W. W. Lester and Wm. J. Bromwell (Columbia, 1864), 57–61.

to come home and got hier to a place called webster and met with some of the militia started out to ketch up conscrips and they stopt us hier and wont let us go."[120]

But there was political pushback. As the Confederate Congress considered the measure, a representative from Mississippi proposed an amendment: "Be it further enacted, That nothing in this act contained shall be so construed, as in its practical operation to impair, in least degree, the separate State sovereignty and independence of the Confederate States, or as calling into question their right, by separate State action, to interpose for the purpose of arresting, within its own limits, any act deemed by itself palpably unconstitutional and oppressive, or to deprive said States, or either of them, of the essential means, as well in war as in peace, of defending from infraction its own reserved rights, or of employing to this end the whole military strength properly appertaining to it."[121]

The amendment failed, but it was an omen of worse to come. Take the governor of North Carolina's riposte in September 1863:

> In addition to sweeping off a large class whose labor was, I fear, absolutely necessary to the existence of the women and children left behind, the hand of conscription has at length laid hold upon a class of officials without whose aid the order and well-being of society could not be preserved nor the execution of the laws enforced, and whose conscrip-

120. Daniel Revis to Sarepta Revis, 15 August [1863], http://cdm16062.contentdm.oclc.org/cdm/ref/collection/p15012coll8/id/1261 (last visited 3 June 2018).

121. Representative Henry S. Foote (TN), *Journal of the Congress of the Confederate States of America* (14 April 1862).

> tion is as insulting to the dignity as it is certainly a violation of the rights and sovereignty of the State. Having heretofore exerted the utmost powers with which I am entrusted, and even exceeded them, according to a recent decision of the Chief Justice of the State, in the execution of this law, at this point I deem it my duty not only to pause, but to protest against its enforcement.[122]

Next year, the governor of Georgia chimed in: "We should keep constantly in view, the great principles upon which we entered into the unequal contest, and should rebuke every encroachment made upon them by our own Government. We have made fearful strides since the war began to a centralized government with unlimited powers. Governor Brown advocates State sovereignty and for the State negotiating her own terms of peace."[123] (A Hawaii newspaper reported the comments and added dryly that the governor was "on the rampage.")[124] The two governors weren't chattering idly. They managed to exempt 92 percent of their own state officials from the ostensibly universal draft.[125]

122. Z. B. Vance to Jefferson Davis, 11 September 1863, in *Executive and Legislative Documents: Extra Session's 1863–64* (Raleigh, NC, 1864), 73.

123. "Significant Message of Gov. Brown, of Georgia," *Nashville Daily Union* (17 November 1864). Contrast "Speech of Hon. Warren Akin: Speaker of the House of Representatives of Georgia: In Reply to Mr. Stephens of Hancock, on the Conscript Law," *Southern Recorder* (16 December 1862).

124. *Pacific Commercial Advertiser* (10 December 1864).

125. James M. McPherson, *Battle Cry of Freedom: The Civil War Era* (New York: Oxford University Press, 1988), 431. See http://docsouth.unc.edu/imls/warfeb22/warfeb22.html (last visited 3 June 2018) for February 1865 Confederacy correspondence on 8,229 Georgia officials claimed to be exempt from the draft.

Such figures learned the lessons of state sovereignty all too well, at least for Davis's purposes. Imagine how plaintive he must have sounded in moaning to his House of Representatives in February 1864 that "public meetings have been held, in some of which a treasonable design is masked by a pretense of devotion to State sovereignty, and in others is openly avowed." He denounced a "too strict regard to the technicalities of the law" permitting the rogues at those meetings to escape treason charges.[126] Imagine the battle fatigue with which he saluted his fellow citizens of South Carolina in October 1864—the Confederacy had just won a minor battle at Saltville, but otherwise had been on a run of stinging losses, not least at Opequon—and offered, "You who have so long been the advocates of State Rights have never raised a clamor against the laws which seem to invade them. . . . Understanding the means of preserving your State Governments, you have not been frightened by the clamor of those who do not breathe the pure air of state sovereignty."[127] One might have thought those recalcitrant governors were the ones breathing that pure air. One might have thought the prospect of states thriving by shedding some of their authority would invite an argument for divided sovereignty—but no Confederate actors dared flirt with that, lest they surrender the political ground they were fighting on. That same month, a much-reprinted letter from Alexander Stephens, the Confederacy's vice president, promised "easy and perfect solutions to all present troubles," solutions that lay in "simple recognition of the fundamental principle and truth upon which all American constitutional liberty

126. *Journal of the Congress of the Confederate States of America* (3 February 1864).

127. "Speech at Columbia," 4 October 1864, in *Papers of Davis*, 11:85–86.

is founded, and upon the maintenance of which alone it can be preserved—that is, the sovereignty, the ultimate absolute sovereignty of the States."[128] Whether proposed in effrontery or cluelessness, these terms somehow didn't tempt the Union. "We have heard of trying to cure a sufferer from hydrophobia by administering 'a little hair of the dog that bit him,'" quipped an Ohio newspaper, "but who, before Aleck., ever insisted that the patient should eat the entire dog?"[129] No wonder that in the middle of the Civil War, one book diagnosing its causes devoted a chapter to sovereignty, with discussions of Vattel and Blackstone.[130] No wonder that in the middle of the war, a future president rose in Congress and lamented that "no man will ever be able to chronicle all the evils that have resulted to this nation from the abuse of the words 'sovereign' and 'sovereignty.' What is this thing called 'State sovereignty'? Nothing more false was ever uttered in the halls of legislation than that any State of this Union is sovereign." Triumphantly, he

128. "The Peace Question in Georgia: Views of Mr. Stephens," *Weekly National Intelligencer* (20 October 1864). See too, for instance, *Chicago Tribune* (15 October 1864); *New York Times* (15 October 1864, reprinted 16 October); *Cleveland Morning Leader* (19 October 1864).

129. *Cleveland Morning Leader* (21 October 1864). See too "Negotiations with Rebels the Necessary Preliminary," *New York Times* (16 October 1864).

130. George Junkin, *Political Fallacies: An Examination of the False Assumptions, and Refutation of the Sophistical Reasonings, Which Have Brought on This Civil War* (New York, 1863), chap. 4. No wonder, too, that Madison marveled, "Who can tell" how Vattel and his ilk would have made sense of American government? Madison to William Cabell Rives, 12 March 1833, in Madison, *Writings*, ed. Rakove, 864. Compare *Arizona v. United States*, 567 U.S. 387, 417 (2012) (Scalia, J., dissenting): "As a sovereign, Arizona has the inherent power to exclude persons from its territory, subject only to those limitations expressed in the Constitution or constitutionally imposed by Congress. That power to exclude has long been recognized as inherent in sovereignty." Scalia goes on to quote Vattel.

brandished Blackstone's language—"supreme, irresistible, absolute, uncontrolled"—and found the states wanting.[131]

After the Civil War, Davis kept doggedly pressing his vision of state sovereignty. (The United States decided not to prosecute even the leaders of the Confederacy.) He saw the same continuities with the War of Independence and the struggle over the Constitution that I want to underline. In 1871, he instructed an Atlanta audience, "You went to war upon the same question for which your ancestors and theirs contended in the first revolution against the government of Great Britain—the right of communal independence, or State sovereignty. You secured it in that first war, and State sovereignty must again be restored or else the republic of America is a failure." In 1873, a Memphis newspaper interviewed him. "The cause for which the war was waged by the south was the rights which were asserted to be inalienable in the declaration of independence and which the constitution was framed to secure," he explained. "The sovereign States when they entered into union reserved, or thought they reserved, all powers of sovereignty, and only delegated functions to a general agent. . . . In view of the usurpations of the last ten years and the present prostration of sovereign States, is it a crime to look hopefully to the restoration of their powers, or is it not rather a slavish abandonment of the rights for the preservation of which the Union was formed to look silently on while tyranny destroys constitutional government?"[132] In his history of the Confederacy, running—sauntering—some fifteen hundred pages, he denied that the Civil War was fought over slavery. Instead he set out "to show that the Southern States had right-

131. Representative James Garfield (R-OH), *Congressional Globe* (1 April 1864).

132. *Papers of Davis*, 13:31 (27 May 1871), 157–58 (30 August 1873). See too 14:307–9 (29 April 1886).

fully the power to withdraw from a Union into which they had, as sovereign communities, voluntarily entered; that the denial of that right was a violation of the letter and spirit of the compact between the States; and that the war waged by the Federal Government against the seceding States was in disregard of the limitations of the Constitution, and destructive of the principles of the Declaration of Independence."[133]

These debates are not safely squirreled away in our remote past. By the 1950s, not just "states' rights" but also state sovereignty, in its full-blown form, furnished an arsenal for opponents of *Brown v. Board of Education* and federal civil rights legislation. In 1957, James Kilpatrick recurred to a familiar narrative about the founding. "These infant States *were* sovereignties, and the people within them were proudly jealous of the fact. They saw themselves, in Blackstone's phrase, 'a supreme, irresistible, absolute, uncontrolled authority.'" With hat tips to Calhoun, Stephens, Davis, and others, Kilpatrick offered this nicely etched gem: "sovereignty, like chastity, cannot be surrendered 'in part.'" And it certainly hadn't been surrendered in whole.[134] Kilpatrick went on to embrace "massive resistance," the campaign to maintain racial segregation of public schools and more.[135]

133. Jefferson Davis, *The Rise and Fall of the Confederate Government*, 2 vols. (New York, 1881), vol. 1, preface, n.p. For the denial about slavery, see, for instance, chap. 1, esp. 1:13–14; also Davis, *A Short History of the Confederate States of America* (New York, 1890), chap. 1, esp. 9. Stephens too kept it up after the war: see Alexander H. Stephens, "Our Government," *Georgia Weekly Telegraph* (18 June 1869), reprinted in other papers around that time, also in Stephens, *The Reviewers Reviewed* (New York, 1872), 45–46.

134. James Jackson Kilpatrick, *The Sovereign States: Notes of a Citizen of Virginia* (Chicago: Henry Regnery, 1957), 10, 14.

135. On Kilpatrick's career, see William P. Hustwit, *James J. Kilpatrick: Salesman for Segregation* (Chapel Hill: University of North Carolina Press, 2013). Champions of popular constitutionalism—I'm thinking in part of

Later that year, fresh from his campaign to hang a portrait of Calhoun in the Senate's reception room as one of five outstanding senators, Strom Thurmond would conduct the longest filibuster of American history: over twenty-four hours on the floor. He was trying to block passage of the 1957 Civil Rights Act—this one was an effort to secure blacks' voting rights—and he too had state sovereignty on his mind: "it is almost an insult to the States." He read much of Kilpatrick's book into the record, not just to pass the time, as if he were obstinately droning his way through the phone book, but also with great admiration. "I wish every American could read this book. . . . This man is a great writer, a true patriot, and a great American."[136]

Again, I think Madison was right that American federalism divides sovereignty. And again, there's a sense in which that view has become standard or official. But some continue forlornly to crave unified sovereignty—and even more might

---

friends of mine—need to wrestle with the implications of the campaign. See Larry D. Kramer, *The People Themselves: Popular Constitutionalism and Judicial Review* (Oxford: Oxford University Press, 2004); Elizabeth Beaumont, *The Civic Constitution: Civic Visions and Struggles in the Path toward Constitutional Democracy* (Oxford: Oxford University Press, 2014).

136. *Congressional Record* (29 August 1957). The year elicited many other feverish defenses of state sovereignty: see, for instance, "A Few Reverses in the War," *Richmond News Leader* (24 July 1957). But again, there is more in the appeal to sovereignty than a wilted fig leaf not quite concealing purulent racism. Consider French theorist Bertrand de Jouvenel, that same year, insisting that "a body politic" must be "tied by an undisputed allegiance to a single Sovereign" (*Sovereignty: An Inquiry into the Political Good*, trans. J. F. Huntington (Chicago: University of Chicago Press, 1957), 4). Contrast Thurmond's later proposal that a commission investigate the jurisdiction of the federal courts: "The Commission would study the jurisdiction and limited sovereignty of the United States in relation to the jurisdiction and limited sovereignty of the States" (*Congressional Record* (10 March 1981)).

be surreptitiously relying on it. Think of the ardent affection on the right for state measures denying the authority of federal law, of the Supreme Court too, when it comes to same-sex marriage.[137] Think of the ardent affection on the left for state measures decriminalizing or legalizing marijuana even though the Feds list it as a Schedule I drug.[138] You can hold either view without insisting on full-blown state sovereignty: you can say that the Feds have overrun their jurisdiction or that they have the right to insist on their view but you hope they won't. But not everyone rallying to these causes wants to make such concessions.

Colonies and Britain, states and the new federal government, Confederate states and the Confederacy: in all these cases, it's not just tempting but also sensible to chart a jurisdictional division of labor. Theorists of federalism have long appealed to subsidiarity, externalities, and the like as organizing principles to describe what sorts of tasks should be assigned to local units, what to national. These maneuvers are not novel; only the lingo is. Take Washington again: "competent powers for all *general* purposes should be vested in the Sovereignty of the United States."[139] Or take Noah Webster: "in all the affairs that respect the whole, Congress must have the same power to enact laws and compel obedience throughout

137. Most dramatically, the combative posture of Chief Justice Roy S. Moore of Alabama's Supreme Court: *Ex parte State ex rel. Ala. Policy Inst.*, 2015 Ala. LEXIS 35 (Ala. Mar. 10, 2015), and *In re King*, 200 So. 3d 495 (Ala. 2016). Moore of course was previously in the news, and removed from office, for insisting on displaying the Ten Commandments in his courthouse despite a ruling that the display violated the establishment clause. See *Glassroth v. Moore*, 335 F.3d 1282 (11th Cir. 2003).

138. 21 U.S.C. § 812(c).

139. George Washington to John Augustine Washington, 15 June 1783, in Washington, *Writings*, 527.

the continent, as the legislatures of the several states have in their respective jurisdictions. . . . Such a power would not abridge the sovereignty of each state in any article relating to its own government."[140] Or take Jefferson: "the states should severally preserve their sovereignty in whatever concerns themselves alone, & that whatever may concern another state, or any foreign nation, should be made a part of the federal sovereignty."[141] Or take Teddy Roosevelt, who pressed the point without even nodding toward sovereignty: "The State must be made efficient for the work which concerns only the people of the State; and the nation for that which concerns all the people."[142] These theorists of federalism take for granted that we can divide sovereignty: that's a good thing, because we can. Will the jurisdictional lines be contestable and contested? Of course. I don't want to underplay the difficulties of figuring out, to descend for a moment from the invidiously high level of abstraction a lot of sovereignty talk gets played out on, when we should think the federal government enjoys implicit preemption of state laws, or, for a more specific example yet, when the dormant commerce clause kicks in. But we should embrace those fruitful difficulties, not flee from them into

140. Noah Webster, Jr., *Sketches of American Policy* (Hartford, 1785), 38, and see 43.

141. Jefferson to George Wythe, 16 September 1787, in *Works of Jefferson*, 5:340. See too Cato, *State Gazette of South-Carolina* (26 November 1787); "Remarks on President Sullivan's Message," *Independent Chronicle and the Universal Advertiser* (4 February 1790); Nathaniel Chipman, *Sketches of the Principles of Government* (Rutland, VT, 1793), 248–49; Polybius to the Republicans of the County of Orange, II, *Republican Watch-Tower* (6 June 1806).

142. "The New Nationalism" (31 August 1910), in Theodore Roosevelt, *Letters and Speeches*, ed. Louis Auchincloss (New York: Library of America, 2004), 811.

the clutches of the fatally embarrassing ones awaiting us if we insist that one government or another must enjoy undivided sovereignty.

Today, to put it bluntly, state courts must hear and enforce claims arising out of federal law.[143] But the federal government may not require state legislatures to pass laws to implement federal policy.[144] Nor may the federal government commandeer state officials to implement federal policy.[145] If you cling to undivided sovereignty, it's going to be awfully difficult to make sense of those distinctions.[146] If you wrest free of that commitment, nothing is easier.

World Government?

I turn finally to disputes about "supranational" government—the League of Nations, the United Nations, and the European Union. Here too the view that sovereignty must be indivisible confuses matters and polarizes debates. Recall my retail/wholesale distinction: instead of (this is retail) arguing on the merits about what level of government ought to exercise particular bits of jurisdiction, opponents and proponents alike (this is wholesale) fall into thinking that either the United Nations, say, will be sovereign or the nation-state will. But there's no reason to conjure up an all-or-nothing choice. The issues are tough enough without apocalyptic imagery. But they're also familiar: we've already worked through examples of the same abstract puzzle.

143. Testa v. Katt, 330 U.S. 386 (1947).

144. New York v. United States, 505 U.S. 144 (1992).

145. Printz v. United States, 521 U.S. 898 (1997).

146. Compare Anthony J. Bellia, Jr., "Federal Regulation of State Court Procedures," *Yale Law Journal* (April 2001).

Yes, there's a tradition of thinking that sovereignty has an inward and outward face, that it works one way in national politics and another way in world politics.[147] I should say at once that I don't believe a word of it. The city of Ann Arbor to the state of Michigan, the state of Michigan to the United States, the United States to the United Nations: all those relationships pose the same structural issues. Yes, it happens to be American law that the municipality is the creature of the state.[148] But whether that makes any sense can't sensibly be underwritten by arguments about state sovereignty, any more than the jurisdictional boundaries of the states and the federal government can be. And it happens to be British constitutional law that Parliament is omnicompetent. It can vote to repeal Magna Carta. Shades of Charles I: it can vote to jail a randomly chosen individual without charges and refuse to permit habeas corpus. No, it won't do those things, for political reasons. But formally it's allowed to.[149] The question is why anyone in her right mind would see that as a feature, not a bug.

147. David A. Lake, "The New Sovereignty in International Relations," *International Studies Review* (September 2003), 304–5; Ned Dobos, *Insurrection and Intervention: The Two Faces of Sovereignty* (Cambridge: Cambridge University Press, 2012). For even more splintering, see Stephen D. Krasner, *Sovereignty: Organized Hypocrisy* (Princeton, NJ: Princeton University Press, 1999), chap. 1. For internal and external sovereignty as logically complementary, see F. H. Hinsley, *Sovereignty*, 2nd ed. (Cambridge: Cambridge University Press, 1986), 158.

148. Mr. Francis cautioned against "erecting and constitutionalizing petty states or principalities, with independent and dangerous powers, within the body of our commonwealth," that is, New York State, in *Proceedings and Debates of the Constitutional Convention of the State of New York, Held in 1867 and 1868, in the City of Albany*, reported by Edward F. Underhill, 5 vols. (Albany, 1868), 4:3131.

149. Thanks to Chris McCrudden for confirming the extent of this constitutional principle. This is the right context for appraising Dicey's views.

Still, do international law and politics really pose the same structural issues? Doesn't the prospect of armed intervention at the international level change everything? Well, no: I fondly recall George Wallace, governor of Alabama, sending a telegram to President John F. Kennedy urging him to withdraw federal troops. Alabama, said the governor, could deal with its "rioting mobs of Negroes," so the president had "disregarded the sovereignty of the State of Alabama."[150] *Of course* war is different, and of course a distinction in degree can amount to a distinction in kind: how we characterize matters is just a question of what's useful or illuminating. However you cast the difference between JFK's troops and, say, full-scale invasion of another country, that goes to the justifiability and limits of norms of nonintervention on the merits, in a properly local or retail argument. My interest at the moment is in invoking sovereignty to cut off the possibility of such argument—or, less strategically but more ominously, in letting sovereignty obscure or preclude any reasonable assessment of our problems and possibilities.

Dicey held that "'limited sovereignty,' in short, is, in the case of a Parliamentary as of every other sovereign, a contradiction in terms," but also that "the method by which Federalism attempts to reconcile the apparently inconsistent claims of national sovereignty and of state sovereignty consists of the formation of a constitution under which the ordinary powers of sovereignty are elaborately divided between the common or national government and the separate states." There's much to say about that "attempts to," but not here. See A. V. Dicey, *Introduction to the Study of the Law of the Constitution*, 3rd ed. (London, 1889), 65–66 n., 133–34. Compare the discussion of Blackstone and federalism in Frederick Pollock, *A First Book of Jurisprudence for Students of the Common Law* (London, 1896), 258–61; and compare Pollock, *An Introduction to the History of the Science of Politics* (London, 1890), 80–81.

150. Governor George C. Wallace to President John F. Kennedy, 13 May 1963, at http://digital.archives.alabama.gov/cdm/singleitem/collection/voices/id/2969/rec/225 (last visited 4 June 2018).

In February 1915—World War I was well under way, though the United States wouldn't enter for over two more years—the Massachusetts legislature (the General Court, as it's called) adopted this striking resolution:

> Whereas the incalculable cost and calamity of the European war have caused a strong public sentiment for the end of all war: Therefore be it
>
> *Resolved*, That the General Court of Massachusetts hereby respectfully requests the Congress of the United States to make a declaration in substance as follows:
>
> The United States of America affirms the political unity of all mankind.
>
> It affirms the supremacy of world sovereignty over national sovereignty.
>
> It promises loyal obedience to that sovereignty.
>
> It believes that the time has come for the organization of the world government, with legislative, judicial, and executive departments.
>
> It invites all nations to join with it in the formal establishment of that government.[151]

Just four days later, the state's senior senator, Henry Cabot Lodge, duly introduced the resolution to be inserted into the *Congressional Record*.[152]

151. *Journal of the House of Representatives of the Commonwealth of Massachusetts* (26 February 1915). More apocalyptic was W. N. Ewer, "War or Revolution," *Tribunal* [London] (8 November 1917): "there is no way out but this—the destruction of State sovereignty and the overthrow of capitalism," which would require "European revolution."

152. *Congressional Record* (2 March 1915).

This unlikely bit of proposed self-immolation of course met its indignant mirror image. "Shall We Risk Our Sovereignty Forever and Police the World with Our Soldiers?" demanded a contributor to the *Manufacturers Record* in 1919. "Shall the price of victory for America be the abjuration of her sovereignty and her traditions, her institutions and her processes of thought and government?"[153] Soon after, another contributor warned, "when history will record the sorrows and joys of our national family, these men who kept for us our undivided sovereignty will be the great ones of American tradition."[154]

Once again, sovereignty talk made the stakes cosmic; once again, more phlegmatic observers tried to deflate the melodrama. "The most persistent argument used against the League of Nations is that it limits and restricts the sovereignty of the United States," agreed a journalist. But "absolute sovereignty is non-existent." All nations were already abridging their alleged sovereignty through international law and by signing treaties. "To be an absolute sovereign, a government must be either an international despot or an international pariah."[155] It's easy to say that sovereign states are always free to bind themselves by signing a treaty. But it's too easy: it sails blithely past the classic theory's conviction that the sovereign can't ever bind itself. And it ignores the pregnant bit of international law

153. P. H. Whaley, "Shall We Risk Our Sovereignty Forever and Police the World with Our Soldiers?" *Manufacturers Record* (3 July 1919).

154. Ida M. H. Starr, "Have They Forgotten That the Sun Rises in the East? Southern War Mother Asks if Administration Senators Have Wandered So Long in Dusky Twilight That They Cannot See the Sunlight of Facts That Reveals the Iniquity of League of Nations Covenant," *Manufacturers Record* (11 December 1919).

155. "Sovereignty and the United States," *Trenton Evening Times* (28 February 1919).

traveling under the Latin tag *jus cogens* or peremptory norms: norms so fundamental that they bind sovereign states whether or not they agree.

Defenders of the League in Congress took much the same line. "The opponents of the league contend for the absolute and unlimited sovereignty of the United States," commented a Kentucky representative in 1919. But such American sovereignty might collide with "the absolute, unlimited sovereignty of another great power." So the real choice was to settle such conflict with "an international tribunal" or to go to war, where "thousands and probably millions of American lives will be sacrificed."[156] A Delaware senator groaned in battle fatigue: "It is stated, iterated, and reiterated, time and time again, by opponents of this league that our sovereignty is impaired, because the league sets up a supergovernment or superstate, which is vested with a power to lay down law for the United States, and to compel the United States to obey its commands." Were that so, he countered, no one would be supporting the League. But opponents had conjured a phantasm. "Under this league nothing in the way of action by the United States can be forced upon us."[157] What was the senator thinking? After all, the League offered no special veto power to the United States. But the League's Covenant said, "Except where otherwise expressly provided in this Covenant or by the terms of the present Treaty, decisions at any meeting of the Assembly or of the Council shall require the agreement of all the Members of the

156. Representative William Fields (D-KY), *Congressional Record* (9 June 1919). Compare John H. Dietrich, "The World Not Yet Made Safe," *Christian Register* (28 November 1918), inveighing against the role of "*absolute and unlimited sovereignty*" in the debate over the League.

157. Senator James Wolcott (D-DE), *Congressional Record* (1 October 1919).

League represented at the meeting."[158] (If there was something invidiously idealistic about the League, surely it was the failure to realize that this unanimity requirement would effectively stop the member states from acting on anything remotely controversial. "But alas!" lamented Keynes. "Does not this provision reduce the League . . . into a body merely for wasting time?")[159] Nor does that "except" clause give away the game. It seems to refer only to procedures permitting member states to submit disputes to arbitration or a proposed Permanent Court of International Justice, or all other members of the League's Council or Assembly agreeing that one of the states in the dispute was in the wrong. Amendments to the Covenant could be adopted by majority rule, but "no such amendments shall bind any Member of the League which signifies its dissent therefrom, but in that case it shall cease to be a Member of the League."[160]

Once again, some contemporaries saw clearly enough that sovereignty could be divided, that it didn't make sense to think that establishing an international organization with limited jurisdiction meant abrogating U.S. sovereignty. While World War I raged on, an Oklahoma senator introduced a joint resolution. He wanted Congress to resolve "that international government, supported by international force, should be immediately organized to take the place of the existing international anarchy." He envisioned an international military devoted to protecting member states' territorial integrity. Without shifting gears or stumbling, without mentioning

158. Covenant of the League of Nations, Art. 5, at http://avalon.law.yale.edu/20th_century/leagcov.asp (last visited 11 June 2018).

159. John Maynard Keynes, *The Economic Consequences of the Peace* (London: Macmillan, 1919), 242.

160. Covenant, Art. 26.

sovereignty, he also wanted to affirm that "every civilized and informed people should have the unquestionable right of internal self-government, with exclusive control within its own territory over immigration, emigration, imports, exports, and all internal affairs, with the right to make its own political and commercial affiliations."[161] The implicit nod to colonialism is neither here nor there for our purposes. What matters is seeing a jurisdictional division of labor, abstractly the same as the suggestion that Britain have the right to impose external taxes, the colonies internal taxes; abstractly the same as the suggestion that the new federal government would handle general concerns, the states local ones. Just like these other proposed divisions of labor, the League of Nations, or any such supranational government, might or might not be a good idea. Even if it's a good idea, it might or might not be a good idea to assign any particular task to it. With those questions I have nothing to do. For all I care about here, a Missouri senator might have been entirely correct in both complaining that the League of Nations would "strip this nation of partial sovereignty" and holding that the United States should maintain "partial sovereignty" over the Philippines.[162] Regardless, he belongs in the camp of those who see that sovereignty can be divided. Here I want only to insist that conceiving of sovereignty as indivisible confuses matters. Perhaps that confusion is why the Okla-

161. Senator Robert Owen (D-OK), S. J. Res. 94, 65th Cong., 1st sess. (15 August 1917). In Paris negotiations, President Wilson rejected a French proposal for the League to have its own army: "'Unconstitutional and also impossible,' said Wilson." Margaret MacMillan, *Paris 1919: Six Months That Changed the World* (New York: Random House, 2001), 93.

162. "Senator Reed Attacks League of Nations Idea," *Idaho Daily Statesman* (31 October 1918); Senator James Reed (D-MO), *Congressional Record* (2 February 1916).

homa senator's resolution disappeared after being referred to the Committee on Foreign Relations.[163]

The same confusions haunted the debate over the United Nations—and they still do. Weeks after the UN was born, a Mississippi representative was as pugnacious as ever. Quoting, or misquoting,[164] the astonishingly prolific Mortimer Adler as saying, "We must do everything we can to abolish the United States"—and, ah innocence! letting the House know that even though Adler's speech sounded like a foreigner must have delivered it, the *Jewish Who's Who* revealed that Adler was from New York—the representative fumed, "what they want is a world government to which the United States will be subordinate." "I am not willing to surrender the sovereignty of my own country," he continued, "and set up some super government to be run by a gang of long-nosed internationalists to intervene in the affairs of every country in the world."[165]

There's doubtless much to say about the unsavory links between anti-Semitism and hatred of world government, not least in the long-standing image of Jews as rootless cosmopolitans and the echoing of that trope in antiliberal attacks on individualism: but I wistfully shove that topic aside. Once again, anxious fury at eradicating American sovereignty met

163. 65 Bill Profile S. J. Res. 94 (1917–1919), at http://congressional.proquest.com (last visited 5 June 2018).

164. Joseph Preston Baratta, *The Politics of World Federation: From World Federalism to Global Governance* (Westport, CT: Praeger, 2004), 490.

165. Representative John Rankin (D-MS), *Congressional Record* (23 November 1945). Rankin was an old hand at leering anti-Semitism. Several years earlier, Rankin's assault on "Wall Street and a little group of our international Jewish brethren" had provoked a vehement denunciation from Representative M. Michael Edelstein (D-NY), who left the chamber to cheers and promptly died of a heart attack: *Congressional Record* (4 June 1941); "Edelstein Dies after House Talk," *New York Times* (5 June 1941).

its mirror image in giddy glee at the sovereignty of a new world government. Though more premonitory than jubilant, one author warned in 1946, "only through a world sovereignty could war be abolished, and civilization preserved."[166] But a San Francisco newspaperman snorted at the stupidity of such claims. "The isolationists are trying to confront us with the dilemma of a postwar world, in which we either merge our identities into a world super-state, or else retain our unconditional sovereign separateness. . . . The whole 'either or' should belong to the high school debating society, unless, as is likely, present-day high school students have risen intellectually above it. Certainly it belongs nowhere in dealing with reality."[167] Bingo.

But it's not as though those insisting on the indivisibility of sovereignty never heard their opponents. Sometimes they did. They just didn't believe them. In 1952, the American legal counsel to the UN's secretary-general, himself an "enthusiastic

166. Raymond Swing, *In the Name of Sanity*, 2nd ed. (New York: Harper & Brothers, 1946), vi. I've silently corrected a typographical error. See too Vernon Nash, *The World Must Be Governed* (New York: Harper & Brothers, 1949), 32–33, 45–46. For belief in sovereignty as a clinical disorder, see William S. Sadler, *Prescription for Permanent Peace* (Chicago: Wilcox and Follett, 1944), 68–70.

167. Chester Rowell, "Trick Agitation Is Mask for Strategy," *San Francisco Chronicle* (20 February 1943). Rowell's earlier debates with Senator William Borah (R-ID) are instructive. See Rowell, "The World Court: Debate with Senator Borah, before the Idaho Bar Association: Lewiston, Idaho, September 3–5, 1925," Chester H. Rowell Papers, 1887–1946, carton 3, Bancroft Library, University of California at Berkeley, typescript, 14. Borah later made contrived arguments that Rowell conceded he then hadn't: see, for instance, *Congressional Record* (24 January 1935). Appealing to the hazards of nuclear war, Anthony Eden urged "that we all abate our present ideas of sovereignty," but acknowledged that "the world has not, so far, been ready to abandon, or even really to modify, its old conceptions of sovereignty" (*Hansard* (22 November 1945)).

advocate" of the body, urged that "international co-operation can exist only if states are willing to yield some portion of their sovereignty for the common good." "Bit by bit, national sovereignty has been eroded, but it still holds a most potent and formidable power over men's minds."[168] Indeed it did: a Reverend Claude Bunzel warned the American Council of Christian Churches of California "that UNESCO is educating the masses for eventual world government." Disdainfully quoting that legal counsel, he demanded, "How can sovereignty be divided? If we give up some portion of our national sovereignty, and bow to a higher power, we are no longer sovereign—unless words have lost all meaning. We go on to say that the latest political heresy is that sovereignty can be divided. Sovereignty cannot be divided. It can only be relinquished."[169] You might recall that I'm skeptical of the tradition of political theology. It's not what that tradition has in mind, but it is instructive to see a minister pronouncing anathema on a conceptual modification. Or try it this way: it's easy to smirk at the ostensible paranoia of critics with such overheated worries about the United Nations, let alone poor UNESCO. Better to diagnose the source of their febrile denunciations: and that's the view that sovereignty can't be divided. Reverend Bunzel's maneuver is embarrassingly transparent: he wants to rail against UNESCO action by complaining about the meaning of a word. But it doesn't make sense to secure a substantive position by jumping up and down about the dictionary, even

168. A. H. Feller, *United Nations and World Community* (Boston: Little, Brown, 1952), vii, 12.

169. *Hearings before a Subcommittee of the Committee of the Judiciary: United States Senate: Eighty-Third Congress . . . on S. J. Res. 1 . . . and S. J. Res. 43* (Washington, DC: U.S. Government Printing Office, 1953), 260 (6 November 1952).

if authorities as canonical as Bodin, Grotius, Hobbes, Blackstone, and the rest used the term that way. The classic theory can't be secured by making it an allegedly analytic or linguistic truth, lest opponents be free to respond easily, "Well, we don't need sovereignty in *that* sense."

Somehow plenty of people fall for the seductive power of dictionary definitions—or remain convinced of the merits of what is more or less the classic theory. Transfer sovereignty to a world government? Horrors, think some on the right. (Horrors, I suppose, think plenty on the left, too, but they seem more prone to realize that's not in the cards.) The American Sovereignty Restoration Act, a perennial long sponsored by Ron Paul, was most recently sponsored by Representative Mike Rogers (R-AL) with eight Republican co-sponsors.[170] It would withdraw the United States from the United Nations. The bill discreetly disappears once it's referred to the Foreign Affairs Committee, but it canters along in conservative circles and online. (Check out #amexit on Twitter or the group Amexit on Facebook.) Abandoning the Paris climate agreement, President Trump declared, "our withdrawal from the agreement represents a reassertion of American sovereignty."[171]

You'll be forgiven for noticing how closely these arguments track those over Brexit. Once again, some of the arguments there were properly local or retail, though for all that they

170. H.R. 193, at http://www.congress.gov/bill/115th-congress/house-bill/193 (last visited 5 June 2018). There's also a House Sovereignty Caucus: see the remarks of Representative Doug Lamborn (R-CO), *Congressional Record* (17 May 2016). For worries that the United Nations' actions "compromise your Viagra," see Representative James Traficant (D-OH), *Congressional Record* (22 July 1988).

171. "Statement by President Trump on the Paris Climate Accord," 1 June 2017, available at http://www.whitehouse.gov/the-press-office/2017/06/01/statement-president-trump-paris-climate-accord (last visited 30 July 2018).

might have been utterly meretricious. That's how I'd describe those buses trundling around the countryside emblazoned with this message: "We send the EU £350 million a week / let's fund our NHS instead / Vote Leave." (Boris Johnson appeared in front of posters making the claim more explicit: "Let's give our NHS the £350 million the EU takes every week.") But those buses also said, "Let's take back control."[172] Right, no mention there of sovereignty. But it's lurking in the margins—and was often made vociferously central in the campaign to leave the European Union. "Above all," declared the leader of the House of Commons, "it is a campaign to restore the sovereignty of our nation."[173] Prime Minister David Cameron assured the House of Commons that he would "put beyond doubt that this house is sovereign." Yes, he wanted to remain in the EU: he wanted only to restrict the volume of legislation coming from Brussels, to let Britain tend to properly national affairs.[174] But subsidiarity wasn't going to satisfy those bent on reclaiming sovereignty. (Back to the feature-or-bug point: parliamentary supremacy was indeed compromised by EU membership, as

172. "Nathan Gill: 'I Don't Know Anything' about £350m NHS Pledge," ITV Report, 24 June 2016, at http://www.itv.com/news/wales/2016–06–24/nathan-gill-i-dont-know-anything-about-350m-nhs-pledge (last visited 6 June 2018). Johnson hasn't backed down; he later said the figure should have been £438 million: "Leave Campaign's £350m Claim Was Too Low, Says Boris Johnson," *Guardian* (15 January 2018). Contrast Chuka Umunna, "It's Official: There's a £200m Hole in the Brexit Bus Promise," *New Statesman* (8 August 2017).

173. "Top Tories Announce Drive to 'Restore Britain's Sovereignty,'" *Daily Mail* (20 February 2016).

174. "EU Deal: Cameron Vows to Put Commons Sovereignty 'beyond Doubt,'" *Guardian* (3 February 2016). See too David Cameron to Donald Tusk, 10 November 2015, at http://assets.publishing.service.gov.uk/government/uploads/system/uploads/attachment_data/file/475679/Donald_Tusk_letter.pdf (last visited 6 June 2018).

the *Factortame* decision confirmed.[175] But it doesn't follow that EU membership is a bad idea.) Nor would they be deterred by patient and lucid explanations that the actual choice confronting Britain wasn't sovereign autonomy or capitulating to rules promulgated in Brussels.[176] The real choice was between having no seat at the table in the formulation of those rules or having a right to participate: so retrieving sovereignty from Brussels meant *reducing* the scope of British political agency. As one journalist put it, "to take back sovereignty can be to surrender control."[177] (Imagine an American state protecting its sovereignty by refusing to elect representatives to Congress. Or, as a perceptive critic of South Carolina's commitment to nullification noted, the state couldn't possibly withdraw from the union and "remain sovereign, independent and free." "She would be obliged, from her own imbecility, to throw herself upon the mercy of some mighty potentate for protection.")[178] You might think it undignified for celebrated politician Chris Patten to have snarled at "all this ideological crap about sovereignty and taking back control."[179] But maybe he was onto something.

175. R (Factortame Ltd) v. Secretary of State for Transport (No 2) [1991] 1 AC 603. See H. W. R. Wade, "Sovereignty—Revolution or Evolution?" *Law Quarterly Review* (October 1996).

176. For instance, "Boris Johnson Is Wrong: In the 21st Century, Sovereignty Is Always Relative," *Economist* (21 February 2016); "The Sovereignty Argument for Brexit Is a Myth," *Newsweek* (10 May 2016).

177. "Boris Johnson Is Wrong: Parliament Has the Ultimate Authority," *Financial Times* (25 February 2016).

178. Helvidius, *Charleston Courier* (24 August 1832). See too the lucid account of how the Bretton Woods agreement could enhance U.S. autonomy in Leo M. Churne, "Bretton Woods—A Cornerstone of Lasting Peace," in *Bretton Woods Agreement Act: Hearings before the Committee on Banking and Currency, House of Representatives . . . on H.R. 2211*, 2 vols. (Washington, DC: U.S. Government Printing Office, 1945), 2:1333.

179. "Brexit: 'Ideological Crap about Sovereignty and Taking Back Control,'" *Irish Times* (22 July 2017).

After the vote, Sarah Palin embraced news of Brexit by joining the party: “The Brexit referendum is akin to our own Declaration of Independence. May that refreshed spirit of sovereignty spread over the pond to America’s shores! Congratulations, smart Brits. Good on you for ignoring all the fear mongering from special interest globalists who tend to aim for that apocalyptic One World Government that dissolves a nation’s self-determination and sovereignty . . . the EU being a One World Government mini-me. . . . May UN shackles be next on the chopping block.”[180] Nor did the drearily acrimonious and spectacularly unproductive negotiations over Brexit puncture the faith of the hardcore true believers. (“Project Fear on speed,” sniffed Tory hardliner Jacob Rees-Mogg at government contingency plans for severe economic dislocation.)[181] I don’t introduce any of this evidence to mock the cause. I don’t happen to want to join the Home School Legal Defense Association in “fighting against the ratification of dangerous treaties like the United Nations Convention on the Rights of Persons with Disabilities,” nor in solving such alleged problems in one fell swoop by bailing out of the UN, but I’m open to arguments on the merits: real arguments, retail arguments, not daunting invocations of the indivisibility of sovereignty.[182] Likewise, if the American Sovereignty Restoration Act is a shorthand name for arguments on the merits, I’ve got no worries about it here. But if the thought is that the UN is

180. http://www.facebook.com/sarahpalin/photos/a.10150723283643588.424640.247187735587/10154310627508588, 24 June 2016 (last visited 6 June 2018). More sedately, the John Birch Society (yes, they’re still around): http://www.facebook.com/JohnBirchSociety/posts/1256177637755400, 30 September 2016 (last visited 6 June 2018).

181. “Brexit Doomsday Debunked,” *Daily Express* (4 June 2018).

182. “Heard about Brexit? Is It Time to Talk Amexit?” *States News Service* (18 July 2016).

bothersome or worse precisely because it guts American sovereignty, well, count me out.

Coda

You'll have noticed that most of my champions of undivided sovereignty are pursuing unhappy, even repellent, political causes. They want to wage war; they want to maintain chattel slavery; and so on. So you might suspect I'm impeaching, or lampooning, undivided sovereignty by suggesting it has lousy policy consequences. I want to disavow that, at least in the most straightforward reading of "policy." But I do hold that a commitment to indivisible sovereignty gets in the way of seeing the world clearly.

Sovereignty can be divided. The best evidence that something is possible is that it's actual. American federalism works. The United Nations, like it or not, issues rules that can bind member states. So does the European Union. But surprise! national governments haven't disappeared. Opponents of all these regimes might sensibly worry about this and that exercise of authority by the higher-level government, or for that matter about the scope of their authority.

But what they can't say sensibly is that the nature of sovereignty makes such schemes impossible, that we must be recklessly sliding toward anarchy. If they are inclined to say something like that, they should think about the historical record, about how just that view of sovereignty created and fomented conflict. (If *you're* inclined to say something like that, so should you.) The hundreds of thousands of corpses of America's Civil War, to say nothing of the lower casualty count of the American Revolution and the vastly higher one of the twentieth century's world wars, are a bitterly ironic counterpoint to the millions of corpses of the early modern wars of religion. Back then, you could plausibly argue that sovereignty would salve the horrific wounds of endless war. But after the Civil War? For real?

Every political community, we were solemnly instructed, needs a locus of authority—call it sovereign—that would be unlimited, undivided, and unaccountable. So far I've explored struggles showing that we can and do both limit and divide sovereign authority, and that those might be precious developments. So the count is two strikes. Next up: accountability.

4
Accountable

Time to explore attempts to hold sovereign actors accountable. I mean legally accountable, not just accountable to God; not just politically accountable, whether in elections or riots in the streets or insurrections; not just accountable in the eyes of future historians: though I suppose all of those might actually rein in some of the pernicious excesses of sovereign actors.[1] But legal accountability is precisely what the classic theory of sovereignty rules out—and precisely what people have struggled for, in episode after episode. I'll also explore startling cases where mere criticism is reviled as an outrageous affront to sovereignty. These two matters are tied: legal accountability turns out to be another kind of affront.

The struggle is ongoing, the battlefield treacherous. It would be rash to predict unconditional victory for the forces of accountability. But it wouldn't be rash to wish for it.

1. Consider the apparent ambivalence of *Englands Monarch, or A Conviction and Refutation by the Common Law, of Those False Principles and Insinuating Flatteries of Albericus* (London, 1644), 7.

Royal Thrust and Parry

When we last saw Charles I, he had angrily ordered Parliament to adjourn. But the Commons had insisted on taking a vote he wanted to prevent, had even rammed a sobbing Speaker of the House into his chair to continue its proceedings. Charles had capitulated on the Petition of Right—Coke, remember, was "half dead for joy"—but he was also adamant that he had an absolute right to adjourn or dissolve Parliament, indignant that he'd been reproached about raising tonnage and poundage funds, furious that the House of Commons had tried to "give law to Sovereignty." He would rule for eleven years without convening Parliament. How did he manage without relying on Parliament to vote him taxes? With constitutional improvisations, not least the radical extension of the tradition of raising ship money. The conventional understanding was that the crown could exact charges from port towns in time of war; Charles made it clear that he thought he could raise those funds anywhere across the realm, in times of peace too. Though he managed to extract approval from the courts, in the later 1630s the scheme proved rickety, officeholders and subjects alike sometimes truculent in refusing.[2]

When Charles finally convened a Parliament again in 1640, not much had changed. By 1642, he would congratulate himself on his restraint in not seizing the papers of his parliamentary opponents—"in cases of high treason there is no privilege of Parliament"—and would denounce a committee's declarations. The members of the committee had flouted "the

2. Henrik Langelüddecke, "'I Finde All Men & My Officers All Soe Unwilling': The Collection of Ship Money, 1635–1640," *Journal of British Studies* (July 2007).

limits of their duty and regard to their Sovereign."[3] And he would attack the thought that Parliament enjoyed a popular trust.[4] No wonder that civil war broke out that year. The war years are crammed full of episodes putting sovereignty into bold relief—and under intense pressure. I think, for instance, of yet another royal progress, this one a dismal caricature of Elizabeth's triumphs: the king showing up in town after town to raise troops, often with only desultory results. "A mighty Confluence of People" came to see Charles in Kingsmore, July 1644, "and there saluted His MAJESTY with general Shouts and Acclamations." Charles diligently made his pitch, but only those already signed up drew together to serve. The rest, "having seen their Sight, went home again."[5] One thing to seize an opportunity to gawk at Charles, even to cheer for him; another to risk their lives in defense of him or his views—or monarchy itself, if it came to that. Parliament was of course also raising troops, also with mixed success: "such Rake-Hells as they could scrape together . . . all fit Instruments of Hells, to hew down the Cedar of Monarchy," sniffed a later critic.[6] I confess to sneaking admiration for the Clubmen, organized to repel both sides of the war from penetrating their territory.[7] And

3. *Cal. S. P., Charles I, 1641–3*, 246–47 (8 January 1642).

4. *His Majesties Answer, to a Printed Book, Intituled, A Remonstrance or The Declaration of the Lords and Commons Now Assembled in Parliament, 26 May 1642* (London, 1642), 6–7.

5. Edward Walker, *Historical Discourses, upon Several Occasions* (London, 1705), 43–45. I owe the reference to David Underdown, *Somerset in the Civil War and Interregnum* (Newton Abbott, UK: David & Charles, 1973), 75–76. See too Anthony J. Fletcher, *The Outbreak of the Civil War* (London: Edward Arnold, 1981), 322–33.

6. [William Assheton], *The Cry of Royal Innocent Blood, Heard and Answered* (London, 1683), 108.

7. For the 5 March 1645 Declaration of Clubmen at Woodbury, see *The Diary and Papers of Henry Townshend, 1640–1663*, ed. Stephen Porter et al. (Bristol: Worcestershire Historical Society, 2014), 183.

I think of one aggrieved royalist's scolding of his opponents' claim to be patriots: "Have you not carried yourselves towards our natural Prince in all ways of hatred, contention and disobedience? Have you not abandoned his Authority and gone about to take away his absolute Sovereignty from him?"[8]

Reluctantly, though, I'm zooming past the spectacular years of civil war. Here's a terse wrap-up of the close. A Scottish army holding Charles handed him off to Oliver Cromwell and the Puritans for £100,000. (Apparently Charles thought they'd "sold him at too cheap a rate."[9] What price the sovereign? What price sovereignty?) Parliament was reconfigured: probably not at Cromwell's orders—the military leader dragged his feet on his way to London—Colonel Pride had stood on Parliament's steps with a list of insufficiently zealous members of the House of Commons. Some were arrested, some turned away, and as word trickled out some never showed up.[10] Indeed, two members already inside the House were "called forth by feigned Messages sent in by some Officers under other Mens Names, and there violently pulled out of the door."[11] After "Pride's purge," a "Rump" Parliament remained: this body in January 1649 put Charles on trial for his life, charging him with violating the fundamental laws of England. (The House

8. Edw[ard] Symmons, *A Vindication of King Charles* ([London], 1648), 277–78.

9. Patrick Maul[e], Earl of Panmure, to [Archibald Johnston], Lord Wariston, 23 January 1647, in [David Dalrymple], *Memorials and Letters Relating to England in the Reign of James the First*, 2nd ed. (Glasgow, 1766), 191.

10. David Underdown, *Pride's Purge: Politics in the Puritan Revolution* (Oxford: Clarendon, 1971), chap. 6.

11. Theodorus Verax [Clement Walker], *Anarchia Anglicana: or, The History of Independency: The Second Part* (n.p., 1649), 30. Compare *The Parliament under Power of the Svvord* (London, 1648), 3; [William Prynne], *Articles of Impeachment of High-Treason, Exhibited by the Commons of England, in a Free Parliament* (London, 1648), 7.

of Lords balked at the measure; the Commons decided it was law anyway.) I suggest we see this as a bid to establish the legitimacy of the action. So too we should see the publication of a trial transcript as an appeal to the public.[12] If you're feeling dour, you can substitute: as an attempt to instruct the realm. If you're feeling dourer yet, you can substitute: as a way of notifying lowly subjects what nauseating new political comestibles would soon be crammed down their throats. Dour myself, at least ordinarily, I'm not inclined to see this move in terms as bleak as that last.

Regardless, the transcript seems reasonably faithful, not least because Charles acquitted himself credibly. (Reasonably faithful, though not complete. We learn from an account published decades later that "insolent soldiers" blew tobacco smoke at Charles—and that one spat in his face.)[13] Indeed, sometimes I think that this was the first and last excellent performance of his ignominious career. The king took pains not just to argue against the legitimacy of the proceedings, but also to radiate contempt. When they marched him into the courtroom, "after a stern looking upon the Court, and the people in the Galleries on each sides of him," Charles sat, "not at all moving his Hat, or otherwise showing the least respect to the Court."[14] When the charges against him rang out—"*Charles*

12. I draw here on remarks I made in a different context in my *Happy Slaves: A Critique of Consent Theory* (Chicago: University of Chicago Press, 1989), 122.

13. *A True Copy of the Journal of the High Court of Justice, for the Tryal of K. Charles I*, taken by J. Nalson (London, 1684), 103. See too [Hineage Finch], *An Exact and Impartial Accompt of the Indictment, Arraignment, Trial, and Judgment (According to Law) of Twenty Nine Regicides, the Murtherers of His Late Sacred Majesty of Most Glorious Memory* (London, 1660), 39, 263.

14. All the trial quotations are from *King Charls His Tryal: or A Perfect Narrative of the Whole Proceedings of the High Court of Iustice* ([London],

Stuart (to be a Tyrant and Traitor, &c.)"—"he laughed as he sat in the face of the Court." And he demanded over and over to know "by what lawful Authority I am seated here." If they could give him a satisfactory answer, he'd answer the charges.[15] But "in the mean time I shall not betray my Trust; I have a Trust committed to me by God, by old and lawful descent."[16]

1649), short and enchanting enough that I'm not bothering with individual page references. Stop reading this; go read that.

15. Charles's challenging the court's authority is central in the very brief *Collections of Notes Taken at the Kings Tryall* ([London, 1649]).

16. Compare [Chevalier Ramsay], *An Essay upon Civil Government* (London, 1722), 103: "Sovereigns have no Judges upon Earth above them, so as to punish them, but they have always a Law above them, in order to regulate them"; and the bishop of Carlisle's lines in Shakespeare, *Richard II*, act 4, sc. 1:

> And shall the figure of God's majesty,
> His captain, steward, deputy-elect,
> Anointed, crowned, planted many years,
> Be judged by subject and inferior breath,
> And be himself not present? O, forfend it, God,
> That in a Christian climate souls refined
> Should show so heinous, black, obscene a deed!

See too [John Donne], *Psevdo-Martyr* (London, 1610), 168–70; William Hayes, *The Paragon of Persia; or The Lawyers Looking-Glasse* (Oxford, 1624), 21; Huntley's lines in [John Ford], *The Chronicle Historie of Perkin Warbeck* (London, 1634), sig. F2 recto:

> But Kings are earthly gods, there is no meddling
> With their anointed bodies, for their actions
> They only are accountable to Heaven.

For a way of splitting the difference in this debate, consider Junius Brutus [Hubert Languet], *Vindiciae contra Tyrannos* (London, 1648), 46–47. It was easier to cast the king as enjoying a popular trust and as legally accountable after the Glorious Revolution: so, for instance, R[ichard] Claridge, *A Second Defence of the Present Government under K. William, and Q. Mary, Delivered in a Sermon, Preached October the 6th 1689* (London, 1689), 22, 25–26. See too A Divine of the Church of England [Richard Claridge], *A Defence of the Present Government under King William and Queen Mary* (London, 1689), 7;

John Bradshaw, the lord president of the court, must have anticipated that Charles might play that card, so he had a ready response: the court acted "in the name of the People of *England*, of which you are elected King." Let's agree that this last claim was, shall we say, eccentric. Eccentric, not novel: Samuel Rutherford, for instance, already had described monarchy as a popular trust and argued that the king was legally accountable.[17] And a much-rehearsed if opportunistically selected bit of the thirteenth-century legal authority, Bracton, suggested that the law was the king's superior and if he slipped out of its confines, his nobles could bridle him.[18] The lord pres-

"Reflections upon the Advice from Rome, and Italy," *Present State of Europe* (September 1701); [Charles Lucas], *A Tenth Address to the Free Citizens, and Free-holders, of the City of Dublin* (Dublin, 1748), 5.

17. Samuel Rutherford, *Lex, Rex: The Law and the Prince* (London, 1644), 148, and see generally 230–51.

18. Bracton, *De Legibus et Consuetudinibus Angliae; On the Laws and Customs of England*, ed. George E. Woodbine, trans. Samuel E. Thorne, 4 vols. (Cambridge, MA: Belknap Press, Harvard University Press, 1968–77), 2:110. For appeals to this bit of Bracton during the civil war, see, for instance, *Maximes Unfolded* (n.p., 1643), 41–42; *A Disclaimer and Answer of the Commons of England* (London, 1643), 19; William Prynne, *A Plea for the Lords* (London, 1648), 22. For similar appeals to Fortescue, *A Remonstrance of the Un-lawfulnesse of the Warre* (Paris, 1652), 177–78; A Minister of London [George Hickes], *Jovian, or, An Answer to Julian the Apostate* (London, 1683), 210–11. Responding to Hickes, see *An Answer to a Late Pamphlet Intituled, The Judgment and Doctrine of the Clergy of England concerning One Special Branch of the King's Prerogative* (London, 1687), 8–9; Samuel Johnson, *Julian's Arts to Undermine and Extirpate Christianity* (London, 1689), 170–72. And see the pugnacious and electric *Passive Obedience in Actual Resistance: or, Remarks upon a Paper Fix'd Up in the Cathedral Church of Worcester, by Dr. Hicks* (London, 1691). For typical appeals to the force of the coronation oath, see A True Lover of the Queen and Country [Daniel Defoe], *The Judgment of Whole Kingdoms and Nations, concerning the Rights, Power, and Prerogative of Kings, and the Rights, Privileges, and Properties of the People* (London, 1710), 28; T[homas] Rutherford, *Institutes of Natural*

ident also alluded to "what was hinted to" Charles when he first entered: I suppose this referred to the court's sadly opaque invocation of "that Debt and Duty they owe to Justice, to God, the Kingdom, and themselves, and according to the Fundamental Power that rests in themselves." "If you acknowledge not the Authority of the Court," declared the lord president, "they must proceed." Charles wasn't buying it. "*England* was never an Elective Kingdom," he snapped, "but an Hereditary Kingdom for near these thousand years." You can generate grave doubts about whether Charles had notice, whether this was a properly legal proceeding at all.[19]

Sometimes the exchange became a risible caricature of peremptory assertion. A cartoonist could have drawn them sticking out their tongues at one another. "We are satisfied with our own Authority," said the lord president. "You have shewn no lawful Authority to satisfy any reasonable man," shot back the king. "That is in your apprehension, we are satisfied that are your Judges," replied the lord president. But those in the court knew their project would work better if they could get Charles to take up his role as defendant and participate. So they adjourned more than once, hoping that he'd return—penitent, bullied, delirious, or even, God knows how, persuaded—and plead on the merits. That didn't work. Instead Charles improved his lines.

Some of his remarks hewed closely to English constitutional law. "The Commons of England was never a Court of Justice," he observed: and indeed the House of Lords had

---

Law: Being the Substance of a Course of Lectures on Grotius de Jure Belli et Pacis, 3rd ed., 2 vols. (Philadelphia, 1799), 2:150–51.

19. For a defense focused more on the trial of Louis XVI, see *Regicide and Revolution: Speeches at the Trial of Louis XVI*, ed. Michael Walzer, trans. Marian Rothstein (Cambridge: Cambridge University Press, 1974), 1–89.

played that role for centuries. But other remarks shifted the register of the argument. "A King," Charles announced, "cannot be tried by any Superior Jurisdiction on Earth."[20] For a while, this claim made the court sputter, but eventually it came up with a lofty claim of its own: "Justice knows no respect of persons." The thought of course is not that justice is properly disrespectful; it's that justice is blind to whether your social status or official rank is low or high. No matter that Charles was a king; like the lowliest subject, he would have to answer to the law. "The Law is your Superior," as the court put it later, underlining the point this way: "the Sovereign, and the High Court of Justice, the Parliament of England . . . are not only the highest Expounders, but the sole Makers of the Law."[21]

But the court went on to declare, "there is something that is superior to the Law, and that is Indeed the Parent or Author of the Law, and that is the People of England. . . . They gave Laws to their Governors, according to which they should govern." Perhaps the court thought better of the earlier claim that Parliament was sovereign. Perhaps the court was muddleheaded. Perhaps it thought these claims cohered. Regardless, it disdained Charles's conviction that he was accountable only to God. The end of government, the responsibility of all officeholders, was "the enjoying of Justice." Any officeholder, including the king, who "will go contrary to the end . . . must

20. See too [Jean d'Espagne], *Anti-Dvello: The Anatomie of Dvells* (London, 1632), 18: "Sovereign powers are exempt from justifying their actions before any Tribunal"; [Philip Hunton], *A Treatise of Monarchie* (London, 1643), 15–16.

21. See too John Cook, *King Charls His Case* (London, 1649), 6–7. For a scathing later attack on Cook's view, see Samuel Butler, *The Plagiary Exposed, or, An Old Answer to a Newly Revived Calumny against the Memory of King Charles I* (London, 1691), 2–3.

understand that he is but an Officer in trust, and he ought to discharge that trust," lest he expose himself to "animadversion and punishment."[22] We are not tiptoeing toward social contract theory. We are squarely in its terrain, and if you'd like more explicit textual evidence, here you go: "there is a contract and a bargain made between the King and his People." The court promptly reverted to feudal categories—the "Liege Lord" and the exchange of protection for subjection—but those too offer a contractual understanding of political authority. Imagining contract theory as distinctively modern is painfully mistaken. And this framing led the court straightaway to this forbidding conclusion: "if this bond be once broken farewell Sovereignty."

Charles never budged, never pled. So the court did what any court does when confronted with an uncooperative defendant. It proceeded to convict him and sentence him to death. The grim pageantries and argument continued during Charles's execution. He made his way to the scaffold "walking on foot," "bareheaded." Stripped of his imposing royal regalia, he was plain old Charles Stuart, a man who had so betrayed the demands of political office that he'd earned the death penalty: or so the Rump Parliament wanted onlookers to believe. Still stubborn, Charles denied that the people of England were anything like what we would call citizens. They were subjects, on the receiving end of political authority. "Having share in Government . . . is nothing pertaining to them. A Subject and a Sovereign, are clean different things." But the time for argument was past. After some fussing about the placement of his hair, Charles "laid His Neck upon the Block," and "the Executioner at one blow, severed his head from his Body": he "held

22. Compare [James Stewart], *Jus Populi Vindicatum* (n.p., 1669), 170.

it up, and showed it to the Spectators."[23] Over a century later, Blackstone looked back and shuddered. His disapproval was typical enough, though surely not universal. But the terms in which he voiced it are still instructive: "the popular leaders (who in all ages have called themselves *the people*) began to grow insolent and ungovernable: their insolence soon rendered them desperate: and, joining with a set of military hypocrites and enthusiasts, they overturned the church and monarchy, and proceeded with deliberate solemnity to the trial and murder of their sovereign."[24]

You can flatten the drama into a titanic combat: a royal sovereign, above the law and accountable only to God, against a parliamentary court acting in the name of the people, perhaps even of popular sovereignty, and insisting that everyone, including the highest officeholder, is accountable at law for his conduct. The flattening isn't exactly stupid, but it eliminates intriguing wrinkles worth noting: not just in the name of historical fidelity, already a plenty sufficient justification, but also in noticing how malleable these political concepts are, how the vicissitudes of actual political conflict shape and reshape which appeals political actors make, which are persuasive, which unpersuasive. I shouldn't have to add, but I will, that we can and should keep that sort of thing in focus without beginning to

23. *King Charls His Speech Made upon the Scaffold* (London, 1649), 3, 4, 9–10, 14. On subjects and sovereigns, see too *The English Realm a Perfect Sovereignty and Empire, and the King a Compleat and Imperial Sovereign* (n.p., 1717), 15–17.

24. William Blackstone, *Commentaries on the Laws of England*, 4 vols. (Oxford, 1765–69), 4:431. Blackstone's famous cadences on sovereignty were inverted in John Barnard Byles, *A Discourse on the Present State of the Law of England* (London, 1829), 17: "here, where no person is above the law, where the sovereign himself is its subject, and the law reigns alone universal, uncontrollable, irresistible!"

imagine that all arguments are pretextual or mere strategic maneuvering. If they were *that*, no one would ever bother pressing such arguments in the first place, because everyone else would just chuckle and move on. If they were that, paying attention to arguments would be a rube's game, and self-styled behaviorists and realists would actually have a plausible research agenda, not a confused tribute to a zany picture of science.

So here are some of the wrinkles. No longer was Charles denouncing Parliament for trying to "give law to Sovereignty," if that meant that the sovereign had to be above the law, as articulated and defended by the command theory of law. Now he was arguing that the fundamental laws of England were on his side. There need be no practical space between these two pictures: English law might have defined the monarch as unaccountable or might have said that Parliament couldn't revamp his role. But at least atmospherically, they sure do sound different. Likewise, we've seen even that staunch defender of the Petition of Right, John Eliot, disclaim any subversive strategy and proudly insist, "all that I spoke was in all duty and loyalty to the king." It might have seemed a dizzyingly, enticingly, frighteningly open question whether Parliament meant to punish Charles or eradicate monarchy, though several months after Charles's execution, Parliament—that is, the Rump of the Commons—would make it brutally clear by enacting legislation declaring England to be a "a Commonwealth and Free-State . . . without any King or House of Lords."[25] So here's a last wrinkle. As it turned out, members of Parliament

25. "An Act Declaring and Constituting the People of England to Be a Commonwealth and Free-State," in *Acts and Ordinances of the Interregnum, 1642–1660*, ed. C. H. Firth and R. S. Rait, 3 vols. (London: His Majesty's Stationery Office, 1911), 2:122 (19 May 1649). See too *Journal of the House of Commons* (4 January 1649).

hadn't merely executed Charles. They'd done their best to execute monarchy. But that doesn't begin to suggest they'd tried to execute sovereignty.

Their intentions aside, a few glimpses of popular culture suggest the stakes. After the English civil war broke out, a woman in Norfolk grumbled that "now there is no King, no laws, nor no justice . . . because the King was not where he should be."[26] Just after Charles I's execution, Sarum assizes saw a man "indicted for saying *there was no Law, and that a company of Rogues had beheaded the King, and therefore there was no Law*." He was found guilty, fined a whopping £100, and imprisoned without bail until he could pay.[27] Just after that, some poachers "killed and wounded many of the King's deer" in Waltham Forest, "saying they came for venison and venison they would have, for there was no law settled at this time."[28] The command theory of law, no arcane fixation of theorists, was also a central prop in the view that you can't hold the sovereign accountable. The Puritans faced an uphill struggle.

As you surely have surmised even if you've never glanced at English history, the regicides didn't kill monarchy, either.

26. David Underdown, *Revel, Riot, and Rebellion: Popular Politics and Culture in England, 1603–1660* (Oxford: Clarendon, 1985), 218–19.

27. [Bulstrode Whitelocke], *Memorials of the English Affairs* (London, 1682), 431. I owe the reference to J. S. Morrill and J. D. Walter, "Order and Disorder in the English Revolution," in *Order and Disorder in Early Modern England*, ed. Anthony Fletcher and John Stevenson (Cambridge: Cambridge University Press, 1985), 137.

28. Affidavit of John Peacocke, 2 May 1649, in *Fifth Report of the Royal Commission on Historical Manuscripts* (London, 1876), 20. I first stumbled on this episode thanks to Fletcher, *The Outbreak of the English Civil War*, 376–77. For context, see Daniel C. Beaver, *Hunting and the Politics of Violence before the English Civil War* (Cambridge: Cambridge University Press, 2008), chap. 3.

Not institutionally, and not in popular culture. Reluctantly again, I zoom right by the heady days of the interregnum and the collapse of the Puritans' republic; I return to the tale with Charles II's triumphant return to London in 1660. Sailing the king back, Pepys jotted down, "the shouting and joy expressed by all is past imagination."[29] "Diverse maidens" petitioned the mayor to greet the monarch "clad in white Waistcoats, and other ornaments of triumph";[30] "a triumph of above 20,000 horse and foot, brandishing their swords and shouting with inexpressible joy; the ways strew'd with flowers, the bells ringing, the streets hung with tapestry, fountains running with wine," recorded Evelyn on the king's thirtieth birthday, the day of his procession through the streets of London; several days later he added that "the eagerness of men, women, and children to see his Majesty and kiss his hands was so great, that he had scarce leisure to eat for some days." These eager subjects were streaming in from all over the kingdom.[31] So too emissaries streamed in from abroad: "there was no Prince nor State in *Europe* who sent not, or were not sending their Ambassador upon this wonderful occasion."[32] On that same birthday, a curate sedulously instructed the faithful, "Christ, I told you, is King; the King is Christ's Vicegerent."[33] "All the world in a

29. *The Diary of Samuel Pepys: A New and Complete Transcription*, ed. Robert Latham and William Matthews, 11 vols. (London: Bell, 1970–83), 1:158 (25 May 1660).

30. *Mercurius Publicus* (24–31 May 1660).

31. *Memoirs Illustrative of the Life and Writings of John Evelyn*, ed. William Bray (London, [1871]), 265 (29 May 1660, 4 June 1660).

32. James Heath, *A Chronicle of the Late Intestine War in the Three Kingdoms*, 2nd ed. (London, 1676), 456. I've silently omitted a stray indefinite article.

33. William Towers, *A Thanksgiving Sermon: For the Blessed Restauration of His Sacred Majesty Charles the II* (London, 1660), 7. Compare [Edward

merry mood because of the King's coming," recorded Pepys after Charles's arrival.[34]

All the world? Surely some were principled republicans: for instance, during the civil war one radical embraced the people's "absolute Sovereignty," with which they'd "empowered their Body Representative."[35] Even Grotius and Bodin could be enlisted to defend the proceedings against Charles, if the people were sovereign.[36] And it's not dyspeptic to suspect that some of those celebrating were anxiously trying to cover their tracks, worried about reprisals. Surely the ringleaders had something to fear. Some rushed out of the country. The new regime came down hard on those who remained. If this was first and foremost a bid to renew monarchy, it also redounded on understandings of sovereignty.

We have another trial transcript, an emphatic counterpoint to that of Charles's 1649 trial, its publication too a bid to consolidate a view of legitimate authority—by renewing an old one. This transcript is from 1660, when the new regime tried twenty-nine regicides for murder. Presiding, the lord chief baron announced, "I must deliver to you for plain, and true Law; That *no Authority, no single person, no community of*

Hyde, Earl of Clarendon], *Transcendent and Multiplied Rebellion and Treason, Discovered, by the Lawes of the Land* (n.p., 1645), 1–3.

34. *Diary of Pepys*, 1:165 (31 May 1660).

35. Richard Overton, *An Arrow against All Tyrants and Tyranny* (Printed at the backside of the Cyclopian Mountains, by Martin Claw-Clergy, Printer to the reverend Assembly of Divines, and are to be sould at the signe of the Subjects Liberty, right opposite to persecuting Court, 1646), 5. See too [Henry Parker], *Observations upon Some of His Majesties Late Answers and Expresses* ([London, 1642]), 20; John Lilburne, *The Prisoners Plea for a Habeas Corpus* (n.p., [1648]), 8 n. c; [Stewart], *Jus Populi Vindicatum*, 170.

36. [John Canne], *The Golden Rule, or, Justice Advanced* (n.p., [1649]), 1, 6 (Grotius), 32 (Bodin).

persons, not the people collectively or Representatively have any coercive power over the King of England."[37] If Charles had been obdurate in refusing to play along at his trial, so were some of the regicides at this one. An unrepentant Thomas Harrison started arguing that kings were accountable, that Charles had begun the war, that "God is *no respecter of Persons*"—and the court tried to cut him off. Still Harrison persevered, and this time a prosecutor interrupted: "Methinks he should be sent to *Bedlam,* till he comes to the *Gallows,* to render an Account of this. This must not be suffered. It is in a Manner a New Impeachment of this King, to justify their Treasons against his late Majesty." A lawyer representing the royal family chimed in: "My Lords, This Man hath the *Plague* all over him, it is pity any should stand near him, for he will infect them."[38] Symptoms of insanity or pathology, Harrison's views were now officially not up for reasoned debate, but reprehensible poison, anathema to be censured. Surprise! he was found guilty. A regicide who'd fled to Switzerland condemned the "hasty Verdict" against Harrison. "That the Inhumanity of these Men may the better appear, I must not omit, that the Executioner in an ugly Dress, with a Halter in his Hand, was placed near the Major General, and continued there during the whole time of his Tryal, which Action I doubt whether it was ever equall'd by the most barbarous Nations."[39]

Harrison was hanged—but, by design, not long enough to kill him. When "half dead, he was cut down by the common Executioner, his privy members cut off before his eyes, his Bowels burned, his Head severed from his Body, and his Body

37. [Finch], *Accompt,* 10; and see 280.

38. [Finch], *Accompt,* 48–49.

39. *Memoirs of Edmund Ludlow, Esq,* 2nd ed., 3 vols. (London, 1720–21), 3:62–63. This last volume is titled *Memoirs of Lieutenant General Ludlow.*

divided into Quarters."[40] (Go ahead, dig in and feast on bitter irony: the defenders of sovereignty solemnly recapitulated the crazed excesses of the wars against religion, the very excesses that sovereignty was supposed to eliminate. Who needs berserk soldiers when they have legal proceedings?) A later tradition has it that after being sliced open, Harrison pulled himself up and punched his hangman in the ear.[41] I don't credit the tradition, and not only because of the heroic physiological feat: a detailed contemporaneous account doesn't mention it, though it does show how sunny and serene he was.[42] His head was "set on a Pole" on top of Westminster Hall, the parts of his body placed on various city gates.[43] Other regicides got the same treatment and were left to linger for gruesome dramatic effect. The next year, a Dutch traveler noted "many limbs of traitors or accomplices of Oliver Cromwell . . . displayed on stakes," some twenty "heads on stakes" to boot.[44]

40. [Finch], *Accompt*, 286.

41. [Bartholomew Shower], *Cases in Parliament Resolved and Adjudged* (London, 1698), 136.

42. *The Speeches and Prayers of Major General Harison, Octob. 13 . . . Together with Several Occasionall Speeches and Passages* (n.p., 1660). Gallows speeches make for a notoriously unreliable genre, but if anything the impetus would be to make Harrison sound contrite. See too George Bates, *Elenchus Motuum Nuperorum in Anglia: or, A Short Historical Account and Rise of the Late Troubles in England* (London, 1685), pt. 3, 54: "with the same madness and obstinacy as he had behaved himself at his trial, the cruel Traitor affecting an undauntedness at his death, was hang'd and quarter'd, as he well deserved."

43. [Finch], *Accompt*, 286.

44. *The Journal of William Schellinks' Travels in England, 1661–1663*, trans. and ed. Maurice Exwood and H. L. Lehmann (London: Offices of the Royal Historical Society, 1993), 51 (15 August 1661), 48 (14 August 1661). I owe the reference to Crawford Gribben, *John Owen and English Puritanism: Experiences of Defeat* (Oxford: Oxford University Press, 2016), 210.

The spectacular theatrics hadn't yet drawn to a close. Parliament decreed that the corpses of Puritan leaders Cromwell, Ireton, Bradshaw, and Pride be exhumed, hanged, and buried ignominiously under the gallows.[45] Somehow Pride escaped the indignity, but the other three dutifully plummeted from Westminster honor to Tyburn infamy—and the hanging lasted a full nine hours.[46] Their decapitated heads were displayed on poles high up in (or on top of?) Westminster Hall, with Bradshaw's—no accident—"over that part where that monstrous High Court of Justice sat."[47] Some regicides facing life in prison were first carted to Tyburn "with Ropes about their Necks" before being returned to the Tower of London.[48]

45. *Journal of the House of Commons* (4 December 1660). For a later dubious tale, see Senex, "Oliver Cromwell," *Times* [London] (31 December 1874).

46. DNB, s.v. "Pride, Thomas"; *Memoirs of Evelyn*, 271 (30 January 1661).

47. *Mercurius Publicus* (31 January–7 February 1661). This paper says the heads were "set upon poles on the top of *Westminster Hall*," which might sound like it's over the roof; but Pepys has the heads "set up upon the further end of the hall," which sounds like inside (*Diary*, 2:31 (5 February 1661)); and *Diary of Townshend*, 297 (29 January 1661), ambiguously has them "set up over Westminster Hall." The editors of *Diary of Pepys*, 5:297 n. 2, report that Cromwell's "head remained for display at Westminster Hall for about 25 years, when it was blown down in a storm." Their abbreviated citation led to the wonderfully grisly and detailed accounts in "Proceedings at Meetings of the Royal Archaeological Institute: 1st February, 1911," *Archaeological Journal* (1911), 233–53, which left me less confident than the editors. I'm with Mr. W. H. St. John Hope at 253: "It was difficult to come to any satisfactory conclusion as to whether the head was fixed outside or inside the Hall." And there's plenty of room for doubting the claim that, wherever it was, it lasted twenty-five years.

48. *Journal of the House of Commons* (1 July 1661). For a brief narrative of the punishment, see *The Traytors Pilgrimage from the Tower to Tyburne* (London, 1662).

Some thought this forbidding performance was going to be renewed every year, but the legislation doesn't mandate that.[49]

The Speaker of the House of Commons assured Charles II that he hoped "to meet your Majesty as our Sovereign, with the Duty of Subjects." Then he gushed, "If the Affections of all Englishmen can make you happy; if the Riches of this Nation can make you Great; if the Strength of this warlike People can make you considerable at Home and Abroad, be assured you are the greatest Monarch in the World. Give me leave to double my Words and say it again, I wish my Voice could reach to Spain, and to the Indies too, You are the greatest Monarch in the World!"[50] (Picture yourself delivering these vehement lines. Better yet, strike a proudly self-abasing posture and read them aloud: but I won't require that you do so in formal dress, standing before a distinguished and powerful audience in one of the world's most imposing halls. No giggling, please.) While the courts of King's Bench and Common Pleas were in session in Westminster Hall, the "common Hangman" ceremoniously burnt the 1649 act setting up the court to try Charles I and

49. *Diary of Pepys*, 3:19 (27 January 1662); Francesco Giavarina, Venetian Resident in England, to the Doge and Senate, 10 February 1661, *Cal S. P., Venice*, 33:106; 13 Car. II c. 15 s. 4 (1660).

50. *History and Proceedings of the House of Commons* (5 May 1661), also in *Journal of the House of Lords* (10 May 1661). See too the Earl of Manchester's address to Charles, *Journal of the House of Lords* (29 May 1660). Publications are overupholstered with this sort of thing, with and without explicit appeals to sovereignty. See, for instance, Aurelian *Cook, Titus Britannicus: An Essay of History Royal* (London, 1685), 251: "the Person of the Prince they had Murder'd, was beyond any Parallel, being most Virtuous, most Innocent, most Religious; and that his Judges were for the most part mean and desperate Persons, whose Hands were lifted up by Ambition, Sacrilege, Covetousness, and success against the Life of that incomparable Prince, whose lamented and barbarous death God would not suffer to go unrevenged."

a couple of other legislative abominations, interregnum measures to strip Charles II of his "pretended title" and safeguard Cromwell.[51] Not enough to notice that these laws were obsolete; not enough to repeal them. These people knew how to kill a bill. Ten years after the restoration, Charles II's birthday still produced effulgent tributes: "God hath set him upon a Hill, made his Sovereignty to be recognized. Here is no co-ordinate, co-equal, co-rival power of Parliaments . . . No Sovereign Authority of the People above him. . . . No Blaspheming of our Earthly God is allowed."[52]

The regicides' trial, the grisly executions, and the rest were acts in a drama designed to renew the magic of monarchy. I'll say it again: it flattens the story to think of the Rump Parliament as opposing sovereignty. But certainly Charles claimed to be sovereign and claimed that as a result he couldn't be held legally accountable for his actions. Certainly at the Restoration Parliament wanted to acknowledge Charles II's sovereignty, and certainly the regicides' trial was designed to make the very idea of holding a sovereign king legally accountable seem utterly repulsive. No surprise that decades later, we find facile invocations—incantations—of the view Charles insisted on in vain: "the *King* has the *Supreme Power,* and is *Sovereign,* and therefore Above the *Law,* and cannot be *Tried* by it."[53] But of course views like Harrison's survived, too. Here's Bentham: "In

51. *Mercurius Publicus* (23–30 May 1661).

52. John Lake, *A Sermon Preached at Whitehal upon the 29th Day of May, 1670 Being the Day of His Majesties Birth and Happy Restoration* (London, 1670), 36–37.

53. [Charles Leslie], *The Finishing Stroke: Being a Vindication of the Patriarchal Scheme of Government* (London, 1711), 137 (Mr. Higden in dialogue); the same with incidental variations in [Charles Leslie], *A New Farce; Represented in a Battle-Royal between Three Cocks of the Game* (London, 1716), 12. See William Higden, *A View of the English Constitution, with Respect to the*

whatever place you see dignity, especially dignity in company with crown—in a word royal dignity, think not in that place to see justice."[54]

The Scene Changes

Let's again sail across the Atlantic. On the hundredth anniversary of Charles I's execution, a Congregationalist minister in Boston inveighed against casting Charles as a saint or martyr, against treating the anniversary "as a day of fasting and humiliation." Parliament's resistance, he urged, was "a most righteous and glorious stand, made in defense of the natural and legal rights of the people, against the unnatural and illegal encroachments of arbitrary power." Charles had sought "to exercise a wanton licentious *sovereignty* over the properties, consciences and lives of all the people"; he deserved what he got.[55] Decades later, an elderly John Adams saluted the minister's sermon. "It was read by everybody," he declared, and if you wanted to understand "the principles

---

Sovereign Authority of the Prince, and the Allegiance of the Subject, 3rd ed. (London, 1710), 60.

54. Jeremy Bentham, *Official Aptitude Maximized: Expense Minimized*, ed. Philip Schofield (Oxford: Clarendon, 1993), 389. The immediately following passage is a stinging attack on Blackstone. See generally Laophilus Misotyrannus, *Mene Tekel, or, The Downfall of Tyranny* (n.p., 1663), 44–45; James Burgh, *Political Disquisitions*, 3 vols. (London, 1774–75), bk. 3, chap. 3; *The Trial of Maurice Margarot, before the High Court of Justiciary, at Edinburgh* (London, [1794]), 25; John Young, *Essays on the Following Interesting Subjects*, 4th ed. (Glasgow, 1794), 43; Thomas Wood, *Essays on Civil Government, and Subjection and Obedience* (Wigan, 1796), 11; Richard Dinmore, *Of the Principles of the English Jacobins*, 2nd ed. (Norwich, 1797), 30.

55. Jonathan Mayhew, *A Discourse concerning Unlimited Submission and Non-resistance to the Higher Powers* (Boston, 1750), 49, 48, 44, 46.

and feelings which produced the Revolution," you had to read it.[56]

There is something majestic—I don't mean that he was the king—about Charles I's fulminating against his unruly Parliaments, defending even his right to jail men without charges by pronouncing, "without overthrow of sovereignty we cannot suffer this power to be impeached." Rather less majestic, I'll suggest, are the overheated complaints of Rhode Island's delegates to the Congress of the Confederation, also the pugnacious conduct of a South Carolina governor on the stump at the close of the nineteenth century and his pugnacious defense of it. These episodes show that Bentham was onto something.

Rhode Island first. A 1787 news story published in Newport recounted the state legislature's wrestling with what to do about the state's war debts and devalued paper currency.[57] Other papers reprinted this stultifyingly bland story more or less verbatim: so much was routine practice in the day's newspapers.[58] A Massachusetts paper ran the same bland story, but under the inflammatory title, "Quintessence of Villainy!"[59] Then a New York paper ran it with that title, too.[60] Rinse and

56. John Adams to H[ezekiah] Niles, 13 February 1818, in *The Works of John Adams*, ed. Charles Francis Adams, 10 vols. (Boston, 1850–56), 10:288; Adams to William Tudor, 5 April 1818, in *Works*, 10:301. For the more immediate context of Mayhew's *Discourse*, see Chris Beneke, "The Critical Turn: Jonathan Mayhew, the British Empire, and the Idea of Resistance in Mid-Eighteenth-Century Boston," *Massachusetts Historical Review* (2008). Thanks to Hank Miller for leading me to this episode.

57. "Proceedings of Government," *Newport Herald* (22 March 1787).

58. "Proceedings of Government," *American Herald* (26 March 1787); *Essex Journal and New-Hampshire Packet* (28 March 1787); "Proceedings of Government," *Salem Mercury* (31 March 1787).

59. "Quintessence of Villany!" *Massachusetts Centinel* (28 March 1787). I've silently corrected this alternate spelling, perfectly acceptable in its day.

60. "Quintessence of Villainy!" *Daily Advertiser* (6 April 1787).

reprint: a soporific story with a sizzling title, but still business as usual. Yet this last publication caught the attention of Rhode Island's delegates (in those years, Congress met in New York City). Irate, they fired off a letter to New York's governor: "This daring insult to a Sovereign State, they consider as the most scan[da]lous of Libels." They demanded that the newspaper's publisher be "reprehended agreeably to the laws of the State over which you preside." New York's legislature promptly instructed the state attorney general to proceed against the publisher if the delegates insisted, though no action followed.[61] With prickly pride, the delegates sent their own governor a copy of their letter to New York's governor. "We could not be silent," they bristled, "when so great an indignity was offered to the highest exercise of Sovereignty in our state. . . . We represent a sovereign state, and will not suffer its honor sullied with impunity."[62] A couple of weeks later, they still bristled. "The peculiarity and delicacy of our situation required an assertion of the dignity of our state, or a submission to the most debasing humility."[63] How touchy their sovereign dignity! The offense was only in the words "Quintessence of Villainy." The offense is daring to criticize sovereignty, if only in a newspaper title.[64] Wrap your head around the idea of lèse-majesté against

61. Rhode Island Delegates to George Clinton, 7 April 1787, in *Letters of Delegates to Congress, 1784–1789*, ed. Paul H. Smith et al., 26 vols. (Washington, DC: Library of Congress, 1976–2000), 24:206 and n. 1.

62. Rhode Island Delegates to John Collins, 7 April 1787, in *Letters of Delegates*, 24:207.

63. Rhode Island Delegates to John Collins, 24 April 1787, in *Letters of Delegates*, 24:256.

64. For context, see Patrick T. Conley, *Democracy in Decline: Rhode Island's Constitutional Development, 1776–1841* (Providence: Rhode Island Historical Society, 1977), chaps. 4–5. Consider here the amendment, echoing Article II of the Articles of Confederation, that Rhode Island sought after

an American state. When you're done doing that, if your head is still pliable, wrap it around the idea of a sister state happy to leap into action to prosecute the offending publisher. The episode suggests that colonial American republicanism was not entirely what some imagine.

My South Carolina governor offers the same perverse surprises. This time, though, there's evidence that onlookers ridiculed his haughty pretensions. The apparent arrogance and frivolity of the governor's appearance on the historical stage depended on how well Americans had embraced legal accountability, not just as rhetoric but as institutional reality. In a world where even a frontier newspaper could celebrate law as "the sovereign of sovereigns," you don't get very far pontificating about how your august status puts you beyond the law.

"A fice dog with its tail cut": when Governor J. Gary Evans lobbed that odd invective at Judge Joseph H. Earle during a campaign debate, the two came to blows.[65] Lively as that day's campaigns could be, the fisticuffs made it to the front page of the *New York Times*.[66] The two were competing in South Carolina's 1896 Democratic primary for the U.S. Senate

---

ratification of the Constitution: *Providence Gazette and Country Journal* (13 March 1790), also in *Public Laws of the State of Rhode-Island and Providence Plantations* (Providence, 1844), 32.

65. The fullest accounts are "The Rowdy Campaigners," *Weekly News and Courier* (29 July 1896) and "Judge Earle Strikes Gov. Evans," *The State* (25 July 1896). The latter has the language I've quoted; for slight variants, "A Blot on the State's Escutcheon," *Manning Times* (29 July 1896); "At Last!" *Daily Charlotte Observer* (25 July 1896); "A Product of Tillmanism," *Washington Post* (27 July 1896). Today's spelling for the dog is *feist*, and there's some evidence the dog is the etymological source for *feisty* as well as for the older sense of *fist* as breaking wind.

66. "Hits Gov. Evans in the Face," *New York Times* (25 July 1896).

and tensions were already high. Evans had "promised to rip Judge Earle up the back" before one debate; at another the two rose and shook their fingers at one another. "Judge Earle appeared more angry than I have ever seen him. His face was white, while that of Evans was red."[67] Eventually Evans pummeled Earle and bloodied his face, though Earle's story was that he'd been hit by a member of the audience.[68] (The next day, Evans "laughingly" recalled "the underhanded lick that he let loose" at Earle. "I could have beaten him into a pulp were I so inclined," he boasted. "He was as easy to handle as a child, and completely at my mercy.")[69] Earle landed a blow on Evans, too. In ensuing days on the stump he conceded that as a judge he shouldn't break the law, but proudly maintained that as a man he would never "permit a man to insult me without resenting it."[70] One newspaper found the spectacle so "disgraceful and humiliating" that it called for abolishing primaries.[71] "The campaign can hardly sink any lower," moaned another.[72] Still the politicking remained rowdy.[73]

67. "Resuming the Campaign," *The State* (12 July 1896); "How's This for High?" *Journal and Review* (29 July 1896). For other sharp exchanges between the two, see "Earle and Evans," *Journal and Review* (22 July 1896); "Coffee or Pistols?" *The State* (22 July 1896); "Do It at Your Peril," *Journal and Review* (29 July 1896); "Politics Getting Warm" and "A Political Sensation," *Manning Times* (29 July 1896).

68. "Interview with Judge Earle," *Greenville Mountaineer* (5 August 1896).

69. "The Governor Discusses the Fight," *Weekly News and Courier* (29 July 1896); "Interview with Judge Earle," *Greenville Mountaineer* (5 August 1896). See too "The Campaign Outlook," *The State* (26 July 1896).

70. "Quiet Meeting at Barnwell," *Weekly News and Courier* (29 July 1896). See too "A Very Serious Charge," *Manning Times* (5 August 1896); "The Old Grind in Greenville," *Weekly News and Courier* (19 August 1896).

71. "The Row at Florence," *The State* (25 July 1896).

72. "The Rowdy Campaigners," *Weekly News and Courier* (29 July 1896).

73. "Heelers Howled," *The State* (5 August 1896); "Howling at Winnsboro," *Greenville Mountaineer* (8 August 1896); "Looks like a Conspiracy," *Weekly News and Courier* (12 August 1896).

The chief of police in Florence, scene of the combat, served Judge Earle with a warrant for disorderly conduct. He had a warrant for Governor Evans, too, but the governor refused it out of hand. The governor claimed "that it could not be legally served upon him, and if it was served, he would forcibly arrest and would moreover take charge of the Florence police force." The chief of police huddled with the mayor; contrite, cowed, or cautious, the two met the governor at the train station before he left town and "assured him that they meant no disrespect, and had simply been ill advised by the city attorney."[74] Disrespect? Well, the governor said that he wanted the warrant returned "with the contempt it deserves," that he "considered it an insult."[75] (Not just any old insult. "He considered it a great insult," the chief of police told another paper.)[76] Bloodied candidates for federal office and dismissive defiance of the law: no wonder newspapers all over the country picked up the story.[77]

74. "Judge Earle Strikes Gov. Evans," *The State* (25 July 1896).

75. "The Governor Liable to Arrest," *Greenville Mountaineer* (5 August 1896).

76. "The Governor above the Law," *Weekly News and Courier* (29 July 1896).

77. *Philadelphia Times* (25 July 1896); *Bradford Era* (25 July 1896); *Norwalk Daily Reflector* (25 July 1896); *Nebraska State Journal* (25 July 1896); *Philadelphia Inquirer* (25 July 1896); *Oil City Derrick* (25 July 1896); *Omaha World Herald* (25 July 1896); *Portsmouth Daily Times* (25 July 1896); *Steubenville Daily Herald* (25 July 1896); *Roanoke Daily Times* (25 July 1896); *New Brunswick Daily Times* (25 July 1896); *Frederick News* (25 July 1896); *Semi-Weekly State Journal* [Indiana] (28 July 1896); *Upper Des Moines* (29 July 1896); *Indiana State Journal* (29 July 1896); *Anita Republican* [Iowa] (29 July 1896); *Ames Times* (30 July 1896); *Galveston Daily News* (30 July 1896); *Appomattox and Buckingham Times* (30 July 1896); *Marion Sentinel* [Iowa] (30 July 1896); *Wilkes-Barre Weekly Times* (30 July 1896); *New Haven Register* (30 July 1896); *Roland Record* [Iowa] (31 July 1896); *Newton Record* [Iowa] (31 July 1896).

So the head of the state—or the executive branch, anyway—was insulted to think he could be served with an arrest warrant. "Makes Himself Ridiculous," jeered one headline. "No man is so high that he is not amenable to the law of the land and Governor Evans makes himself ridiculous when he refuses to be arrested by the proper authorities." "A Monarchical Jumping Jack," sneered another. "Since when has a Governor become above the law? Are we living under a monarchical or a republican form of government? Which?"[78] "Governor or Autocrat?" leered yet another. Did Evans imagine he couldn't be arrested for murder? His view of the law was "as untenable and monstrous as it is new."[79] Not new, exactly: Charles I and Blackstone could have embraced the thought. But new enough—and repugnant—in the United States. In the press, this governor was earning raucous raspberries, not devout deference. Could that serene regicide Harrison have peered across the ocean and into the future, he'd have felt profoundly vindicated.

Newspapers reprinted and discussed the careful analysis Florence's city attorney provided to the city council. In his capacity as governor, argued the attorney, Evans couldn't be hauled into court to answer for his political conduct. But one J. Gary Evans could most assuredly be held legally accountable for slamming another man in the face, and Evans couldn't escape legal responsibility for that action by pleading that he was the governor. The governor's contemptuous—contemptible—rejection of that view betrayed "total ignorance of the first principles of republican government," if not "dementia."

78. Both quoted in "A Whole State Disgusted," *Weekly News and Courier* (5 August 1896).

79. "Governor, or Autocrat?" *Weekly News and Courier* (29 July 1896).

(Another point on the scoreboard for Harrison. Who's crazy now?) The governor seemed to appeal to "the theory of 'kingly prerogative,' inherited from the sovereigns of England": "he informed the mayor that he could no more be arrested than the 'king (sovereign) of England' . . . forgetting at the moment of this ridiculous assumption of 'kingly prerogative,' that the doctrine of the 'king can do no wrong' has no place among republican simplicity." If the attorney bobbled the distinction between prerogative and the dispensing power, still he was onto something deep—and precious. No less was at stake than equality under the law.[80] The *Washington Post* agreed with the local papers. "In no State . . . is the Governor above the law. He is just as amenable to the statutes as the humblest private citizen."[81]

It's stunning to find an American governor deploying the language of insult and contempt, preening himself on being above the law: as if he were King Charles I, as if the very idea of legal accountability for his actions affronted his august status. The city attorney was right: "republican simplicity" rejects such pernicious poses out of hand. A governor is not a king, is not a sovereign above the law, may not imagine that his rarefied dignity is impeached when the law applies to him, too. The mayor and the chief of police may have been sheepish enough to apologize. But as far as I can tell no one sobbed hysterically

80. "The Governor Liable to Arrest," *Greenville Mountaineer* (5 August 1896). The letter is also in "An Outrage on Decency," *The State* (1 August 1896); "An Outrage on Decency," *Watchman and Southron* [Sumter] (5 August 1896); "The Governor Liable to Arrest," *Laurens Advertiser* (11 August 1896); "The Governor Reviewed," *Abbeville Press and Banner* (12 August 1896); "The Governor Liable to Arrest," *People's Journal* (13 August 1896).

81. "Above the Law," *Washington Post* (30 July 1896). See too William Rawle, *A View of the Constitution of the United States of America* (Philadelphia, 1825), 156.

at the prospect of defying this tinpot governor. And had the governor been convicted of assault, his successor couldn't have taken legal revenge against the actors who handled the case, and no abject mayors would have risen to flatter him as their sovereign, the greatest governor in the world.

What about the tergiversations of Richard Nixon? What passed for bantering in his sordid White House is sobering. In December 1971, Nixon, his aide John Ehrlichman, and others were discussing the revelation that a navy yeoman had been passing thousands of pages of National Security Council records to journalist Jack Anderson. Ehrlichman was going to interview the yeoman. "I want a direct question about homosexuality asked," Nixon instructed Ehrlichman. "You never know what you're going to find." The day after Nixon complained about Henry Kissinger's "intellectual arrogance" and defensiveness ("that's the problem with too much education"), Kissinger joined the discussion. Nixon was rambling. "Now get—take care of the yeoman. We better do something with him, but I don't know what the hell. Have you got any ideas?" "Yeah," said Ehrlichman, "but they're all illegal." "All of them illegal?" asked Nixon. "Hah, hah. That's good." "Put him in a sack and drop him out of an airplane," suggested Ehrlichman. "That would do it," agreed Nixon. "Yeah."[82] But the grumpy president was happier to insist on legal accountability when he suspected that LBJ had wiretapped his campaign plane. Nixon insisted, "The FBI cannot be above the law on this thing."[83]

82. *The Nixon Tapes, 1971–1972*, ed. Douglas Brinkley and Luke A. Nichter (Boston: Houghton Mifflin Harcourt, 2014), 336, 341, 344.

83. *The Nixon Tapes, 1973*, ed. Douglas Brinkley and Luke A. Nichter (Boston: Houghton Mifflin Harcourt, 2015), 78 (16 February 1973). On the wiretapping charge, see Cartha "Deke" DeLoach, *Hoover's FBI: The Inside*

The main event—Watergate—raises further issues about the accountability of government officials, issues that will sharpen my account of how pernicious the claims of sovereignty are. Let's begin a few years after Nixon resigned, with the infamous thought he offered in an interview with David Frost: "when the President does it, that means that it is not illegal." Sounds like Pufendorf's claim from over three hundred years before: "sovereignty or supreme command" has to "be acknowledged *unaccountable*," "exempt from human laws, or, to speak more properly, *above* them." "By definition," deadpanned Frost. "Exactly. Exactly," chorused Nixon. But I don't think he was captivated by some ostensibly logical point. Nor do I think his point was as sweeping as Pufendorf's. Nixon immediately added, "if the President, for example, approves something because of the national security, or in this case because of a threat to internal peace and order of significant magnitude, then the President's decision in that instance is one that enables those who carry it out, to carry it out without violating a law. Otherwise they're in an impossible position."[84]

There's a lot in there and we needn't unravel it all. Nixon is pressing a claim about what it takes for the executive branch to function well. Through the interview, he takes pains to emphasize what he took to be the legitimate grounds on which he acted. (Sometimes he also ponders the crime of obstruction of justice, which requires acting "corruptly," and then he argues that his motives were pure. "I had to . . . keep the peace at home, because keeping the peace at home and keeping support for the war was essential in order to get the enemy to

---

Story by Hoover's Trusted Lieutenant (Washington, DC: Regnery, 1995), 406–9.

84. "Excerpts from Interview with Nixon about Domestic Effects of Indochina War," *New York Times* (20 May 1977).

negotiate.") And—this bit goes to their legal accountability, not his—he wants to say that his subordinates in the huge and sprawling executive branch have to be able to take his orders and act on them, that the machinery of government will sputter to a halt, or be open to sabotage on policy grounds, if they are not just free, but actually required, to second-guess what he does.

Any such view is controversial. So is the thought that any such view adequately defends Nixon. Still, despite how easy it is to lampoon the notorious one-liner—"when the President does it, that means that it is not illegal"—Nixon's view isn't like Pufendorf's. He is not saying that as sovereign he has to be above the law, across the board. Nixon's view isn't like Bodin's. Bodin, remember, had urged that it's paradoxical, impossible, for law to bind the sovereign: "a man may well receive a law from another man, but impossible it is in nature for to give a law unto himself." Nixon's view isn't like Burlamaqui's. Despite his concession that sovereignty could be limited, Burlamaqui had insisted that it was a "characteristic essential to sovereignty . . . that the sovereign, as such, be above all human or civil law."[85] Nothing Nixon says would begin to explain, bizarre contexts aside, why he couldn't be legally accountable for punching George McGovern in the face. Nothing Nixon says would begin to explain why the very thought of being impeached, regardless of the grounds, is a nonstarter.

So too, I think, for Nixon's pleading executive privilege when special prosecutor Leon Jaworski filed a subpoena to get the tapes of White House deliberations. Predictably, Jaworski

85. Jean-Jacques Burlamaqui, *The Principles of Natural and Politic Law*, trans. Thomas Nugent, ed. Peter Korkman, 2 vols. (Indianapolis: Liberty Fund, 2006), 2:46–47.

announced that "despite his extensive powers and even his status as Chief Executive and Chief of State, the President, whether in his personal capacity or his official capacity, is distinct from the United States and is decidedly not the sovereign." "The President, though Chief Executive and Chief of State, remains subject to the law. . . . In our system *even the President* is under the law."[86] But—here's the crux—Nixon's lawyers cheerfully conceded the point in their reply brief. Even with a bit of snark: "The Special Prosecutor states an obvious and important truth when he reminds us that 'in our system *even the President* is under the law.'" They cheerfully conceded the point in oral argument before the Supreme Court, too: "The President is not above the law by any means."[87] They wanted to intimate that Jaworski was pounding the table to no avail. Or, to vary the metaphor, that he was thrashing mightily with these grandiloquent pronouncements, but not landing any blows against the idea of executive privilege. I noticed before that the spatial imagery of "above the law" is puzzling. Nixon's lawyers seized the opportunity to wrestle the image to earth, to start drawing relevant distinctions. If it matters, I'll admit—no, I'll proclaim in stentorian tones, maybe even clad in formal dress—that Nixon got this stuff badly wrong. But his position is still structurally different from the classic theory of sovereignty.

What's the difference between executive privilege and the view Pufendorf and Bodin and Burlamaqui (and Hobbes

86. Brief in U.S. v. Nixon and Nixon v. U.S., nos. 73-1766, 73-1834, in *Special Report of the Joint Committee on Congressional Operations* (Washington, DC: U.S. Government Printing Office, 1974), 20, 68 (of brief; also paginated 43, 91 in this publication).

87. Reply brief for Nixon, in *Special Report*, 31 (456); Oral Proceedings before the United States Supreme Court, 8 July 1974, in *Special Report*, 507.

and Filmer and . . .) had about law and sovereignty? Whether conceived generously or stingily, the claim of privilege runs this way: if or insofar as some laws' application would squarely undercut your ability to get your job done, those laws won't apply to you. If, for instance, the president needs to able to communicate frankly with his advisers in order to set enforcement policies or his foreign policy agenda, then he has a claim of privilege against laws that would otherwise ordinarily require publication of government proceedings, or their availability under Freedom of Information Act requests, or whatever else. (But not: the president can't be required to submit a tax return, because doing so is time-consuming, boring, frustrating, and will impede his ability to make important decisions. Assignment for the reader: why not? Hint: the answer is not that he can hire an accountant.)

The president isn't alone, the executive branch isn't alone, in having privileges. American law is shot through with them. Here's one granted in the Constitution to senators and representatives: "for any Speech or Debate in either House, they shall not be questioned in any other Place."[88] Yes, your representative in Congress can take the floor, name you, and say that she is appalled to learn that you've embezzled money from your employer, diddled small children in the park, and popped kittens into the microwave for fun—and you won't be able to sue her for slander. The Constitution relieves representatives from such legal liability to safeguard full, vibrant debate on the floor. But this privilege too has limits. Senator William Proxmire liked to award Golden Fleece Awards to ridicule wasteful government spending. But when he gave one to the director of research at the Kalamazoo State Men-

88. Art. 1, sec. 6, cl. 1.

tal Hospital—to develop an objective measure of aggression, the director was studying how animals clench their jaws when they're stressed—the director sued him. Yes, Proxmire had taken the Senate floor to present the award. But he'd also discussed it in a TV interview and he'd put it in a newsletter he sent to some one hundred thousand people. Proxmire invoked the Constitution's speech-or-debate clause to repel the lawsuit. The issue made its way to the Supreme Court, which held that while the clause properly extended to, say, committee reports and hearings, it wouldn't extend as far as the interview or the newsletter.[89] So Proxmire couldn't say, "Senators don't answer to lawsuits." He couldn't even say, "Senators don't answer to defamation suits." The privilege was limited.[90]

Not only such poohbahs as presidents and representatives enjoy legal privileges. Lawyers enjoy one just like that of the speech-or-debate clause: they can't be held liable for defamation for what they say in court proceedings. This privilege safeguards vigorous legal representation and, again like the constitutional provision, it extends to court filings, but not to whatever a lawyer says outside the courtroom. And it's about the job being done, not any special dignity of being a lawyer. You might not be a lawyer, but if you're representing yourself *pro se*, you get exactly the same privilege. Farther afield, if you're sued for battery or charged by the prosecutor with assault—suppose you break someone's arm—you can defend yourself by pleading self-defense, if you can show, roughly speaking, that you had a reasonable and actual belief that your life or limb was threatened. Everyone enjoys that privilege. No

89. Hutchinson v. Proxmire, 443 U.S. 111 (1979).

90. Compare the suggestion that it was too severely limited: Josh Chafetz, *Congress's Constitution: Legislative Authority and the Separation of Powers* (New Haven, CT: Yale University Press, 2017), 228–29.

one enjoys any general immunity from the tort of battery or the crime of assault. Or again, if you've made a confidential communication to your spouse, you can't be required to hand it over as evidence: that's to safeguard the privacy and intimacy of marriage.

Here's another way to see the difference between these legal privileges and the legal unaccountability summoned up by the classic theory of sovereignty. The privileges attach to performance in a role. When you're out of that role, the privilege won't apply. When the law doesn't bear on your performance of the role, the privilege won't apply. But if the sovereign is above the law, he (or it, or whatever else) is unaccountable across the board: 24/7, as we say, regardless of what he's doing, regardless of how or whether the particular law bears on what he's doing. For an intermediate case, consider the aristocrats of early modern England. Their status as aristocrats enabled them to quash certain legal proceedings: you couldn't sue them for trespass, for instance. Nor could they be required to serve on juries. Such exemptions had nothing to do with performing a role; it had instead to do with an understanding of their dignity not far removed from, though less than, the immense dignity of the sovereign. But aristocrats' exemptions didn't apply to any and every law, either.[91]

The more sweeping claims of privilege are, the more they will have the same practical force as the thought that the sovereign must be above the law. When Paula Jones sued him for intentional infliction of emotional distress, President Clinton argued that a sitting president doesn't have to answer to *any* tort suit: after all, he's got a constitutionally important

91. For more, see my "Aristocratic Dignity?" in Jeremy Waldron, *Dignity, Rank, and Rights*, ed. Meir Dan-Cohen (Oxford: Oxford University Press, 2012).

and time-consuming job to do. But a unanimous Supreme Court rejected Clinton's "effort to construct an immunity from suit for unofficial acts grounded purely in the identity of his office."[92] (President Trump tried to wriggle out of answering Summer Zervos's defamation lawsuit by arguing that the ruling in Clinton's case applied only to federal courts: Zervos was suing in state court. A New York court found that distinction entirely unpersuasive. It did so because it's entirely unpersuasive.)[93] While it's possible to imagine some privilege with dramatic sweep—both across one's social activities and across the swath of law—I can't think of a single privilege that works that way.

So there isn't merely a logical difference between, say, the structure of Charles's invoking sovereign unaccountability and Nixon's invoking executive privilege. There's an immense practical difference. Here's the last way I'll put it. Justice knows no respect of persons: that slogan was a pointed weapon against Charles; no wonder it struck him and his defenders,

92. Clinton v. Jones, 520 U.S. 681, 695 (1997).

93. Zervos v. Trump, 59 Misc. 3d 790 (S. Ct. of N.Y., 2018). And see the amusingly brief and dismissive *Zervos v. Trump*, 2018 N.Y. Slip Op. 75055 (N.Y. Ct. of Appeals, 2018). But it is still true that immunities might properly apply in some fora, not others. Consider International Court of Justice, *Case concerning the Arrest Warrant of 11 April 2000 (Democratic Republic of the Congo v. Belgium)*, 14 February 2002, ordering Belgium to cancel the arrest warrant for Abdoulaye Yerodia Ndombasi, then the minister of foreign affairs of the Democratic Republic of the Congo. Belgium had wanted to try Yerodia for violations of the Geneva Convention and crimes against humanity on the basis of acts he committed before becoming minister, not least speeches inciting attacks on the Tutsis of Kinshasa. The ICJ ruled that the doctrine of state immunity made an action in a Belgian court a nonstarter. The decision leaves open the possibility of prosecuting Yerodia in an international tribunal. For worries about the opinion's dictum that states can't prosecute other states' officials for official acts even after they're out of office, see Steffen Wirth, "Immunity for Core Crimes? The ICJ's Judgment in the *Congo v. Belgium* Case," *European Journal of International Law* (2002).

then and later, as ludicrous. He was above the law across the board, above any and every law, all the time, regardless of what he was doing, precisely because of who he was, the status he occupied: that of king, of sovereign. But the slogan is completely compatible with all kinds of legal privileges. They don't attach to persons, to anyone's status. They attach only to performance within a role.

One last complication could soften the contrast between Nixon and Charles, president and king. The grand jury investigating Watergate was keen to indict Nixon. One day, nineteen of the twenty-three members were present. All nineteen raised their hands to vote to indict him, "and some of us raised both hands." Jaworski's legal team agreed and drafted a six-page indictment. But Jaworski wasn't sure it was legal to indict a sitting president. He worried too about "the trauma of the country," and "what happens if he surrounds the White House with the armed forces."[94] So he refused to sign any indictment. What is more remarkable, he didn't return to the grand jury after Nixon resigned and his team again recommended indictment. Can a sitting president be indicted before being impeached and convicted? The question is a staple of constitutional lawyers' parlor games, and leading political actors have debated it from the republic's beginning. In a 1789 Senate debate, William Grayson held, "the President is not above the law; an absurdity to admit this idea into our government."[95] That same year Senator William Maclay mocked the view that the president could be prosecuted only after being impeached

94. *20/20*, "Watergate: An Untold Story," ABC, 17 June 1982. The grand jury's foreman wrote to Jaworski after Ford pardoned Nixon: he wanted to challenge the pardon. That was legally unpromising, but Jaworski didn't even respond.

95. See "Notes of a Debate in the Senate," in *Works of John Adams*, 3:409; the debate seems not to be in *Gales & Seaton's Register*.

and removed from office. Maclay echoed Grayson: "although President he was not above the laws." Then he sharpened the point: what if the president murders someone, or "continues his Murders daily," while Congress isn't in session to impeach him?[96] A 2000 memo from the Office of Legal Counsel argues that a sitting president is constitutionally immune.[97] If a president can't be indicted, he is closer to enjoying the sweeping legal immunity that the classic theory of sovereignty insists on. Closer, but not yet there. Charles and his supporters would never have agreed that he could be deposed, then prosecuted. But everyone agrees the president can be impeached, then prosecuted. Hamilton seized on the point to underline the difference between the president and the king of England.[98]

I wish I could report that sovereign immunity is a relic of the past. It's not. Let's turn to it.

Georgia on Their Minds

During the American Revolution, American troops outside Savannah needed supplies. Georgia contracted with Robert

96. *The Diary of William Maclay and Other Notes on Senate Debates*, ed. Kenneth R. Bowling and Helen E. Veit (Baltimore: Johns Hopkins University Press, 1988), 168 (26 September 1789). Contrast Jefferson to George Hay, 20 June 1807, in Thomas Jefferson, *Writings*, ed. Merrill D. Peterson (New York: Library of America, 1984), 1179–80. Brett M. Kavanaugh, "Separation of Powers during the Forty-Fourth Presidency and Beyond," *Minnesota Law Review* (May 2009), 1459–62, proposes that Congress pass a statute deferring civil and criminal actions against the president while he is in office; Kavanaugh says he "strongly agree[s]" that "no one is above the law in our system of government" (1462).

97. Office of Legal Counsel, "A Sitting President's Amenability to Indictment and Criminal Prosecution," 2000, at http://www.justice.gov/sites/default/files/olc/opinions/2000/10/31/op-olc-v024-p0222_0.pdf (last visited 10 July 2018).

98. *Federalist* no. 69.

Farquhar, a Charleston merchant, who duly delivered a whopping amount of merchandise. But the state's agents didn't pay him the almost $170,000 he was due. Years later, Farquhar drowned. His daughter stood to inherit the money—if it could be collected. Her husband petitioned the legislature, but it spurned him: the state's agents had the money; the family was free to pursue them.

Alexander Chisholm, an executor of Farquhar's estate, sued the state in federal court. The governor responded that Georgia was "a free, sovereign and independent State," so it couldn't be forced to answer a lawsuit: not "before any Justices of the federal Circuit Court for the District of Georgia" and not, for that matter, "before any Justices of any Court of Law or Equity whatsoever."[99] The two judges—one was Justice Iredell of the Supreme Court, sitting on circuit—dismissed Chisholm's suit.

Chisholm turned to the Supreme Court. One of Chisholm's lawyers was Edmund Randolph, who happened to be U.S. attorney general. The local federal marshal summoned the governor and the state attorney general, but they didn't appear before the Court. In fact, no one appeared to represent the state. The case was put off for some six months, yet once again no one appeared to represent the state. Just as the court trying Charles inexorably proceeded when he refused to cooperate, the Court ruled anyway. Justice Iredell still thought Chisholm's case was hopeless, but the Court's other four members ruled in Chisholm's favor.

99. Doyle Mathis, "*Chisholm v. Georgia*: Background and Settlement," *Journal of American History* (June 1967), 22. I've relied on this article for my account of the case's history; see too *The Documentary History of the Supreme Court of the United States, 1789–1800*, ed. Maeva Marcus et al., 6 vols. (New York: Columbia University Press, 1985–94), 5:127–37.

Justice Wilson—this was James Wilson, the distinguished author and law professor who'd signed the Declaration of Independence and the Constitution, no Johnny-come-lately to constitutional structure and law—shredded the thought that Georgia's sovereignty placed it above the law. We've already seen Wilson mocking sovereignty and he kept at it here, with the same textual observation Lincoln would offer. "To the Constitution of the United States the term SOVEREIGN is totally unknown."[100] It didn't even refer to popular sovereignty. It's not a great argument: compare the occasional rogue suggestion that the Constitution's blushing reference to "other persons" indicates the Founders' covert commitment to abolishing slavery. But Wilson went on to argue that there was nothing invidious or paradoxical about any group of men, including a state, binding themselves by law. It would be pernicious to allow them to unbind themselves by invoking sovereignty.[101]

Georgia's House of Representatives promptly took up legislation making it a felony—and imposing the death penalty, "without benefit of clergy, by being hanged"—for anyone, federal marshals included, to respond to the Supreme Court ruling by levying the state's property or treasury, or the governor or attorney general's property, to pay Chisholm or anyone else for "any debt or pretended debt" owed by Georgia. The draconian measure wasn't driven by the thought that Chisholm still ought to be pursuing those agents of the state. The bill was entitled "An Act Declaratory of Certain Parts of the Retained Sovereignty of the State of Georgia." It went to a third reading in the

100. Chisholm v. Georgia, 2 U.S. 419, 454 (1793). Senator Lewis Cass (D-MI) liked this argument, too: see *Congressional Globe*, appendix (12 August 1850); *Congressional Globe* (11 December 1856).

101. *Chisholm* at 456. For further bafflement about the role of sovereignty here, see Wilson's notes in *Documentary History*, 5:215–17.

House[102] but seems to have disappeared after being reported to the state Senate.[103] The case resonated across the country. The Massachusetts legislature got as far as framing language urging its congressional delegation to "use their utmost influence" to make sure the vexing provision enabling such lawsuits to be "either wholly expunged from the Constitution, or so far modified and explained, as to give the fullest security to the States."[104] Massachusetts's stance is yet another reason to reject the claim that state sovereignty was just a pretext for defending slavery.

Chisholm wasn't alone in posing a question about where or whether states might have to answer to lawsuits.[105] William Vassall had fled Massachusetts at the outset of the revolution. Though he maintained that he wanted only to avoid "Noise, Tumult & War," the state treated him as a loyalist. It forbade him to return to Massachusetts and took control of his lovely Boston house. To raise money during the war, the state mortgaged the house and sold his furniture. The ensuing machinations over title are complicated, but happily not germane for our purposes. Eventually Vassall's lawyer filed suit in the Supreme Court—and Massachusetts failed to appear. Just as Georgia had, Massachusetts believed state sov-

102. *Augusta Chronicle* (23 August 1793); the measure is also in *Congressional Record* (21 February 1831).

103. *Augusta Chronicle* (7 December 1793); *Documentary History*, 5: 237 n. 2.

104. *General Advertiser* (4 July 1793); *Gazette of the United States* (6 July 1793).

105. For a lengthy review, see Kurt T. Lash, "Leaving the *Chisholm* Trail: The Eleventh Amendment and the Background Principle of Strict Construction," *William and Mary Law Review* (April 2009). Or see the cases and materials collected in vols. 5 and 6 of *Documentary History*. For the basic narrative of *Vassall*, I've relied on *Documentary History*, 5:352–69. Two states jousted about *Chisholm* in an illuminating border dispute: see *Rhode Island v. Massachusetts*, 37 U.S. 657 (1838), along with *Argument in the Case Rhode-Island against Massachusetts* (Providence, 1838).

ereignty precluded federal jurisdiction in the case. In 1793, Sam Adams drafted a letter circulated to the other states. "The claim of a Judiciary Authority over a State possessed of *Sovereignty*, was of too much moment to be submitted to, without the most serious deliberation." On mature consideration, the Massachusetts legislature had decided federal jurisdiction was "dangerous to the peace, safety & independence of the several States, & repugnant to the first principles of a Federal Government." And here Adams scared up the phantom Madison had sought assiduously to exorcise: "the power claimed, if once established, will extirpate the federal principle, & procure a consolidation of all the Governments."[106] Adams was echoing the state's attorney general, who'd already weighed in: "Sovereignty must, in its nature, be absolute and uncontrollable by any civil authority." "The states, as states, were not liable to the civil process of the supreme judicial of the Union; and no one pretended to say, that if the states were so liable, there was not a consolidation of all the governments into one."[107] We can go back further. In the *Federalist*, Hamilton had assured his readers, "It is inherent in the nature of sovereignty not to be amenable to the suit of an individual WITHOUT ITS CONSENT."[108]

106. For the episode, John K. Alexander, *Samuel Adams: The Life of an American Revolutionary* (Lanham: Rowman & Littlefield, 2011), 290–92. The text of the letter is not in *The Writings of Samuel Adams*, ed. Harry Alonzo Cushing, 4 vols. (New York: G. P. Putnam's Sons, 1904–8); instead see *Records of the Governour and Council of the State of Vermont*, 8 vols. (Montpelier, 1873), 4:427–28. For the manuscript version, see *Documentary History*, 5:442–43. The judge who sat with Iredell in the first court to hear Chisholm's complaint also worried about consolidation: Edmund Pendleton to Nathaniel Pendleton, 10 August 1793, in *Documentary History*, 5:232.

107. James Sullivan, *Observations upon the Government of the United States of America* (Boston, 1791), 22, 30; see generally 22–37.

108. *Federalist* no. 81. Story closely followed Hamilton's language: Joseph Story, *Commentaries on the Constitution of the United States*, 3 vols. (Boston, 1833), 3:538. See too *Beers v. Arkansas*, 61 U.S. 527, 529 (1857): "It is an

Alarmed at what some took to be the overweening role of federal courts, the states ratified the Eleventh Amendment: "The Judicial power of the United States shall not be construed to extend to any suit in law or equity, commenced or prosecuted against one of the United States by Citizens of another State, or by Citizens or Subjects of any Foreign State." Though the initial text of the Constitution had granted federal jurisdiction over "Controversies . . . between a State and Citizens of another State,"[109] a provision underwritten by the First Judiciary Act,[110] Madison had argued in Virginia's ratifying convention that federal jurisdiction would obtain only "if a state should condescend to be a party."[111] (*Condescend* here means graciously lower itself from its dignified status to deal with a lowly inferior on as-if terms of equality.)[112] And Madison commented decades later that the amendment "may as well import that it was declaratory, as that it was restrictive of the meaning of the original text."[113] I've no interest in fussing over the

established principle of jurisprudence in all civilized nations that the sovereign cannot be sued in its own courts, or in any other, without its consent and permission; but it may, if it thinks proper, waive this privilege, and permit itself to be made a defendant in a suit by individuals." For the suggestion that a foreign sovereign can be invited to appear, *Manning v. State of Nicaragua*, 14 How. Pr. 517 (N.Y. Sup. Ct. 1875).

109. Art. 3, sec. 2, cl. 1.

110. 1 Stat. 73, sec. 13 (1789), granting the Supreme Court "original but not exclusive jurisdiction" in controversies "between a state and citizens of other states, or aliens."

111. *The Debates in the Several State Conventions on the Adoption of the Federal Constitution*, collected by Jonathan Elliot, 2nd ed., 4 vols. (Washington, [DC], 1854), 3:533 (20 June 1788).

112. For more on this sense, see my *Poisoning the Minds of the Lower Orders* (Princeton, NJ: Princeton University Press, 1998), 206–10.

113. Madison to Spencer Roane, 6 May 1821, in *The Republic of Letters: The Correspondence between Thomas Jefferson and James Madison, 1776–1826*, ed. James Morton Smith, 3 vols. (New York: Norton, 1995), 3:1873. See too

original understanding, though sanity demands noticing the abundant evidence that the appeal to state sovereignty to resist federal jurisdiction was hotly contested. We've already seen Wilson's staunch view in *Chisholm* and his role in the founding, not to mention the Judiciary Act, which after all made it through Congress when state legislatures were still choosing senators. I'll add just one bit of pungent sarcasm, from a 1793 letter to a Boston newspaper: "Does not every body know that *sovereignty* consists in doing *injustice* with impunity? Has it not in all ages been one of the darling prerogatives of royal sovereignty, and is not republican sovereignty entitled to the *right* of doing *wrong* without answering for it, as much as any crowned villain that ever existed?"[114] Such deep controversy in the originalist sources suggests that at least we should get used to thinking of original understandings, plural, and then deciding how to adjudicate among them—if or insofar as we care about original understandings. The case that it's normatively dubious shoved firmly aside, originalism is a meretricious Tower-of-Babel fantasy. It's just not true that once upon a time, people agreed about what the Constitution means, and only later got confused. They disagreed immediately: on the Alien and Sedition Acts, on the Bank of the United States,[115] and more. Some patrons claim that originalism yields clear results, but the theory can't deliver the goods.[116]

Agrippa to the People, *Massachusetts Gazette* (11 December 1787); Hampden, *Massachusetts Centinel* (26 January 1788); *Forms of Government* (Annapolis, 1827), 133.

114. "From Correspondents," *Mercury* [Boston] (26 July 1793).

115. There's an especially amusing speech by Henry Clay, *Debates and Proceedings in the Congress of the United States* (15 February 1811).

116. My objection isn't novel, and indeed leading originalists at least implicitly concede the gist of it. For a thoughtful examination, see Richard H.

Instead of fencing with originalists, though, I want to distinguish different views swirled together in these discussions. Is the problem letting a state be sued by a citizen of another state? or hauling a sovereign state into federal court against its will? Is it those conditions jointly? (The federal courts play an everyday role in so-called diversity jurisdiction: if you sue a citizen of another state, we worry that neither your state courts nor hers would be suitably impartial.) Or is it making a sovereign state answerable in any court at all? And whichever view you choose, what exactly is the problem with permitting lawsuits against states?

The case law is haunted by appeals to sovereign dignity, as if it were an insult to haul a state into court against its will—as if an American state were King Charles I.[117] In 1887, the Supreme Court declared, "The very object and purpose of the Eleventh Amendment were to prevent the indignity of subjecting a state to the coercive process of judicial tribunals at the instance of private parties."[118] In 2002, nothing had changed: "The preeminent purpose of state sovereign immunity is to accord States the dignity that is consistent with their status as sovereign entities."[119] Despite the plain text of the Eleventh

---

Fallon, Jr., "Judicially Manageable Standards and Constitutional Meaning," *Harvard Law Review* (March 2006), 1317–20.

117. For more extended treatments, with varying degrees of skepticism and approval, see Ann Althouse, "On Dignity and Deference: The Supreme Court's New Federalism," *University of Cincinnati Law Review* (Winter 2000); Evan H. Caminker, "Judicial Solicitude for State Dignity," *Annals of the American Academy of Political and Social Science* (March 2001); Scott Dodson, "Dignity: The New Frontier of State Sovereignty," *Oklahoma Law Review* (Winter 2003).

118. In re Ayres, 123 U.S. 443, 505 (1887), approvingly quoted in *Puerto Rico Aqueduct and Sewer Authority v. Metcalf & Eddy, Inc.*, 506 U.S. 139, 146 (1993).

119. Federal Maritime Comm'n v. S.C. State Ports Auth., 535 U.S. 743, 760 (2002).

Amendment, in 1890 the Supreme Court decided that citizens couldn't even sue their own states in federal court.[120] (Ordinarily federal courts also have jurisdiction when a case poses significant questions of federal law.) Nor can Congress use its Article I powers to eliminate the states' ability to invoke sovereign immunity. Here's Justice Kennedy, writing for the Court: "Federalism requires that Congress accord States the respect and dignity due them as residuary sovereigns and joint participants in the Nation's governance. Immunity from suit in federal courts is not enough to preserve that dignity, for the indignity of subjecting a nonconsenting State to the coercive process of judicial tribunals at the instance of private parties exists regardless of the forum."[121] States enjoy "a substantial portion of the Nation's primary sovereignty, together with the dignity and essential attributes inhering in that status."[122]

I know people who discard such language as pious flapdoodle, the sort of poetic rhapsody to which Justice Kennedy was prone now and again. But Justice Kennedy isn't alone in the doctrine, and the appeal to sovereign dignity has a

120. Hans v. Louisiana, 134 U.S. 1 (1890). However quixotically, Justice Brennan remained staunchly opposed to this doctrine: see, for instance, *Edelman v. Jordan*, 415 U.S. 651, 667–68 (1974) (Brennan, J., dissenting).

121. Alden v. Maine, 527 U.S. 706, 709 (1999). On the scope of this rule, see too *Seminole Tribe of Fla. v. Florida*, 517 U.S. 44 (1996). But Congress can still use its powers under section 5 of the Fourteenth Amendment in this domain: *Fitzpatrick v. Bitzer*, 427 U.S. 445 (1976). For cautions about the scope of *Fitzpatrick* after *City of Boerne v. Flores*, 521 U.S. 607 (1997), see *Florida Prepaid Postsecondary Ed. Expense Bd. v. College Savings Bank*, 527 U.S. 627 (1999).

122. *Alden* at 714. The hits just keep on coming: See too *Franchise Tax Bd. of Cal. v. Hyatt*, 587 U.S. __ (2019), overruling *Nevada v. Hall*, 440 U.S. 410 (1979) and enlisting "Each State's equal sovereignty and dignity" (slip op. at 13) to hold that states cannot be hauled into other states' courts, either. "The States' sovereign immunity is a historically rooted principle embedded in the text and structure of the Constitution" (*Hyatt*, slip op. at 16).

distinguished lineage. No wonder that in a scathing dissent, Justice Souter reviewed Bodin, Pufendorf, Blackstone, and more. No wonder that after quoting Blackstone's rhapsody to royal dignity, Souter sounded just like the newspapers so exasperated with Governor Evans's professing insult at being presented with an arrest warrant: "It would be hard to imagine anything more inimical to the republican conception, which rests on the understanding of its citizens precisely that the government is not above them, but of them, its actions being governed by law just like their own."[123]

The problem is not that states aren't the sort of entities that might have dignity or might be insulted.[124] If you drag a state flag through the mud while jeering at the state's ugly capitol, you express contempt for the state: that's easy. The problem is why we should construe having to answer to a lawsuit as an invidious insult. Not for the first time, the telltale emptiness of the appeal to sovereignty lies innocently on the surface. It's in Hamilton's appeal to sovereignty's inherent nature, in Kennedy's to its essential attributes—each as vacuous as Burlamaqui's assertion that it's an essential characteristic of sovereignty to be above the law. The question-begging language points not

123. *Alden* at 802 (Souter, J., dissenting).

124. Henry Paul Monaghan, "Comment: The Sovereign Immunity 'Exception,'" *Harvard Law Review* (November 1996), 132, scoffs at the Court's invoking "indignity" in *Seminole Tribe*: "The idea that a state, an utterly abstract entity, has feelings about being sued by a private party when 'its' highest officials are regularly so sued surely strains credulity." So too Michael C. Dorf, "The Supreme Court 1997 Term: Foreword: The Limits of Socratic Deliberation," *Harvard Law Review* (November 1998), 61, scoffs at the Court's appeal to "the dignity of the states—as if they were natural persons that could experience hurt feelings beyond those of their residents." But—their mistake is sadly common—dignitary harms aren't a matter of hurt feelings. They are, as I've said before, public, objective, sociological: see my *Defaming the Dead* (New Haven, CT: Yale University Press, 2017), especially 215, 229.

to any feature of the world, but to the meaning of a concept. But it is an open question whether states ought to enjoy legal immunity. That question can't be settled by reminding us what hallowed theorists have said about sovereignty, because once again we are free to respond that we don't want states to be sovereign in that sense.

The historical record is peppered with outraged complaints about sovereign immunity. In the 1840s, Mississippi stopped making payments on some of its bonds; later the state simply repudiated some.[125] A Boston lawyer denounced "this stupendous fraud," "this atrocious fraud," "an act which would make the cheek of an Arab burn with shame." (Insert deep sigh here.) But what was to be done? "By its independent sovereignty it defies the national judiciary."[126] In the 1870s, Tennessee wrestled with a familiar debtor's problem, what to do about bonds it couldn't make payments on. Proposed schemes included simply refusing to pay.[127] A Tennessee newspaper waxed indignant: the legislators "as a last resort are always ready to say to the public creditor, You can't sue us, so go ahead and crack your whip, we'll button our pockets and you may help yourselves. . . . Honest men can only hold down their heads in shame and hope for better times."[128]

Eleventh Amendment jurisprudence has focused on dragging states into federal court. But modern American law also permits the federal government to refuse to be sued in

125. Clifford Thies, "Repudiation in Antebellum Mississippi," *Independent Review* (Fall 2014).

126. A Member of the Boston Bar [Ivers James Austin], *An Account of the Origin of the Mississippi Doctrine of Repudiation* (Boston, 1842), 22.

127. Robert B. Jones, *Tennessee at the Crossroads: The State Debt Controversy, 1870–1883* (Knoxville: University of Tennessee Press, 1977).

128. "The Legislature on the Debt," *Clarksville Weekly Chronicle* (22 March 1879).

tort in its own courts—and permits states to refuse to be sued in tort in their own courts. That's the background or default rule, though governments can graciously condescend to be sued by specifying the circumstances under which they'll permit it. (The federal government didn't permit *any* tort actions against itself until 1946.)[129] One standard twentieth-century reference work puts it this way: "The rule is well established that a state is not liable for the negligence or misfeasance of its officers or agents, except when such liability is voluntarily assumed by its legislature."[130] Branding it "unfair and unsuited to the times," Pennsylvania's high court abolished the doctrine of sovereign immunity.[131] Scant weeks later—American democracy isn't all that sclerotic—the state legislature reimposed it.[132] We sometimes say, unilluminatingly, that sovereign immunity in tort stems from the common law. Sure, but more specifically it comes from the same hoary insistence that the sovereign is above the law.[133] Brood over this bit from Oliver Wendell

129. Federal Tort Claims Act, 60 Stat. 842. For discussions of British law from the same period, see "They Can Do No Wrong," *Courier and Advertiser* [Dundee] (5 May 1938); "Justice," *Daily Mail* [Hull] (10 April 1942); "A Long-Delayed Reform," *Western Daily Press and Bristol Mirror* (18 April 1942).

130. *Ruling Case Law*, ed. William M. McKinney and Burdett A. Rich, 28 vols. (Northport, NY: Edward Thompson, 1914–21), 25:407, cited in legal sources as 25 R. C. L. 407. See too Herbert Broom, *A Selection of Legal Maxims* (London, 1845), 13, 50, 200.

131. Mayle v. Pennsylvania Dep't of Highways, 479 Pa. 384 (1978).

132. 1 Pa.C.S. § 2310.

133. See, for instance, Alpheus Todd, *On Parliamentary Government in England*, 2 vols. (London, 1867–69), 1:168. Harold J. Laski, "The Responsibility of the State in England: To Roscoe Pound," *Harvard Law Review* (March 1919), reprinted in Laski, *The Foundations of Sovereignty and Other Essays* (New York: Harcourt, Brace, 1921), is both a helpful analysis of the background and a polemic. For the history, the state of the law about a century ago, and an indispensable critique, see the series by Edwin M. Borchard,

Holmes, expressing the ubiquitous insistence for the Supreme Court: "Some doubts have been expressed as to the source of the immunity of a sovereign power from suit without its own permission, but the answer has been public property since before the days of Hobbes. (Leviathan, c. 26, 2.) A sovereign is exempt from suit, not because of any formal conception or obsolete theory, but on the logical and practical ground that there can be no legal right as against the authority that makes the law on which the right depends. '*Car on peut bien recevoir loy d'autruy, mais il est impossible par nature de se donner loy*.' Bodin, Republique, 1, c. 8."[134] Holmes went on to cite John Eliot, whose work we've glanced at, and Baldus, whose work we haven't. This battery of venerable sources gives away the game. Holmes's contrast between "formal conception or obsolete theory" and "logical and practical ground" is illusory, because the bit from Bodin and the associated citations are merely formal or logical claims. Yet again, this picture of sovereignty and law doesn't capture or illuminate anything in the

---

"Government Liability in Tort" (and variant titles), *Yale Law Journal* (November 1924, December 1924, January 1925, November 1926, April 1927, June 1927), *Columbia Law Review* (May 1928, June 1928). For a more recent peremptory polemic urging that the doctrine is unconstitutional, see Erwin Chemerinsky, "Against Sovereign Immunity," *Stanford Law Review* (May 2001).

134. Kawananakoa v. Polybank, 205 U.S. 349, 353 (1907). See too *American Banana Co. v. United Fruit Co.*, 213 U.S. 347, 357–58 (1909); *Ex parte United States*, 257 U.S. 419, 432–33 (1922); Holmes to Harold Laski, 29 January 1926, in *Holmes-Laski Letters: The Correspondence of Mr. Justice Homes and Harold J. Laski, 1916–1935*, ed. Mark DeWolfe Howe, 2 vols. (Cambridge, MA: Harvard University Press, 1953), 2:822–23. Holmes and Laski amiably fenced over the decision for years, but Holmes never budged: "I categorically and brutally think that one who doesn't think it right (I mean in the general aspects) simply doesn't understand what he is talking about" (Holmes to Laski, 3 January 1926, in *Holmes-Laski Letters*, 2:817).

world, in our available political and legal options. It reminds us of the structure of a concept. That won't do.

There are countless cases where plaintiffs' suits are dismissed because of sovereign immunity. Working in a quarry, Carl Koehler was injured when a rock came flying his way from a blast in the next quarry, operated by the state, and hit him in the head. To recover about $3,000 paid him in workmen's compensation but also to win him more adequate damages, his employer sought $20,000 from the government, but the state high court found no legislative action authorizing such a suit.[135] Connecticut law requires prospective litigants to play a curious version of "Mother, may I?" with the state's Claims Commissioner. "Whenever the Claims Commissioner deems it just and equitable, the Claims Commissioner may authorize suit against the state on any claim which, in the opinion of the Claims Commissioner, presents an issue of law or fact under which the state, were it a private person, could be liable."[136] The rule, if you can call it that, is strikingly reminiscent of unstructured sovereign grace. To put it mildly, it raises due process worries; a state court rejected a challenge to it as an unconstitutional delegation of authority under the state constitution.[137] Here's an example of how it works for Connecticut litigants. Susan Brik gave birth to Vayle Nelson in a private hospital. Vayle was having trouble breathing and her blood was acidotic. The doctor decided she needed to be transferred. But the state transport team was late in getting her to a state hospital: Vayle ended up with severe brain damage. The commissioner denied the aggrieved parties' application to sue because

135. Wisconsin Granite Co. v. State, 54 S.D. 482 (1929).

136. Conn. Gen. Stat. § 4-160(a). For the legislature's oversight role, see § 4-159.

137. State v. Charlotte Hungerford Hosp., 133 Conn. App. 479 (2012).

they hadn't complied with the usual discovery requirements. They got a new lawyer and tried again. The commissioner granted the claim—but in court the state argued successfully that he didn't have authority under the statute to reverse his initial judgment.[138]

The legal thickets can be daunting. Veteran David Muir died after participating in clinical drug trials run by the University of Cincinnati Medical Center and the Cincinnati Veterans Administration Medical Center. He had been badly burned, he was severely depressed, and he had hepatitis C. Filing a flurry of claims, his sister wanted to argue that his death was caused by medical malpractice. But the Eleventh Amendment, sovereign immunity, and her failure to file on time under the Federal Torts Claim Act meant that she never got to present her case on the merits.[139] Had the rock slamming into Koehler come from a privately operated quarry, had a private transport firm delayed getting Nelson to another private hospital, had Muir died after treatment in a private hospital, their lawsuits would have sailed forward effortlessly. Of course plaintiffs might have won or lost. But they would have had a

138. This is a partial rendition of long-running, complicated litigation, which later took up a retroactive amendment of the relevant statute. See *Nelson v. Dettmer*, No. X07CV075012152S, 2008 Conn. Super. LEXIS 1926 (Super. Ct. July 30, 2008); *Nelson v. Dettmer*, 2008 Conn. Super. LEXIS 2853 (Super. Ct. Nov. 13, 2008); *Nelson v. Dettmer*, 2009 Conn. Super. LEXIS 479 (Super. Ct. Feb. 11, 2009); *Nelson v. Dettmer*, 2009 Conn. Super. LEXIS 1546 (Super. Ct. June 4, 2009); *Nelson v. Dettmer*, 2009 WL 6383056 (December 10, 2009); *Nelson v. Dettmer*, 305 Conn. 654 (2012); *Nelson v. Dettmer*, 2015 Conn. Super. LEXIS 1326 (Super. Ct. Mar. 12, 2015). I've drawn too on various pleadings in the case, at least some of which are publicly available despite a motion to seal introduced at one point. Conn. Gen. Stat. § 4-156 is the disputed provision on rehearings; § 4-158 is the amended provision.

139. Sykes v. United States, 507 Fed. Appx. 455 (6th Cir. 2012).

chance. Defendants would not have been permitted to wriggle free of the charges by appealing to sovereignty.

Today torts professors routinely tell their students that every jurisdiction has a torts claim act specifying the conditions under which the sovereign will permit itself to be sued. Well, not quite. Tennessee legislation imposes a blanket ban.[140] The legislature is obviously free to reverse or modify that, though I see no reason to believe it will. Not so in Arkansas, whose constitution has provided since 1874 that "the State of Arkansas shall never be made defendant in any of her courts."[141] Official bodies have proposed changes,[142] but the provision stands. Matthew Andrews sued under the state's minimum wage act: he was the bookstore manager for Rich Mountain Community College and the college had stopped paying him overtime. And indeed the act explicitly provided for suing the state or its subdivisions.[143] But the state supreme court ruled, perfectly sensibly, that the legislature didn't have the authority to evade the constitutional ban.[144]

Remember that all I want to urge in this book is that we learn to think about these matters without relying on the con-

140. Tenn. Code Ann. § 20-13-102.

141. Ark. Const. Art. 5, § 20. Louisiana's constitution sets the default rule as full liability in tort, but permits the legislature to limit it: La. Const. Art. XII, § 10. Wash. Const. Art. I, § 12 provides, "No law shall be passed granting to any citizen, class of citizens, or corporation other than municipal, privileges or immunities which upon the same terms shall not equally belong to all citizens, or corporations." So what's so special about municipal corporations?

142. Arkansas Constitutional Revision Study Commission, *Revising the Arkansas Constitution* (Little Rock: n.p., 1968), 42; *A Report to the People of the State of Arkansas by the Seventh Arkansas Constitutional Convention* (Little Rock: n.p., 1970), 70.

143. Ark. Code Ann. § 11-4-218(e).

144. Bd. of Trs. of the Univ. of Ark. v. Andrews, 2018 Ark. 12 (2018).

cept of sovereignty. So officially I have nothing to say about whether the rules of sovereign immunity are justifiable absent any hand-waving about how the sovereign must be above the law. I will, though, permit myself to blurt out that the Eleventh Amendment and sovereign immunity in tort are laughably bad rules, patent affronts to equality under the law. And I will permit myself to glare with a jaundiced eye at a typical argument for immunity, this version offered at Illinois's sixth constitutional convention. That state's constitution had had the same flat ban on suing the state that Arkansas's still does.[145] Now an amendment was being proposed: the default rule would be that the state would be liable in tort, but the state legislature would be permitted to impose restrictions.[146] Mr. Foster was opposed: "It's all very well to say fair is fair and the state should stand like other people, but the state's charged with the responsibility of protecting persons and property. It does things nobody else does. It sends policemen out with guns on their hips; it sends firemen out; it operates prisons, jails, and hospitals. It is responsible far more than any other individual, and to say it should have no greater standing in court than someone else is just plain, to me, silly."[147] Yes, the state does lots of more or less unique things that might turn out to injure its citizens. (Though I wonder what rule Mr. Foster would recommend for private prisons and hospitals.) So

145. Ill. Const. (1870), Art. IV, § 26.

146. The new provision was adopted: Ill. Const. (1970), Art. XIII, § 4. The legislature reimposed plenty of immunity: Ill. Rev. Stat., Ch. 127, ¶ 801 (1973), now 745 Ill. Comp. Stat. Ann. 5/1. See *Williamson Towing Co. v. Illinois*, 534 F.2d 758 (7th Cir. 1976), sorting out a tangle about the relationship between this statute and the Eleventh Amendment.

147. *Record of Proceedings: Sixth Illinois Constitutional Convention*, 8 vols. (Springfield: Secretary of State, 1972–88), 5:3952. For more general discussion of the new provision, 6:633–90.

does General Motors. I can round up the other usual suspect arguments quickly enough. Like the state, or anyway Mr. Foster, GM might love to point out that its budget would suffer if it had to pay out tort judgments and settlements. Like the state or Mr. Foster, GM might like to huff and puff about how busy and important it is, and how fielding tort complaints will distract it from making whizbang cars, a socially important task. But we don't let GM press such arguments.[148] If such arguments are, to use a learned term of art, just plain silly when applied to GM, why aren't they just plain silly when applied to the government? Don't say it's because the government is sovereign, lest you find yourself flailing and strangling in a vanishingly tight circle.

Just an Old Sweet Song

Let's return to Georgia, several decades after it lost *Chisholm*—but gained the Eleventh Amendment. The state was once again squabbling with the federal government over sovereignty, this time with another contestant in the match, the Cherokee tribe or nation, and no, there isn't a politically or legally neutral category here. The story begins with Georgia's arrest, prosecution, and conviction of George (or Corn) Tassels (or Tassel) for murder. Tassels had murdered another Native American at Talking Rock, in Cherokee territory, but there he was in Hall County, being found guilty in a Georgia court. Did Georgia have jurisdiction in the case? The county superior court briskly rejected the claim that it didn't. Not just prior American case law, but

148. On crushing liability as a reason to relieve actors of liability, contrast *Strauss v. Belle Realty Co.*, 65 N.Y.2d 399 (Ct. of App. N.Y. 1985) with *Stevens v. Owens-Corning Fiberglas Corp.*, 49 Cal. App. 4th 1645 (1996).

that distinguished theorist of sovereignty, Vattel, proved that Georgia held the land the Cherokees resided on as property. "It is difficult to conceive how any person, who has a definite idea of what constitutes a sovereign State, can have come to the conclusion that the Cherokee Nation is a sovereign and independent State."[149]

There were state laws on point, too—if they were legally valid. Georgia had been moving against the Cherokees for some time. In 1825, the governor had warned against an overweening federal role in dealing with the Cherokee and Creek tribes alike. Professing "devotion to the Union," he denounced a "consolidation"—we've seen that fateful word—and a perverted union that would leave the states with but "a shadow of sovereignty."[150] In 1827, the state had extended the state's criminal jurisdiction over part of Cherokee territory, though not apparently over Talking Rock.[151] In 1828, the state had prohibited members of the tribe from entering Georgia.[152] The next year, it had decreed that "no Indian, or descendant of Indian" of the Creek or Cherokee nations could appear as a competent witness in any suit "to which a white man may be a party."[153] Also in 1829, it had extended the state's criminal jurisdiction over all the Georgia lands occupied by the Cherokee. It had

149. State v. George Tassels, 1 Dud. 229 (Hall Superior Court, September 1830). Vattel also provides authority in "The Legislature," *Constitutionalist* [Augusta] (23 November 1830).

150. "Governor's Message," *Daily Georgian* (14 November 1825). For the state's protest against federal spending to support the American Colonization Society, *Resolutions of the Legislature of Georgia, in Relation to the American Colonization Society, February 4, 1828* (Washington, DC, 1828).

151. *Laws of the Colonial and State Governments, Relating to Indians and Indian Affairs, from 1633 to 1831* (Washington City, 1832), 195.

152. *Laws*, 197–98.

153. *Laws*, 199.

also expanded the boundaries of Hall County to include territory claimed by the Cherokees, but the new boundaries didn't reach as far as Talking Rock.[154]

Chief Justice Marshall of the Supreme Court sent down a writ of error to hear Tassels's case. The governor presented it to the legislature, which responded with a 22 December 1830 resolution: "The right to punish crimes, against the peace and good order of this State, in accordance with existing laws, is an original and necessary part of sovereignty which the State of Georgia has never parted with." So it somberly expressed the "deepest regret" about the chief justice's "interference." Meanwhile, full speed ahead: the governor should instruct Hall County's sheriff—"by express," no less—to proceed with the execution.[155] American bureaucracy isn't always all that sclerotic, either: Tassels was hanged just two days later. Soon,

154. *Laws*, 199–200. For the changing map of Georgia, see http://publications.newberry.org/ahcbp/map/map.html#GA (last visited 16 July 2018). The 1829 statute expands Hall County; the maps show no change until 1831, when it shrinks. I haven't sorted this out, because the jurisdictional statute is doing the work that matters here. The state's measures were noticed elsewhere: consider, for instance, the sardonic "Georgia Indians," *Charleston Mercury* (20 January 1830), acknowledging the concern of New Yorkers: "The State of Georgia is infinitely indebted to them for their kind interference in her domestic regulation, and for the friendly disposition which they manifest to decide the relative rights of the general government, of the State of Georgia, and of the Indians within her limits"; and see the sustained follow-up in *Charleston Mercury* (23 January 1830). Later the paper replaced the sardonic prose with scathing denunciation: "We have never regarded the Indian meetings of the North in any other light than that of impertinent interference in the internal regulations of the Southern States" (3 April 1830).

155. *Acts of the General Assembly of the State of Georgia, Passed in Milledgeville at an Annual Session in October, November and December 1830* (Milledgeville: By Authority, 1831), 282–83. Note too "Governor's Message," *Georgia Journal* (23 October 1830), also in *Southern Recorder* (23 October 1830) and *Federal Union* (23 October 1830). For a sympathetic overview,

New York papers excoriated the Southern papers exulting in the deed.[156] But the glee lingered. "We have heard it repeatedly asked, where will all this end? The answer seems to us very plain. *Why, with the Death of the Indian!* The Supreme Court says, You, State of Georgia, shall not hang the Indian. The State of Georgia says, I will *hang* the Indian. Well the Indian is hung!—what then! To whom is the State of Georgia answerable? To the Supreme Court? Surely not! Is she not a sovereign, free and independent State, and knows no master save disposing Heaven!"[157] Then again, an Alabama newspaper wrote, "the 'poor Indian' who is scorned and scoffed at by a certain set of political zealots in our country, when supplicating justice from the Supreme Court, will be just as sure of the protection of his rights, as if he were the proudest nabob in the land."[158]

Though Tassels's case was arguably moot, Georgia was doubling down: the month before the Supreme Court ruled, legislation kicked in criminalizing Cherokee self-govern-

---

see "The Tribunal of Dernier Resort," *Southern Review* (November 1830), 421–512.

156. "Georgia and the Supreme Court," *Commercial Advertiser* (6 January 1831); "Georgia and the Supreme Court," *New-York Spectator* (11 January 1831).

157. "Important from Georgia," *Southern Recorder* (15 January 1831), attributed to the *Charleston Mercury*, from an issue I've not located: in the relevant weeks some issues are missing, some illegible. Tocsin, "Well Done, Georgia!" *Charleston Mercury* (30 December 1830), is self-explanatory; "George Tassels," *Charleston Mercury* (1 January 1831), reprints the *Georgia Athenian* to report Tassels's execution. The language I've quoted above is quoted again, as part of a lengthy response, in A Georgian, "For the Cherokee Phoenix," *Cherokee Phoenix, and Indians' Advocate* (12 February 1831). It is also in the two New York newspaper stories just cited. Contrast the muted tones of "Execution of an Indian," *Western Luminary* (2 February 1831).

158. Florence, Alabama *Gazette*, quoted in "Georgia and the Indians," *Cherokee Phoenix* (5 March 1831). I have not located the original story.

ment.[159] One observer noticed "the exceeding desire of Georgia to extend her sovereignty over the lands of the Cherokees."[160] So the Cherokees sought an injunction preventing Georgia from enforcing its laws in their territory. Georgia again sent no lawyer to represent it before the Supreme Court. The Eleventh Amendment doesn't compromise the constitutional grant of federal jurisdiction in cases "between a State . . . and foreign States."[161] But were the Cherokees a foreign state in the relevant sense?

No, ruled Chief Justice Marshall for the Court. Among other observations, he made deft use of the constitutional grant of power to Congress to "regulate commerce with foreign nations . . . and with the Indian tribes."[162] This is the familiar canon that we not render legal language as "mere surplusage": it would be weird to include the latter clause if the tribes already qualified as foreign nations. And then Marshall argues that "foreign nation" and "foreign state" have the same referent in these two different clauses of the Constitution. So the Cherokees weren't a foreign nation: "They may, more correctly, perhaps, be denominated domestic dependent nations . . . in a state of pupilage. Their relation to the United States resembles that of a ward to his guardian."[163] And that meant the federal courts had no jurisdiction.

159. *Laws*, 220–23.

160. "Georgia and the Cherokees," *Niles' Weekly Register* (8 January 1831).

161. Art. 3, sec. 2.

162. Art. 1, sec. 8, cl. 3. The opinion confusedly refers here to "the eighth section of the third article" (*Cherokee Nation v. Georgia*, 30 U.S. 1, 18 (1831)). This isn't an error in the Lexis transcription; it appears that way in the print edition, *Reports of Cases Argued and Adjudged in the Supreme Court of the United States: January Term 1831*, reported by Richard Peters (Philadelphia, 1831), 162.

163. *Cherokee Nation* at 17–20. Compare Akhil Reed Amar, "Intratextualism," *Harvard Law Review* (February 1999), whose thesis seems to be that

Justice Johnson's opinion is listed as a dissent, but he too would deny relief. And he agrees that "in no sense can [the Cherokees] be deemed a foreign state, under the judiciary article." So the Court didn't have jurisdiction. But perhaps "in pursuance of my practice in giving an opinion on all constitutional questions," the opposite of the modern rule of avoidance, Johnson presses on and arrives at a version of what we now call the political questions doctrine: the Cherokees' motion was "one of a political character altogether, and wholly unfit for the cognizance of a judicial tribunal." Why? "In the exercise of sovereign right, the sovereign is sole arbiter of his own justice. The penalty of wrong is war and subjugation."[164] "The judicial power cannot divest the states of rights of sovereignty," agrees Justice Baldwin.[165]

Sovereignty plays out differently for Justice Thompson, who really was dissenting: diffident about pronouncing on the constitutionality of Georgia law in the abstract, diffident about trespassing on political questions, he would grant relief. Why? He applies Vattel and finds the Cherokees sovereign: and that means that the Court would have jurisdiction, in turn that Georgia couldn't be permitted to subvert laws and treaties of the United States.[166]

But Tassels was hanged, the Court held it could not issue the injunctive relief that the Cherokees sought, and Georgia kept right at it. The state had also banned white people

---

particular words and phrases (or "very similar" ones, 748) mean the same thing throughout the Constitution, except when they don't. It would be helpful to have criteria for when they do and when they don't.

164. *Cherokee Nation* at 27, 20, 28, 29 (Johnson, J., dissenting).

165. *Cherokee Nation* at 49 (Baldwin, J., dissenting).

166. For the use of Vattel, *Cherokee Nation* at 53 (Thompson, J., dissenting). Thompson was joined by Story (*Cherokee Nation* at 80). For Thompson's rebuttal of Marshall's commerce-clause argument as "mere verbal criticism," see *Cherokee Nation* at 62.

from being in Cherokee territory unless they obtained a permit from the governor (or his agent) and took a loyalty oath.[167] Samuel Worcester, a New England missionary who would translate the Bible for the tribe,[168] ran afoul of that rule; a Georgia grand jury indicted him. Worcester argued that Georgia's law unconstitutionally violated U.S. treaties with the Cherokee. Georgia's court denied that plea. Worcester was convicted and sentenced to four years' hard labor. Once again the Supreme Court issued a writ of error; once again Georgia didn't deign to send a lawyer to represent its case before the Supreme Court.

There is no Eleventh Amendment problem here. Worcester wasn't launching a suit against Georgia; he was appealing his own conviction.[169] Nor does the legal status of the Cherokees pose any jurisdictional problem: they're not a party to the action. So nothing calls for a searching account of whether they qualify as "foreign nations" in the sense at issue in the prior dispute. This time, Marshall readily finds that federal treaties, coupled with the Constitution's insistence that federal law is supreme, mean that the Georgia law at issue is unconstitutional.[170] I suppose his tone about the Indians is more generous, but the substance seems much the same. "The Indian nations were, from their situation, necessarily dependent on some foreign potentate for the supply of their essential wants, and for their protection from lawless and injurious intrusions

167. *Laws*, 221–22.

168. On Worcester's missionary work, see William G. McLoughlin, *The Cherokees and Christianity, 1794–1870*, ed. Walter H. Conser, Jr. (Athens: University of Georgia Press, 1994), 54–83.

169. Cohens v. Virginia, 19 U.S. 264, 405–12 (1821), already had placed the posture of cases such as Worcester's outside the reach of the Eleventh Amendment.

170. Worcester v. Georgia, 31 U.S. 515 (1832).

into their country."[171] "The Indian nations had always been considered as distinct, independent political communities, retaining their original natural rights, as the undisputed possessors of the soil, from time immemorial, with the single exception of that imposed by irresistible power."[172] You can fence about the move from *dependent* to *independent*, but nothing in the case hangs on it. This case really is easier: there's only one dissent, driven by a finicky worry about whether it's okay to have the state court's clerk, not the court itself, respond to the writ of error by sending the record.[173]

If Georgia had less cause to celebrate than it did in the earlier case, still the state refused to comply. The Court's ruling was the occasion of President Jackson's infamous remark: "Well, John Marshall has made his decision, now let him enforce it." The remark is apocryphal, apparently first recorded in 1864.[174] But whether or not he said those words, Jackson's sympathies were obviously with the state throughout.[175] (An 1830 Fourth of July celebration of states' rights in Charleston displayed Jackson's portrait: "Honor and gratitude to his name—he has repulsed the invaders of the constitution.")[176] John Quincy Adams had defeated Jackson in the presidential

171. *Worcester* at 555.

172. *Worcester* at 559.

173. *Worcester* at 562 (Baldwin, J., dissenting).

174. Edwin A. Miles, "After John Marshall's Decision: *Worcester v. Georgia* and the Nullification Crisis," *Journal of Southern History* (November 1973), 519 n. 1, suggests for the first publication Horace Greeley, *The American Conflict: A History of the Great Rebellion in the United States of America*, 2 vols. (Hartford, 1864), 1:106. (Miles used an 1865 edition.) The earliest newspaper report I have found is *Delaware Gazette* (8 February 1867).

175. A *Commercial Advertiser* story that I have not located was reprinted in, for instance, *Daily National Journal* (17 March 1831); *Norwich Courier* (23 March 1831); *Louisville Daily Journal* (30 March 1831).

176. *Niles' Weekly Register* (17 July 1830), reprinted from *Charleston Mercury* (5 July 1830), an issue that seems not to have survived. For an earlier

election of 1824, but lost to him in 1828. From the sidelines, Adams gnashed his teeth: "the Executive of the United States is in league with the State of Georgia. He will not take care that the Laws be faithfully executed. A majority of both Houses of Congress sustain him in this neglect and violation of his duty—There is no harmony in the Government of the Union. The arm refuses its Office—The whole head is sick, and the whole heart faint."[177] But a Georgia congressman vaunted the state's victory—and taunted skeptics by looking back to *Chisholm* and the Eleventh Amendment. "Yes, sir, so well satisfied were the other States that Georgia was right in resisting this attack upon her sovereignty, that they even framed this amendment to the constitution so as to apply to cases already commenced and then pending. I ask, in the most perfect confidence, whether there could be a more decisive concession of the right asserted and maintained by the State of Georgia."[178]

Worcester decided not to persist at law and promised the state that if it released him, he would never return. He left his fate to "the magnanimity of the state." Vaunting "the triumphant ground, which the State finally occupies in relation to this subject, in the eyes of the nation," not least because of Jackson's "overwhelming re-election," Georgia's governor directed Worcester's release. "The State," he crowed, "is free from the menace of any pretended power whatever, to

---

appreciative nod to Jackson's stance, see *Charleston Mercury* (12 January 1830).

177. John Quincy Adams, *Diaries*, ed. David Waldstreicher, 2 vols. (New York: Library of America, 2017), 2:238–39 (4 January 1831); see too 2:294–95 (11 March 1832).

178. Representative Thomas Foster (Whig-GA), *Gales & Seaton's Register* (11 June 1832). For more vaunting of that old victory with an eye to current disputes, see "Speech of Mr. Dawson of Greene, in the Senate of Georgia," *Augusta Chronicle* (17 January 1835).

infringe upon her rights, or control her will in relation to this subject."[179] True, after the Civil War a Georgia court sounded chastened about this sort of thing. Not only was secession illegal, but—this with yet another lavish dollop of Vattel—"the ultimate political sovereignty of the Federal Government resides in the United States of America."[180] Even then, a dissenting judge, also generously sprinkling his opinion with Vattel, wasn't budging on state sovereignty: "I file this dissentient opinion under the strong conviction that the time is not distant, when the legal mind of this country will be found in entire unison with the views I have expressed, and then the wonder will be, that reason had ever been so demented as to deny or ignore their conclusiveness."[181] (Once again, the titillating refrain: opponents aren't wrong, they're crazy.) These matters weren't settled then. I doubt they're settled now.

So much for the mud wrestling between Georgia and the federal government. But as I said, there's another contestant, the Cherokees. Are *they* sovereign? In 1846, learned commentator Henry Wheaton acknowledged that "the denomination of semi-sovereign States is an apparent solecism." Still, that was the status of America's "Indian nations."[182] More generally, international law has worked up other categories for lesser entities: dominions, protectorates, trusteeships,

179. *Federal Union* (17 January 1833), reprinted in *Niles' Weekly Register* (2 February 1833).

180. Chancely v. Bailey, 37 Ga. 532, 539 (1868) (and see 538, 540).

181. *Chancely* at 556 (Harris, J., dissenting).

182. Henry Wheaton, *Elements of International Law*, 3rd ed., rev. and corr. (Philadelphia, 1846), 67, 73. This language is not in the first edition of 1836. On the Philippines Independence Act as bequeathing that same status, see *Congressional Record* (22 March 1934). For worries about "half sovereign states," see John Austin, *The Province of Jurisprudence Determined* (London, 1832), 249–55.

mandates, condominia, and states under suzerainty.[183] I want to notice another way of thinking about dignity and sovereignty, not, that is, the business of insisting one is above the law, or that it's an insult to be summoned to appear in court—not, that is, the business of scorning legal accountability as something for entities of contemptibly lower status. *Semi-sovereign* might sound better than *domestic dependent* or *pupilage* or *ward*, but all of them are decisively stamped as inferior statuses. So we can grasp the campaign for Native American sovereignty as a quest for equality—for dignity in the sense of we too are a fully respectable community.

That sense has surfaced repeatedly in struggles over decolonization, the rights of newly independent nations, and the rights of failed and failing states. Turkey, fighting back against the partition of the Ottoman Empire after World War I, was flexible on many issues in the Lausanne Conference of 1922–23, but not on sovereignty. Britain's foreign secretary ridiculed the Turkish delegation's "exaggerated views" and "obsession." He told its chief negotiator, "You remind me of nothing so much as a music box. You play the same old tune day after day until we are all heartily sick of it—sovereignty, sovereignty, sovereignty."[184] Here's John Red Horse recounting a 1970s episode from the National Indian Youth Council. Roger Jourdain, a Red Lake Reservation leader, met with some students. "'You know there are only three things that tribes have to be concerned about.' The students were getting on the edge of their seats. They were waiting for these magical pieces of wisdom

183. See, for instance, C. H. Alexandrowicz, *The Law of Nations in Global History*, ed. David Armitage and Jennifer Pitts (Oxford: Oxford University Press, 2017), chaps. 9, 16, 19.

184. Joseph C. Grew, *Turbulent Era: A Diplomatic Record of Forty Years 1904–1945*, ed. Walter Johnson and Nancy Harvison Hooker, 2 vols. (Boston: Houghton Mifflin, 1952), 1:524, 525.

to come out, and Roger said, 'Sovereignty, sovereignty and sovereignty.'"[185]

I'm happy to endorse the quest for equality here. Both as a community, or series of communities, and as individuals, Native Americans are and ought to be treated as dignified equals. But slapping the label of sovereignty on for that purpose, standing alone, is exceedingly odd. Better, surely, to reform stigmatizing practices and laws: for instance, to remedy the history of callous and exploitative regulation from the Bureau of Indian Affairs, or for that matter to figure out if we need such a bureau at all, or whether the Feds should be stepping back or disappearing. To demonstrate how stubbornly repetitive I can be, I'll add that discussions of such matters ought to be pursued retail, not wholesale. So, for instance, in 1978 the Supreme Court held that tribal courts do not have jurisdiction over non-Indians, even for crimes committed on tribal lands.[186] Later that same year, though, the Court held that grievances under the Indian Civil Rights Act could be pursued only in tribal courts, not in federal courts.[187] Either decision

185. John Red Horse, "The Concept of Sovereignty and Its Significance for ICWA," in *Sovereignty: The Heart of the Matter: Critical Considerations on the Interface between the Indian Child Welfare Act and the Adoption and Safe Families Act*, ed. Esther Wattenberg (Saint Paul, MN: Center for Urban and Regional Affairs, 2000), 11. For Liberia's teetering government insisting on its "sovereign dignity" and rejecting trusteeship in the aftermath of a civil war where the capital was under siege and the then government controlled perhaps a third of the country, see "Address by His Excellency Mr. Lewis G. Brown, II, Minister of Foreign Affairs of the Republic of Liberia," 2 October 2003, http://www.un.org/webcast/ga/58/statements/libeeng031002.htm (last visited 11 July 2018). The minister spoke on behalf of President Moses Zeh Blah, whose government folded less than two weeks later.

186. Oliphant v. Suquamish Indian Tribe, 435 U.S. 191 (1978).

187. Santa Clara Pueblo v. Martinez, 436 U.S. 49 (1978). See too *Fisher v. District Court of Sixteenth Judicial District*, 424 U.S. 382 (1976) (denying the state of Montana jurisdiction over a tribal adoption dispute).

might be right or wrong. But it is perverse to insist that every single knotty question about a jurisdictional division of labor must have the same answer because of sovereignty. And that's true even if you think Native Americans ought to have full independence from state and federal government. I get that self-government, however understood, is itself a badge of dignity. To demonstrate how belligerently monomaniacal I can be, I'll add that still no one should favor Native American sovereignty if that means establishing some government authority that's unlimited, undivided, and unaccountable.

Federal policies, writes Vine Deloria, "have not been able to solve one single problem of American Indians, because they have taken dignity away from Indians. Until that dignity is restored, no lasting progress can be made by the United States or the respective tribes." That's entirely compatible with his implicitly endorsing "the contentions of the Indian activists at Wounded Knee that the Indian nations have residual right to national existence and self-government which has been violated by the United States," entirely compatible too with his endorsing the views of Justices Thompson and Johnson in *Cherokee Nation* as "valid today in describing many of the present quasi-independent states who have sought the protection of larger nations." Residual right and quasi-independence: "Indians are not seeking a type of independence which would create a totally isolated community with no ties to the United States whatsoever." Instead they seek "clear and uncontroverted lines of political authority and responsibility for both the tribal governments and the United States": that is, a jurisdictional division of labor, just what the classic theory of sovereignty renders as an unthinkable horror.[188] Here and elsewhere, we can

188. Vine Deloria, Jr., *Behind the Trail of Broken Treaties: An Indian Declaration of Independence* (New York: Delacorte, 1974), 262, 118, 162.

sunder this alternative and precious understanding of dignity from the theory of sovereignty.

Little Kings

I return to the arena of international law and politics. My themes here are insult and injury: how diplomats betray—flaunt—remarkably thin skin in resenting insults to sovereign dignity, and how they enjoy immunity to slip away without being held legally unaccountable for sometimes grotesque wrongs.

Grotius was not just a great theorist of sovereignty. He was also an aggrieved ambassador, weighing in on whether England's coach should precede Sweden's and whether he himself should be addressed as "Excellency." There's nothing the least bit idiosyncratic about his prickliness. The English ambassador to Venice protested the impending publication of a book attacking Henry VIII, Elizabeth, and James I "in terms that are not decent." The doge assured him the law guarding against such publications would be enforced. "The Ambassador said he was sure the Republic would see that the dignity of the King of England was respected."[189] That last is better read as a frigid demand than as a satisfied concession.

A tale from distant centuries of absolute monarchy? In 1893—when some residents, mostly American, were trying to overthrow the government and establish a republic—the U.S.

Deloria deploys the term *sovereignty*, but not in the sense I'm pursuing here.

189. "Venice: August 1608," in *Cal. S. P., Venice*, 11:157–58 (16 August 1608). For a bit of tit-for-tat on ambassadors and sovereign dignity, see "Message from Elizabeth to Alexander Hume," *Cal. S. P., Scotland*, 5:534–36 (7 November 1580). For a man jailed "to give content to the French Ambassador," *Cal S. P., Charles I, 1629–31*, 231 (10 April 1630).

ambassador to Hawaii, "laboring under great excitement and anger," confronted the queen's marshal of the kingdom and denounced a news story suggesting he'd been lackadaisical in succoring a shipwrecked American boat. The queen had no connection to the newspaper. Despite marveling at "this most insane and unheard of proceeding" and "his tyrannical and insolent action," Hawaii's cabinet launched criminal libel proceedings against the newspaper. Only then did the mollified ambassador ask that the legal action be dropped.[190]

The American government too could execute depressingly lickspittle stunts to salve wounded ambassadorial dignity. With heated conflict over Britain's role in Ireland—sorry, that doesn't begin to give away the date, does it?—in 1920 a small group in Washington, DC, staged protests in front of the British embassy. The secretary of state responded, "The Government deeply regrets the demonstration. . . . The Government, without delay, will take effective measures to perform its duty of hospitable courtesy to the British Embassy and to preserve its own dignity against conduct which tends in the least degree to a breach of that courtesy to representatives of a friendly Power." It doesn't sound like those in the embassy were all that offended: one invited a protester in for tea. Still, the authorities warned the protesters that they were facing felony charges and a three-year prison term; still they persisted; some were arrested. Next, one protester, actress Mollie Carroll, flew an airplane—the police had no way to pursue her—and dropped

190. "Liliuokalani R. et al. to S. B. Dole, Esq., and Others Composing the Provisional Government of the Hawaiian Islands," 17 January 1893, in *President's Message Relating to the Hawaiian Islands: December 18, 1893* (Washington, DC, 1893), 394–95; "Statement of C. B. Wilson: Facts in Relation to the Revolution of 1893, and the Causes Which Led to It," in *President's Message*, 558.

leaflets across the city. (In jail, another protester offered nonchalantly, "We are following President Wilson's policy in educating the public from the air. You may remember how his speeches were dropped behind the German lines.") The district attorney charged them under a federal statute reaching anyone "who assaults, strikes, wounds, imprisons, or in any other manner offers violence to the person of a public minister in violation of the law of nations." Picketing, went the theory, was offering violence to the ambassador's person. True, Britain was "not at present represented by a resident ambassador." But there was a chargé d'affaires in the embassy, and that was good enough. The indictment claimed that the protesters "had unlawfully and feloniously menaced bodily harm and violence" to the chargé d'affaires and that they "did then and there, at [his] dwelling house . . . affront and insult him, in violation of the law of nations." After a short stint in jail, their protests continued—this time, I should note, with police protection. It looks like the threatened charges came to nothing: soon after Carroll was back onstage in Bernard Shaw's trenchant *O'Flaherty, V.C.*—and telling pointed political jokes about Ireland.[191]

191. "Embassy In Capital Picketed," *Cincinnati Enquirer* (3 April 1920); "'Come in and Have Some Tea,' Urges British Embassy when Pro-Irish Girls Picket Place," *Free Press and Public Ledger* (3 April 1920); "Government Moves to Stop Picketing of British Embassy," *Arizona Republican* (6 April 1920); "British Embassy at Washington Again Picketed," *Atlanta Constitution* (6 April 1920); "Irish Pickets at British Embassy Routed by Women in U.S. Capital," *San Francisco Chronicle* (11 April 1920); "Government Halts Picketing at Embassy of Great Britain; Women Arrested in Capital," *Cincinnati Enquirer* (6 April 1920); "U.S. to Put End to Irish Picketing British Embassy," *Chicago Daily Tribune* (6 April 1920); "Embassy Again Is Picketed; Four Women Are Arrested; Airplane Used in Campaign," *Cincinnati Enquirer* (7 April 1920); "Picketer Scatters Irish Protests from Airplane: Capital Sees Woman Flier Elude Police: Four Arrested on Charge of Offering 'Violence' to Ambassador," *Washington Herald* (7 April 1920); "Irish Pickets

The city saw an encore performance of sorts two years later. Sinn Féin leader Mary MacSwiney was on a hunger strike in prison. In Washington, DC, her sister-in-law Muriel MacSwiney—she had married Mary's brother Terence, Sinn Féin lord mayor of Cork, who'd starved himself to death after being jailed by the British on charges of sedition for his role in the Irish War of Independence of 1920[192]—was spearheading protests in front of the British embassy. The ambassador had left the premises before the protesters arrived, but no matter: a policeman warned the protesters they could walk in front of the embassy only once, but they kept going. So he had them arrested, "the women laughing and chatting with the police who seized their banners," "laughing and joking as they were taken away in three patrol wagons." "'I don't mind being arrested; I am used to it,' replied Mrs. MacSwiney with a smile." She and a couple of other protesters chose to go to jail and refused bond offered on their behalf. (An official pointed out she could be deported.) MacSwiney ridiculed the charges as "absurd"—marching with a placard, she observed, was far from assaulting, wounding, or imprisoning a public minister—and "the defendants laughed openly when the charges were read in court." The commissioner who heard the case—the proceedings were interrupted by laughter from the gallery, too—decided that the law didn't apply, even though the protests were "most embarrassing to this government": that is, to the U.S.

'Bomb' Embassy from the Air," *Sun* (7 April 1920); "Irish Pickets Turn Attack upon Colby," *New York Tribune* (8 April 1920); "Embassy Pickets Accept Freedom," *Evening Star* [Washington, DC] (10 April 1920); "O'Flaherty, V.C., by Bernard Shaw, Satire on Britain," *New-York Tribune* (22 June 1920); "The State of Ballybunion," *Evening Star* (14 November 1920).

192. "MacSwiney Dead," *Nottingham Evening Post* (25 October 1920); "The Late Alderman MacSwiney," *Irish Times* (28 October 1920).

government, which he thought should have done a better job stamping these protesters as wretches and flattering Britain's government. (The commissioner "gave us a good spanking while dismissing the cases," commented a defense lawyer.)[193] Nor was the government alone in denouncing these protests. "The picketing of the British embassy in Washington is an offense that cannot be tolerated," fumed an Oregon newspaper.[194] Not until 1988 would the Supreme Court strike down, as a violation of the First Amendment, the District's ban on the use of banners and the like within five hundred feet of any embassy or other such building "designed . . . to bring into public odium [or] public disrepute political, social, or economic acts, views, or purposes of any foreign government, party or organization."[195] (The United States weighed in with an amicus brief hammering away at the need to safeguard the dignity of

193. "MacSwiney's Widow Arrested in Capital," *St. Louis Post-Dispatch* (14 November 1922); "Cell Door: Is Closed on Widow," *Cincinnati Enquirer* (15 November 1922); "Mrs. MacSwiney Is Arrested Here," *Washington Post* (15 November 1922); "Mrs. MacSwiney Jailed in Capital," *New York Times* (15 November 1922); "Arrest Is Absurd," *Cincinnati Enquirer* (15 November 1922); "Charge Picketed Embassy," *Chickasha Daily Express* (15 November 1922); "Mrs. MacSwiney and 2 Picketers Jailed; 6 Get Bail," *Chicago Daily Tribune* (15 November 1922); "Mrs. MacSwiney Is Arrested," *Boston Daily Globe* (15 November 1922); "Mrs. MacSwiney Is Released from Imprisonment: Charge of Violating the Federal Statute Is Dismissed," *Palatka Daily News* (16 November 1922); "British Embassy Picketers Freed, Cases Dismissed," *Atlanta Constitution* (16 November 1922); "Mrs. MacSwiney and 8 Other Pickets Freed After Hearing," *Evening Star* (16 November 1922); "Exonerated: Of Federal Charge," *Cincinnati Enquirer* (16 November 1922).

194. "Picketing an Embassy," *East Oregonian* (12 April 1920). Contrast, during the Koszta affair, "Washington Gossip," *Daily Republic* (9 August 1853): "These undignified and insulting attempts of a foreign ambassador to muzzle the American press are certainly becoming too frequent for toleration."

195. Boos v. Barry, 485 U.S. 312 (1988).

foreign embassies.)[196] You wouldn't think a ban on what the doctrine sometimes calls core political speech in a traditional public forum would have lasted that long. Its endurance is telling evidence of the subterranean allure of sovereign dignity.

There is more, much more—these tawdry stories too are commonplace—but I'll content myself with one last pair. In 1854, the American ambassador to Spain was on his way to Madrid. Napoleon III's French government stopped him at Calais and told he couldn't pass through French territory. But Vattel had decreed that ordinarily ambassadors should be given free passage! Wheaton had agreed! "The insult to our ambassador is an insult to our government," fumed one newspaper. France backed down.[197] Fifteen years later, a report circulated that Napoleon's government was itself insulted when France's ambassador to China was "slapped in the face by a Chinese Mandarin of high rank in the palace . . . in the very presence of the Chinese monarch." Observers suspected the episode would lead to war if China didn't repent: allegedly France gave the Chinese three days to apologize.[198] The French government said it had no confirmation of the matter.[199] It was then discarded as a "fabulous narrative."[200] Not fabulous, apparently, was the thought that a slapped ambassador could precipitate war.

196. 1987 U.S. S. Ct. Briefs LEXIS 422.

197. "Indignity to Mr. Soule," "The Anglo-French Alliance," and "The Order Denying Mr. Soule a Passage through France Revoked," *Wilmington Journal* (24 November 1854); see too, for instance, *National Era* (23 November 1854).

198. "A War Cloud in the East," *New York Herald* (5 June 1869), reprinted in *Fairfield Herald* (16 June 1869).

199. "Europe," *New York Herald* (6 June 1869).

200. "Miscellaneous," *Chicago Tribune* (14 June 1869). There's no mention of the episode in Molly J. Giblin, "Entangled Empires: The French in China" (PhD diss., Rutgers University, 2015).

No surprise that ambassadors were dubbed "little kings."[201] At issue, though, wasn't only indignity. There was—is—also immunity, which goes back centuries in international law. And I mean sweeping immunity from law across the board, nothing like the carefully limited privileges that actors enjoy so particular laws will not impede their performances in particular roles. You can find exceptions, sometimes caught up in caviling about who is and isn't an ambassador. John Lesley was arguably serving as ambassador to Mary, Queen of Scots, then jailed in England. But when it turned out Lesley was caught up in the Ridolfi plot to assassinate Queen Elizabeth, he found himself in jail, too. His appeal to Elizabeth is sometimes cringing, even maudlin: "I, who used to perform the public duty of ambassador, free by universal right from shame, insult, and the punishment of law, have endured disgrace instead of honor, infamy instead of praise, hatred instead of kindness, and danger instead of safety." He managed both to disavow and to assert claims of legal immunity.[202] But such exceptions are awfully rare and Elizabeth herself sprang into action when France's ambassador ran afoul of proclamations regulating the length of rapiers and was detained at Smithfield.[203] "Even among barbarous nations,"

201. "Ambassadors in London," *Manitowoc Pilot* (14 May 1896); so too *Cardiff Times* (7 December 1895); *Indianapolis Journal* (2 February 1896); *Wichita Beacon* (6 March 1896); *Daily Chronicle* [DeKalb, IL] (31 March 1896); *Fort Wayne Journal-Gazette* (12 April 1896); *Crawfordsville Review* (25 April 1896); *Daily Reporter* [Independence, KS] (30 May 1896); *Logansport Pharos-Tribune* (25 February 1897). I've been unable to track down the original publication, apparently in *Cassell's Family Magazine*.

202. *Oratio* [1574], in John Nichols, *The Progresses and Public Processions of Queen Elizabeth I: A New Edition of the Early Modern Sources*, ed. Elizabeth Goldring et al., 5 vols. (Oxford: Oxford University Press, 2014), 2:154, and see 170–73.

203. John Strype, *Annals of the Reformation*, 4 vols. (London, 1725), 2:619; "Enforcing Statutes of Apparel," 6 May 1562, in *Tudor Royal Proclamations*, ed. Paul L. Hughes and James F. Larkin, 3 vols. (New Haven,

commented Jean Hotman, a French diplomat himself, "the person of an Ambassador hath in all ages been adjudged holy, sacred, and inviolable."[204] In 1698, Dryden put it this way: "The Person of an Ambassador is so Sacred, that it is more inviolable than even that of the Prince himself, who sends him, would be, were he in the Places where he represents him."[205] More measured if more authoritative, Vattel thought a sovereign prince who goes abroad "to negotiate, or to treat about some public affair . . . is doubtless to enjoy all the rights of ambassadors in a more eminent degree." Even when he's simply traveling, "his dignity . . . shelters him from all insult . . . and exempts him

---

CT: Yale University Press, 1964–69), 2:191; "Enforcing Statutes of Apparel," 12 February 1566, in *Tudor Proclamations*, 2:282; "Enforcing Statutes of Apparel," 12 February 1580, in *Tudor Proclamations*, 2:462; "Commanding Honor to Be Shown French Ambassador," 18 April 1581, in *Tudor Proclamations*, 2:484–85, published in briefer form as *By the Queene* (London, 1581).

204. [Jean Hotman], *The Ambassador* (London, 1603), sig. H2 recto. For ambassadors as far better off than dispossessed monarchs, see Mat[thew] Tindal, *An Essay concerning the Laws of Nations, and the Rights of Soveraigns* (London, 1694), 10–12. Then again, one thinks of the political deals cut to encourage tyrants to leave, or of Idi Amin Dada luxuriating in a Saudi hotel after killing hundreds of thousands in Uganda.

205. *Politick Reflections*, in *The Annals and History of Cornelius Tacitus*, 3 vols. (London, 1698), 1:86; with significant variation in John Ayliffe, *A New Pandect of Roman Civil Law* (London, 1734), 257. See *Reflections and Notes on The Annals of Tacitus, Book I: I: Politick Reflections, in The Works of John Dryden*, ed. Edward Niles Hooker et al., 20 vols. (Berkeley: University of California Press, 1956–94), 20:465. For Dryden's role in the translation, see Earl Miner, "Ovid Reformed: Issues of Ovid, Fables, Morals, and the Second Epic in *Fables Ancient and Modern*," in *Literary Transmission and Authority: Dryden and Other Writers*, ed. Earl Miner and Jennifer Brady (Cambridge: Cambridge University Press, 1993), 96. For a contemporary argument about whether ambassadors can be held criminally liable, [William Camden], *Annales: The True and Royall History of the Famous Empresse Elizabeth* (London, 1625), 271–78.

from all jurisdiction."[206] In 1790, Congress granted immunity to foreign ambassadors and ministers and their servants—and added that those suing them "shall be deemed violaters of the laws of nations, and disturbers of the public repose, and imprisoned not exceeding three years, and fined at the discretion of the court."[207] Chief Justice Marshall affirmed such immunity: "A foreign sovereign is not understood as intending to subject himself to jurisdiction incompatible with his dignity."[208]

The tradition is alive and well—invigoratingly, surpassingly, cancerously well—in modern international law. Not just ambassadors but also capacious diplomatic staffs are covered. There are only trivial qualifications to this sweeping immunity in the Vienna Conventions that lay out the basic framework of the current rules.[209] Talk of sovereignty is no longer front and center: each Convention has a passing nod to the UN Charter's invocation of "the sovereign equality of states," but no further mention of sovereignty. (True, a recent State Department manual remarks, "A US ambassador serving abroad symbolizes the sovereignty of the United States."[210] And it is

206. [Emer] de Vattel, *The Law of Nations; or Principles of the Law of Nature*, trans. from the French, 2 vols. (London, 1759), 2:158.

207. Act of April 30, 1790, ch. 9, §§ 25–26, 1 Stat. 117–18. For today's law, see 22 U.S.C. § 254a et seq.

208. The Schooner Exchange v. McFaddon, 11 U.S. 116, 137 (1812). Marshall enlists Vattel as authority at 143.

209. See the Vienna Convention on Diplomatic Relations of 1961 (http://legal.un.org/ilc/texts/instruments/english/conventions/9_1_1961.pdf) and the Vienna Convention on Consular Relations of 1963 (http://legal.un.org/ilc/texts/instruments/english/conventions/9_2_1963.pdf) (last visited 10 July 2018). For a sample of complications about the reach of the relevant principles, see *Khurts Bat v. Investigating Judge of the Federal Court of Germany*, [2011] EWHC 2029 (Admin) [2012] 3 WLR 180.

210. *Protocol for the Modern Diplomat* (Washington, DC: U.S. Department of State, 2005), 12.

endlessly attentive to etiquette, but the concern is ambassadors inadvertently insulting their host states.) It could be that we've taken principles of immunity once resting on the classic theory of sovereignty, removed that theory, and inserted in its place some other rationale that happens to support the same principles. The usual story now would be that any state needs assurances before it sends its officials into the territory of remote and perhaps hostile states, coupled with some tit-for-tat or extended-reciprocity story about how every state is better off if each respects the rules. The argument has the right form: retail, not wholesale. I doubt, though, that it justifies the same old sweeping immunities it's supposed to. In fact, for decades in the United States, the Foreign Sovereign Immunities Act has imposed limits on the traditionally unconditional immunity—and those limits have been ruled retroactive.[211] The sky has not fallen.

Some examples of diplomatic immunity are easy to shrug off as no big deal, even amusing. In 1906, U.S. immigration agents didn't wave the new ambassador from Brazil through the border: they subjected him to "the usual questions." Had he been in jail? an almshouse? an asylum for the insane? Was he an anarchist? a polygamist? The questions were insulting, but anyway the ambassador was entitled to free entry without complying with the usual legal requirements. The secretary of state weighed in.[212] The next year, the State Department apparently intervened when Italy's ambassador ran afoul of the speed limit—of twelve miles per hour.[213]

211. 90 Stat. 2891; 28 U.S.C. §§ 1330, 1602–11 (and see, for instance, *Ashraf-Hassan v. Embassy of France*, 40 F. Supp. 3d 94, 103–4 (D.D.C. 2014), easily discarding an appeal to *The Schooner Exchange*); *Republic of Austria v. Altmann*, 541 U.S. 677 (2004).

212. "Insulted an Ambassador," *Butler Weekly Times* (22 November 1906).

213. "Glen Echo Speed Law," *Evening Star* (3 June 1907).

Some are decidedly less amusing, for instance, these three stories from the U.S. A telex operator at the Egyptian embassy raped a woman in 1983. The son of a Saudi diplomat raped a sixteen-year-old that same year.[214] A secretary to Italy's military attaché was harassing a fourteen-year-old girl in Georgetown; a passerby intervened to try to stop him; the secretary tried to run him down with his car.[215] Unless the diplomats' home countries waive immunity, the government may not bring criminal charges against such offenders. All it can do is expel them from the country. Waivers aren't unheard of. A sixteen-year-old Brazilian was killed in a Washington, DC, car crash caused by a high-ranking Georgian diplomat. He'd been drinking and was careening down Connecticut Avenue at about eighty miles per hour. With the diplomat's consent, Georgia waived immunity; he was convicted of manslaughter.[216] So too when Zaire's ambassador to France, driving almost four times the speed limit on a narrow two-lane road, killed a twelve- and a thirteen-year-old in the French seaside town of Menton. The next day, he left for Zaire. Thousands took to the streets, and eventually Zaire waived his immunity and he returned to face charges. There might be any number of

214. For these cases and more, "Crime by Those with Diplomatic Immunity Rises," *Washington Post* (9 January 1984). On the extension of diplomatic immunity to the children of diplomats, see, for instance, "Brazil and Ambassador's Son Face Lawsuit over Shooting," *New York Times* (12 December 1982).

215. "Diplomats Use Immunity as a Crime Shield," *Houston Chronicle* (4 August 1985).

216. "Love, Anger at Funeral of Girl, 16; Crash Victim's Mother Lashes out at Diplomat," *Washington Post* (8 January 1997); "No 'Justice,' No Rest for Mother of Girl Killed in Crash with Envoy," *Washington Post* (5 February 1997); "U.S. Officially Asks Georgia to Waive Diplomat's Immunity," *Washington Post* (12 February 1997); "Diplomat Pleads Guilty," *Washington Post* (9 October 1997); "Diplomat Sentenced in Teen's Death," *Washington Post* (20 December 1997).

reasons for granting—or refusing—such waivers. You needn't be cynical to notice that Zaire's President Mobutu was getting treated for cancer in France. And you needn't be cynical to notice that prosecutors recommended a feather's tickle on the wrist: a three-year suspended sentence and about a $4,400 fine. In the event, the judge chose a two-year suspended sentence and close to a $10,000 fine. "There was too much privilege for certain people," a leader of the protests had said. "We should all be treated equally."[217] Indeed. Whatever you make of that derisory punishment, it's worth recalling those whose suits simply founder on sovereign immunity. Three domestic workers from India sued, arguing that an attaché to Kuwait's embassy had more or less enslaved them. Defendants pleaded diplomatic immunity; the judge asked the State Department for its view; the department responded that defendants enjoyed immunity; the judge dismissed the action.[218]

So who exactly is disturbing the public repose? Even a telex operator is a little king, as long as he works for the embassy. The social landscape is strewn with tens of thousands of little kings, Charles I action figures, poised to spring into ac-

217. "Zaire Envoy Called Home; French Town Furious," *New York Times* (2 December 1996); "Grieving Town Finds Zaire Diplomatic: Envoy's Immunity Lifted over Accident in France," *Washington Post* (23 January 1997); "Former Zairian Envoy to Face French Justice," *Washington Post* (26 January 1997); "No Jail Proposed for Zairian Envoy," *Washington Post* (26 March 1997); "Zairian Envoy Sentenced in French Auto Deaths," *New York Times* (30 April 1997).

218. Mani Kumari Sabbithi v. Waleed KH N.S. Al Saleh, 605 F. Supp. 2d 122 (D.D.C. 2009). For the judge's letter, see http://www.aclu.org/legal-document/sabbithi-et-al-v-al-saleh-et-al-letter-judge-sullivan-state-department (last visited 11 July 2018). For a follow-up opinion dismissing the case against Kuwait itself on the ground that plaintiffs hadn't properly effected service, see *Mani Kumari Sabbithi v. Major Waleed KH N.S. Al Saleh*, 623 F. Supp. 2d 93 (D.D.C. 2009).

tion and violate whatever laws they like without facing prosecution. Had the same telex operator worked for a private company, Egypt might or might not have tried to intercede on his behalf. But there would have been no doubts about American jurisdiction. No one would have argued that Egypt couldn't securely send its telex operators to work in the United States unless we promised them legal immunity. No one would have argued that our own citizens abroad should then get the same sweeping immunity, regardless of why they're abroad or what they're doing. But you could easily gimmick up that argument. (I just did). How about tourist immunity? Just crank the handle on the reciprocity argument: we can't risk sending our citizens, defenseless with skimpy bikinis and recreational drugs, to foreign resorts and beaches lest they face zany and repellent charges under local law, so we should demand immunity for them and extend immunity to foreign tourists here. Maybe only the brute fact of long-standing practice makes the current rules of diplomatic immunity seem any more plausible.

"Little kings" is exactly right: after all, Charles I or any other sovereign could have graciously submitted to the enforcement of any law—or refused to. Of course actors with legal immunity are inclined to prize what they've got. Pity New York City, the infamously congested home of the United Nations: in one year, diplomats ignored over 134,000 parking tickets and over $5 million in fines. But when the city, cooperating with the State Department, tried to find some scheme to deal with diplomats' parking violations—the audacity!—a UN committee sought to bring the issue to the General Assembly and wondered about bringing in the World Court.[219]

219. "Diplomats Make No Apologies for Immunity," *New York Times* (13 April 1997); "Host Country Committee Delays Action on Recommendation

Swaggering States

Not only diplomats traffic in insult and injury; so too do states. There is a mostly older usage in which an injury is itself an insult. In 1780, Britain's ambassador to the Dutch Republic, unhappy with the Dutch's cozying up to Catherine II of Russia's Armed Neutrality, unhappier with the discovery of negotiations between the Dutch and the rebellious American colonies, fired off "the Complaint of an offended Sovereign" to the Dutch legislature. There'd been "an Attempt against the Dignity of his Crown. The King never imagined that your high Mightinesses had approved of a Treaty with his rebellious Subjects; that would have been a Holding-up of the Shield, a Declaration of War on your Part." Doubtless some irresponsible magistrates were responsible, and the legislature would remedy matters promptly. This ultimatum didn't work: the Fourth Anglo-Dutch War broke out within weeks.[220] The insult lies precisely in the injury, in flouting the interests of a nominal ally, in not according Britain the treatment its dignity demands. Injuries can constitute insults, but there's a causal link, too: an undignified reputation will invite further injuries. That's why President Washington cautioned Congress, "There is a rank due to the United States among Nations, which will be withheld, if not absolutely lost, by the reputation of weakness. If we desire to avoid insult, we must be able to repel it; if we desire to secure peace, one of the most powerful instru-

That General Assembly Consider Parking Issue," Press Release HQ/574 (31 March 1997), at http://www.un.org/press/en/1997/19970331.hq574.html (last visited 11 July 2018).

220. "Foreign Affairs," *St. James's Chronicle or The British Evening-Post* (19–21 December 1780). For context, H. M. Scott, "Sir Joseph Yorke, Dutch Politics and the Origins of the Fourth Anglo-Dutch War," *Historical Journal* (September 1988).

ments of our rising prosperity, it must be known, that we are at all times ready for War."[221]

But sometimes an insult is only an insult: recall the solder who spat at Charles I. No, the problem was not the possibility of communicating a disease. In 1949, the United States wanted Hungary to release an American executive: Hungary claimed he'd confessed to spying and sabotage. The U.S. banned Americans' travel to Hungary. Hungary responded that the ban was "rudely insulting" to its sovereignty.[222] The government was not fretting about lost revenues from tourism. Recently China has taken umbrage at how private firms represent it. Gap, the clothing retailer, was selling a T-shirt with a map of China without Taiwan, some of Tibet, and those little rocks jutting out of the South China Sea over which China has asserted sovereignty. Protests led instantly to Gap's profuse apology and an assurance that it "respects the sovereignty and territorial integrity of China."[223] The kowtowing might be prudent commercial strategy, but you can't understand the full panoply of sovereignty unless you see how China could wax indignant over the marketing of the image.

In 2018, Canada's foreign minister and then the ministry itself took to Twitter to call for the release of imprisoned

221. "Fifth Annual Message to Congress," in George Washington, *Writings*, ed. John Rhodehamel (New York: Library of America, 1997), 848.

222. "Budapest Rejects Protest by U.S.; Says American Confessed Spying," *New York Times* (25 December 1949).

223. "Gap, Wary of Crossing China, Apologizes for T-Shirt's Map," *New York Times* (15 May 2018). See too, for instance, "Marriott to China: We Do Not Support Separatists," *New York Times* (11 January 2018); "'Orwellian Nonsense'? China Says That's the Price of Doing Business," *New York Times* (6 May 2018); "China Tries to Erase Taiwan, One Ally (and Website) at a Time," *New York Times* (25 May 2018); "China Says U.S. Should Tell Airlines to Change Websites in Taiwan Row," *New York Times* (29 June 2018).

human rights activists in Saudi Arabia. Tweeting in response, Saudi Arabia condemned "blatant interference in the kingdom's domestic affairs." Then the dispute bounced out of the Twittersphere. Saudi Arabia expelled Canada's ambassador, withdrew its own ambassador to Canada, announced that Saudi students studying in Canada would have to transfer to other countries, cut off new business with Canada, suspended flights to Canada on its national airline, and announced it would withdraw Saudi doctors working in Canadian hospitals. The Saudis condemned Canada's "attack" and declared they would deter "attempts to undermine the sovereignty" of the kingdom. Back on Twitter, the United Arab Emirates gamely stood with Saudi Arabia "in defending its sovereignty."[224] Here sovereignty is fastidious enough to take garden-variety pixels as an actual attack.

Finally, consider recent U.S. irritation with the UN—first, the fallout of the United States' decision to move the American embassy in Israel to Jerusalem. A Security Council resolution decorously avoided naming the U.S., but said no country should place an embassy in Jerusalem. The U.S. ve-

224. "Saudi Arabia Freezes New Trade, Investment After Canada Demands Activists Be Freed," *Canadian Press* (5 August 2018); "Saudi Arabia Assails Canada over Rights Criticism, Sending Message to West," *New York Times* (6 August 2018); "UAE Says Stands with Saudi Arabia 'in Defending Its Sovereignty,'" *Reuters* (6 August 2018); "Saudi Arabia Escalates Feud with Canada over Rights Criticism," *New York Times* (8 August 2018). Contrast the earlier flap between Mexico and the U.S.: [Anthony] Butler to [Bernardo] Gonzales, 15 February 1833, in *House Executive Documents*, 25 Cong., 2nd sess., XII, doc. 351, 467–68; [Powhatan] Ellis to [John] Forsyth, 26 August 1836, in *Documents*, 601; Wm. Pinkney to Charles E. Hawkins, 20 February 1828, in *Documents*, 631 (the immediately following documents continue the tale). For context, Thomas Maitland Marshall, *A History of the Western Boundary of the Louisiana Purchase, 1819–1841* (Berkeley: University of California Press, 1914), esp. chap. 6.

toed the resolution and American ambassador Nikki Haley addressed the General Assembly before it voted on the matter. She said she was "being forced to defend sovereignty": as though the mere fact of criticism, however solemn and institutional, were unacceptable. "When a nation is singled out for attack in this organization, that nation is disrespected." Then she offered a thinly veiled threat. "The United States will remember this day in which it was singled out for attack in the General Assembly for the very act of exercising our right as a sovereign nation. . . . This vote will make a difference on how Americans look at the UN and on how we look at countries who disrespect us in the UN. And this vote will be remembered."[225] You can think the UN is weirdly hostile to Israel and the U.S. without beginning to cast matters in these terms. Or again: two days after the U.S. withdrew from the UN Human Rights Council, Haley slammed UN special rapporteur Philip Alston's report on poverty in America. "It is patently ridiculous for the United Nations to examine poverty in America," she said. This seems a bit rich, not least because Alston proceeded at the invitation of the Trump administration.[226] Sovereignty here means more than never having to say you're sorry. It means never having to hear criticism in the

225. "U.S. Vetoes U.N. Resolution Condemning Move on Jerusalem," *New York Times* (18 December 2017); "Remarks Before a UN General Assembly Vote on Jerusalem," 21 December 2017, http://usun.state.gov/remarks/8232 (last visited 11 July 2018).

226. "Nikki Haley Calls U.N. Report on Poverty in U.S. 'Misleading and Politically Motivated,'" *Los Angeles Times* (21 June 2018); "Nikki Haley Attacks Damning UN Report on US Poverty under Trump," *Guardian* (21 June 2018); "Statement on Visit to the USA, by Professor Philip Alston, United Nations Special Rapporteur on Extreme Poverty and Human Rights," 15 December 2017, at http://www.ohchr.org/EN/NewsEvents/Pages/DisplayNews.aspx?NewsID=22533 (last visited 12 July 2018).

first place. But surely lèse-majesté ought to have shamefacedly hobbled off the stage by now.

What about holding states, or state actors, accountable? If you hold the command theory of law, if you think coercive enforcement is essential to law,[227] you might think international law is largely notional. Even from that perspective, though, skepticism is readily overplayed. There are reasonably well-functioning regimes in international law: bodies of law, courts settling disputes, and the like. Think, for instance, of the World Trade Organization. Patrons of sovereignty might pounce and point out that such associations are established by treaty, and states are always free to withdraw. Mostly that's right, though it's trickier than many let on. Britain is free to withdraw from the European Union. But the country has to follow the rules it agreed to in the treaty regarding how to trigger the withdrawal process and what the deadline for an agreement would be. It is not at all free to decree that it is no longer bound by those provisions.

The command theory occludes our vision of important features of law, and not just in the international context. It matters enormously that international law is full of critical and justificatory resources, and that states regularly use it to argue.[228] A rogue actor that transgresses doesn't face prosecution conducted by a world government with devastatingly weighty sanctions. But other states and international actors have all kinds of ways of registering their disapproval, and I

227. For a characteristically crisp and spirited view, Frederick Schauer, *The Force of Law* (Cambridge, MA: Harvard University Press, 2015). For a response, see my "Democracy, Law, Compliance," *Law & Social Inquiry* (Winter 2017).

228. Monica Hakimi, "The Work of International Law," *Harvard Journal of International Law* (Winter 2017).

don't mean just pious forms of words. Even those riveted on "behavior" and skeptical of "discourse" should take stock of the evidence that those dynamics have had real impact even in what self-styled realists imagine as the inner sanctum of the pursuit of naked political interest, war.[229]

But what about human rights law? Nuremberg stands for the principle that state actors can be held responsible for war crimes regardless of whether their states ever agreed to the relevant legal principles or to the prosecution or to the authority of the forum. Like the trial of Charles I, the Nuremberg trials raise questions about legality and notice.[230] Regardless of what you make of those, *now* there's notice. And as I noticed before, we now have the idea of *jus cogens* or peremptory norms, principles of international law that bind all states whether they agree or not, indeed even if they disavow them. So what disappears behind the veil of sovereignty in the first place? What exactly are matters of "internal concern" that outsiders have no interest in? Like Saudi Arabia, like Ambassador Haley, China has long trumpeted its own human rights achievements and briskly spurned even criticism from abroad as interference with its internal affairs.[231] It's a dour reminder of how manipulable abstractions are. (China's thunderous

229. Oona A. Hathaway and Scott J. Shapiro, *The Internationalists: How a Radical Plan to Outlaw War Remade the World* (New York: Simon & Schuster, 2017), esp. chap. 16 on "outcasting."

230. Consider Judith N. Shklar, *Legalism* (Cambridge, MA: Harvard University Press, 1964). For more skeptical pressure on reconciling consent and sovereignty in international law, see Jack Goldsmith and Daryl Levinson, "Law for States: International Law, Constitutional Law, Public Law," *Harvard Law Review* (May 2009), 1843–52.

231. Information Office of the State Council of the People's Republic of China, "Human Rights in China," November 1991, at http://www.china.org.cn/e-white/7 (last visited 12 July 2018). See pt. X for the latter.

applause for its own record on religious freedom offers this gem: "Religious groups and religious affairs are not subject to control by foreign countries."[232] I guess that version of autonomy is supposed to explain why the Catholic Church can't appoint Chinese bishops.) After we agree that human rights and noninterference are good things, we have to figure out where to draw the lines.

It's not just China. In March 1971, war broke out in what would become independent Bangladesh, but what was still East Pakistan. Even by the dismal standards of business as usual, it was a nasty war, featuring rape on an industrial scale and genocide. The Nixon administration adopted a hands-off policy.[233] It is rare for American diplomats to register their opposition to government policy, but in April a group working in East Pakistan fired off a telegram to the State Department:

> Our government has failed to denounce the suppression of democracy. Our government has failed to denounce atrocities. Our government has failed to take forceful measures to protect its citizens while at the same time bending over backwards to placate the West Pak dominated government and to lessen likely and deservedly negative inter-

232. Information Office, "China's Policies and Practices on Protecting Freedom of Religious Belief," April 3, 2018, at http://www.china.org.cn/government/whitepaper/node_8004087.htm. For the quotation, http://www.china.org.cn/government/whitepaper/2018–04/04/content_50814494.htm (last visited 12 July 2018).

233. Yasmin Saikia, *Women, War, and the Making of Bangladesh: Remembering 1971* (Durham, NC: Duke University Press, 2011); Gary J. Bass, *The Blood Telegram: Nixon, Kissinger, and a Forgotten Genocide* (New York: Knopf, 2013). On the Nixon administration's posture, see especially Bass, *Blood Telegram*, 102–18.

> national public relations impact against them. Our government has evidenced what many will consider moral bankruptcy, ironically at a time when the USSR sent President Yahya a message defending democracy, condemning arrest of leader of democratically elected majority party (incidentally pro-West) and calling for end to repressive measures and bloodshed. In our most recent policy paper for Pakistan, our interests in Pakistan were defined as primarily humanitarian, rather than strategic. But we have chosen not to intervene, even morally, on the grounds that the Awami conflict, in which unfortunately the overworked term genocide is applicable, is purely internal matter of a sovereign state. Private Americans have expressed disgust. We, as professional public servants express our dissent with current policy and fervently hope that our true and lasting interests here can be defined and our policies redirected in order to salvage our nation's position as a moral leader of the free world.[234]

Does sovereignty include the government's right to slaughter and rape its own people and not be held accountable? If I invited you to feast on the bitter irony of the sovereign's gory execution of Harrison, if that suggested that sovereignty could reproduce in stunning detail the excesses of the wars of religion that it was designed to stop, just what should I say about

234. Telegram from the Consulate General in Dacca to the Department of State, 6 April 1971, http://history.state.gov/historicaldocuments/frus1969-76v11/d19 (last visited 13 July 2018).

this? It didn't take the twentieth century to prove that sovereign states could slaughter their own people. But how hypnotized, what sort of ridiculous Rip Van Winkle, would someone have to be to insist—after Stalin, after Hitler, after Mao, after Pol Pot—that sovereignty is a prerequisite of social order, that sovereign actors must be unaccountable?

If Pakistan's atrocities unfolded today, we could discuss, as a matter of international law, not only whether Pakistan was violating its responsibility to its own people, not just whether the international community was permitted to intercede, but also whether it had an obligation to. The relevant legal language pictures a state failing to protect its citizens from some unnamed atrocious actor. But it extends to a state practicing "genocide, war crimes, ethnic cleansing and crimes against humanity" against its own people.[235]

The scope of sovereignty—of jurisdiction, as I'd rather say—here undergoes a dramatic shift. It's the nail in the coffin to that bewitching map of the globe, where every bit of land mass is in one colored patch or another, governed by one sovereign or another, and each sovereign has total authority over its own colored patch. Jurisdiction is a lot messier than that fantasy permits. States have claims beyond their borders: not just up into the air and several miles out into the water but, for instance, in the treatment of their citizens abroad. States don't have unique authority over whatever happens inside their borders. You can still say that a nation gets to govern its "internal affairs," but you have to concede that that's a normative con-

235. "Resolution Adopted by the General Assembly on 16 September 2005," U.N. Doc. A/RES/60/1, ¶¶ 138–39. On how the responsibility might best be understood going forward, see Monica Hakimi, "Toward a Legal Theory on the Responsibility to Protect," *Yale Journal of International Law* (Summer 2014).

cept, not a geographical one—and you have to worry that the point is tautological.

The responsibility to protect aside, the United Nations plays a funny game with sovereignty. The following phrases are boilerplate in recent Security Council resolutions: "*Reaffirming* its commitment to [the] sovereignty, territorial integrity and political independence of all States"; "*Underlining* its respect for the sovereignty, territorial integrity, political independence, and unity of Somalia"; "*Reaffirming* its respect for the sovereignty, territorial integrity, independence and unity of Iraq."[236] Talk about notional: despite those gestures, the resolutions promptly go ahead and do things. Yes, much of the first one, devoted to combating terrorism, is hortatory: it "*urges*," "*strongly urges*," "*encourages*" states to do this and that. But it also reminds them of their legal obligations and sets up machinery to monitor their compliance.[237] You can decide whether assuring states they're totally independent and then telling them what they should do—and keeping tabs—is fully coherent. You can imagine what Saudi Arabia or Haley or China might say. But the other resolutions are more aggressive. After you're done rolling your eyes at the thought that Somalia enjoyed much territorial integrity, political independence, and unity in the summer of 2017, notice that the resolution "*decides*" what the African Union's peacekeeping mission in the country shall do. The resolution on Iraq calls for an investigative team to collect and preserve evidence of ISIL war crimes. Iraqi judges and other experts, it announces, "will be appointed to the Team to work on an equal footing alongside

236. S/RES/2368 (20 July 2017); S/RES/2372 (30 August 2017); S/RES/2379 (21 September 2017).

237. S/RES/2368, Annex I (a)(1).

international experts." Somalia and Iraq haven't been members of the Security Council since the 1970s.[238] They didn't vote on these resolutions. If these measures respect their sovereignty, you have to wonder what disrespect would look like.

There are other fragmentary or inchoate legal regimes attempting to impose legal accountability on sovereign actors. I'll mention universal jurisdiction: the claim that courts anywhere have a right to try those charged with certain crimes. In 1998, a Spanish magistrate indicted Augusto Pinochet for endless bloody crimes during his rule in Chile; Pinochet was promptly arrested in England. He was held in jail for over a year, and for complicated reasons the prosecution didn't come off. But it wasn't a nonstarter on its face, either.[239]

It's one thing to notice that current arrangements make it possible, sometimes easy, for state actors to get away with murder—literally. It's another thing to insist that this is necessarily so. These matters have a history, shot full of changes large and small, full of political contingency, too. No ritual catechism about sovereignty or the nature of the international order or anything like that can brush that history aside. No ritual catechism can close off future paths, either. So yes, right now state actors can get away with murder. So can garden-variety murderers. In plenty of states around the world, organized crime readily defeats the state. In plenty of states around the

238. http://www.un.org/en/sc/members/elected.asp (last visited 12 July 2018).

239. For an overview, see *The Pinochet Case: Origins, Progress and Implications*, ed. Madeleine Davis (London: Institute of Latin American Studies, 2003). For a more polemical narrative, Geoffrey Robertson, *Crimes against Humanity: The Struggle for Global Justice* (New York: New Press, 2000), chap. 10. For a hauntingly detailed bill of particulars urging the same sort of prosecution against Henry Kissinger, see Christopher Hitchens, *The Trial of Henry Kissinger* (London: Verso, 2001).

world, you need sharper vision—or blurrier and more moralized vision—than I have to distinguish organized crime from the state in the first place. All these problems are similar. None of them become qualitatively different or insoluble because of some cockamamie commitment that the sovereign must be unaccountable or above the law.

A Glimpse of the Future

In 1772, Louis-Sébastien Mercier published a utopian novel of sorts, an exploration of the world in the year 2440.[240] (I don't know why his English translator decided to change it to 2500.)[241] "Absolute sovereignty is now abolished," the wide-eyed reader learned; "the chief magistrate preserves the name of king; but he does not foolishly attempt to bear all that burden which oppressed his ancestors." "The laws reign, and no man is above them, which was a horrid evil in your Gothic government. . . . No one fears man, but the laws; the sovereign himself is sensible that they hang over his head."[242] Mercier thought change was on the horizon, if a distant horizon. Just thirteen years later, William Paley couldn't conceive of change: "there necessarily exists in every government a power from which the constitution has provided no appeal; and which power, for that reason, may be termed absolute, omnipotent, uncontrollable, arbitrary, despotic; and is alike so in all countries."[243] So

240. Louis-Sébastien Mercier, *L'an deux mille quatre cent quarante: Rêve s'il en fût jamais* (Londres [Paris?], 1772).

241. [Louis-Sébastien Mercier], *Memoirs of the Year Two Thousand Five Hundred*, trans. W. Hooper, 2 vols. (London, 1772).

242. *Memoirs*, 2:125, 128–29 (*L'an*, 293, 296).

243. William Paley, *The Principles of Moral and Political Philosophy* (London, 1785), 449.

if there were governments in 2440, they'd have to be the same. But Paley was quite obviously wrong about the alleged necessity. He betrayed his lack of imagination, what it's like to be in the clutches of a theory.

We're part of the way to 2440, and I don't mean chronologically. Maybe we shouldn't get all the way there. Maybe there are good cases for the Eleventh Amendment, sovereign immunity in tort, diplomatic immunity, and the like. Maybe we should decide that Mercier's vision is decadent and shrink from it in horror. But those cases have to be made in retail, not wholesale, terms. They can't be made by gesturing toward the classic account of sovereignty, because that account has been gutted by political struggles and historical changes. We have divided sovereign authority. We have limited it. We have come partway to holding it accountable. I see no reason to pretend to be loftily impartial about those changes, no reason to pretend that critical appraisal is somehow inappropriate. Those changes are all to the good, wildly to the good, and we could use more of them, and we shouldn't wait a few more centuries to achieve them. Sure, I can live without calling the chief magistrate a king. Still: me, I'm rooting for Mercier.

5
Remnants

So where are we?

The classic theory of sovereignty says that to have an orderly society, you have to have a locus of political authority that's unlimited, undivided, and unaccountable. It adds that such sovereign authority is immensely dignified and that law is a matter of sovereign command. The theory, I've suggested, was sensible enough as a response to early modern Europe's wars of religion. But it isn't a timeless bit of political theory, and it has run its course and then some. The point is context, not chronology: even today, the classic theory of sovereignty is plausibly serviceable in some parts of the globe. Take the case of failed states, where the nominal government is a paper entity whose remit barely runs outside the capital city, if even there, where warlords rule some areas and nobody rules others. In such settings, it could be prissy, even perverse, to insist that the locals not invoke sovereignty. "Sovereignty for Somalia!": now there's a slogan I might well get behind.[1]

1. Consider Andrea L. Levy, *Searching for Peace: Views and Comments from Somalia on the Foundations of a New Government* (Washington, DC: National Democratic Institute, 2011).

Sure, I'd worry about making that authority unlimited, undivided, and unaccountable. But it might be—I don't know for sure; the facts matter, and you shouldn't be cavalier about them just because you have normative interests—that it's easier first to build a state and then limit it, divide it, and make it accountable than it is to build in limits, division, and accountability from the get-go. Or that it would be easier to do that in Somalia, if not generally.

But our context, happily, is decidedly different. I offer no apologies for developing my view by canvassing a wide range of historical examples and political struggles, some of them prominent, some illustrative. Theory isn't what you get when you leave out the facts. We've seen political actors made stupid by sovereignty. We've seen political conflicts exacerbated, even created, by it. We've seen cruel and bloodthirsty policies justified by it. Far from securing social order, then, sovereignty has become a threat to social order—or at least to the sort of decent social order we want.

We've also seen actors struggling to domesticate sovereignty: to limit it, to divide it, to hold it accountable. Those struggles, largely successful across much of the West, now have abstract names: constitutionalism, federalism, and the rule of law. They mark decided improvements in our political arrangements. If the theory of sovereignty looks askance at them and predicts they are way stations on the road to anarchy, so much the worse for the theory. The classic theory of sovereignty is an atrocious guide to our problems and possibilities. It fails to pick out what matters about our governments, and it fails so badly that I'm tempted to say it fails even to refer to them. The failure is even worse than that of Locke's odd suggestion that a defining criterion of the concept of *gold* is solubility in aqua regia, when surely most users of the concept, then and now, have no clue whatever about this.[2] Try this: *unicorns* does not actually refer to horses. When we talk about unicorns, we understand we are engaging in folklore or fantasy. We greet the news that maybe once people really believed in them with curiosity, condescension, and contempt. We'd feel sorry for people who mistook horses for unicorns, or we'd wonder whether they were mentally ill. Sovereignty is unicorn government. So . . . ?

Let me remind you of the dilemma facing champions of sovereignty. Prong one: they can yield on one or two of the concept's criteria. They can agree that sovereign power can be limited or divided or held accountable: even some of the great theorists of sovereignty made such concessions. But they can't yield on all three, lest they have a concept with no criteria. That way lies nonsense, quite literally: again, imagine someone who says, "This is a bachelor, but not an unmarried male." Prong two: they can hang onto one or more of the criteria. But why would anyone want to embrace the idea of unlimited or undivided or unaccountable state authority? How many times must we learn that states don't always secure social order, that they sometimes undercut and destroy it? How many political prisoners left to rot in jail with no recourse do we need, how many rape victims, how many living bodies bound and pushed out of helicopters into the ocean, how many grinning

2. Hilary Putnam, *Representation and Reality* (Cambridge, MA: MIT Press, 1991), 22–30. But see too *The Philosophy of Hilary Putnam*, ed. Randall E. Auxier et al. (Chicago: Open Court, 2015), 75–78. Putnam's example comes from Locke's *Essay concerning Human Understanding*, bk. 2, chap. 23 (for instance, § 10: "He, that will examine his complex *Idea* of Gold, will find several of its *Ideas*, that make it up, to be only Powers, as the Power of being melted, but of not spending itself in the Fire; of being dissolved in *Aqua Regia*, are *Ideas*, as necessary to make up our complex *Idea* of Gold, as its Color and Weight").

skulls, how many corpses stacked up, blown up, shoveled into mass graves, left to molder in fields and be picked over by vultures and rats, how many delicate recitals of the filthy business we call ethnic cleansing, to recall that behind such suffocatingly bland phrases as "undercut social order" lies grotesque, unfathomable human suffering? How surprised can you even pretend to be that in cracking down on a Papuan guerrilla movement seeking independence, Indonesia's government has reincarnated the atrocities of the wars of religion? "We were forced to eat shit, drink pee. I was electrocuted in my testicles, bum and legs."[3] How surprised that torture in Pol Pot's prisons including having to eat shit?[4] Don't begin to entertain the fantasy that only far-off or "backward" regimes perform such stunts. Don't airily dismiss the claim from a detainee at Abu Ghraib that one American soldier was "fucking a kid, his age would be about 15–18 years," "putting his dick in the little kid's ass," the kid was "screaming," "and the female soldier was taking pictures."[5] Don't anesthetize yourself with such disgusting Orwellian locutions as "enhanced interrogation techniques." Don't even congratulate yourself on being honest enough to talk about torture, or "acts that can only be described as blatantly sadistic, cruel, and inhuman," as that notorious softy, Secretary of Defense Donald Rumsfeld, put it in testifying before a congressional committee.[6] Instead contemplate pre-

3. Budi Hernawan, *Torture and Peacebuilding in Indonesia: The Case of Papua* (Abingdon: Routledge, 2018), 106.

4. David Chandler, *Voices from S-21: Terror and History in Pol Pot's Secret Prison* (Berkeley: University of California Press, 1999), 110.

5. http://media.washingtonpost.com/wp-srv/world/iraq/abughraib/151108.pdf (last visited 22 July 2018).

6. *Review of Department of Defense Detention and Interrogation Operations: Hearings before the Committee on Armed Services, United States Senate . . . 2004* (Washington, DC: U.S. Government Printing Office, 2005), 6.

cisely what went on at the CIA's "black site" prisons.[7] Instead think as concretely, unflinchingly, pornographically as you can of just what that torture consists in. Isn't this sort of thing precisely what those demanding unlimited or unaccountable authority are in fact demanding? No, of course they don't intend that. But won't it inexorably come in the wake of what they do intend? Hoping to extricate subjects from bloody combat, Hobbes, recall, demanded a "power able to over-awe them all." Surely by now we know decidedly too much about what such a power can and will do.

All too often, the alleged "two faces" of sovereignty—internal and external, domestic and international—are identical twins with the same sadistic, scary scowl: here, too, better to say just one face after all. I know there are more modest and affirmative things to say about the goods we've secured with limits, divisions, and accountability. But a lot of political theory is properly concerned with damage control. We've managed, in large part, to domesticate the state. That we should let it slip its leash is a singularly stupid idea.

You can escape the dilemma by adopting some other account of sovereignty. I'll canvass three notable ones here and explain why I'm not tempted to adopt any of them. But first a challenge: why do we need the concept at all? Ready at hand are the concepts of *state*, *jurisdiction*, and *authority*. They're difficult concepts, for sure. But what extra work needs doing in this terrain that we can't do with those three concepts? One commentator after another concedes that the classic theory of

---

I owe the reference to Seymour M. Hersh, *Chain of Command: The Road from 9/11 to Abu Ghraib* (New York: HarperCollins, 2004), 43.

7. See, for instance, http://www.theguardian.com/us-news/ng-interactive/2017/oct/09/cia-torture-black-site-enhanced-interrogation, with a cascade of nauseating links (last visited 22 July 2018).

sovereignty—they don't frame it quite as I do, but close enough for present purposes—is a baffling and pernicious guide to our problems and possibilities. But then they gesture toward some alternative, however similar to the one it's supposed to replace, or however vague. Take this suggestion from constitutional theorist Neil Walker: "Sovereignty may be defined as the discursive form in which a claim concerning the existence and character of a supreme ordering power for a particular polity is expressed, which supreme ordering power purports to establish and sustain the identity and status of the particular polity *qua* polity and to provide a continuing source and vehicle of ultimate authority for the juridical order of that polity. This definition seeks to address and to answer a number of objections concerning the irrelevance, vagueness, incoherence and normative shortcomings of the concept of sovereignty."[8] Whatever you make of the shift from actual political actors and institutions to discursive frames, the same old difficulties surface instantly, because Walker is hanging onto "supreme . . . power" and "ultimate authority."

Or again: here's the distinguished international lawyer (and my former colleague) John Jackson, testifying before a Senate committee in 1994: "What is happening now, as I am sure you are very aware, is an enormous rethinking of sovereignty generally, the whole concept of sovereignty. And in some ways the concept, certainly the older concept of several centuries ago just does not make any sense in today's world."[9]

8. Neil Walker, "Late Sovereignty in the European Union," in *Sovereignty in Transition*, ed. Neil Walker (Oxford: Hart, 2003), 6, italics removed. For a critical review of the volume, see Neil MacCormick, "Questioning 'Post-Sovereignty,'" *European Law Review* (December 2004).

9. Senate Committee on Finance Hearing, 23 March 1994, "Results of the Uruguay Round Trade Negotiations," in *Hearings before the Committee on*

So where did that enormous rethinking lead? In 2003, Jackson opined that "the world will have to develop something considerably better than either the historical and discredited Westphalian concept of sovereignty, or the current, but highly criticized, versions of sovereignty still often articulated. That something is not yet well defined, but it can be called 'sovereignty-modern,' which is more an analytic and dynamic process of disaggregation and redefinition than a 'frozen-in-time' concept or technique."[10] I'd love to tell you that I grasp what Jackson means by *sovereignty-modern* and that I see how it would be helpful, but I'm afraid I can't. Instead I recommend that you put pressure on his suggestion that "the world will have to develop something considerably better" as an account of sovereignty. Why do we need any account at all? Why not turn sovereignty over to the wizards at Pixar and Disney, so that when they tire of unicorns they can make charming cartoon movies about haughty kings? Yes, sometimes we reinterpret concepts. *Insolence* and *impudence* used to be antonyms, the first the vice of a social superior harsh in exercising his authority, the second the vice of an insufficiently deferential or

Finance: United States Senate: One Hundred Third Congress: Second Session (Washington, DC: U.S. Government Printing Office, 1994), 122. I've moved a wayward comma.

10. John H. Jackson, "Sovereignty-Modern: A New Approach to an Outdated Concept," *American Journal of International Law* (October 2003), 802. Compare Anne-Marie Slaughter, "Disaggregated Sovereignty: Towards the Public Accountability of Global Government Networks," *Government and Opposition* (Spring 2004); Zbigniew Brzezinski, *Between Two Ages: America's Role in the Technotronic Era* (New York: Viking, 1970) ("the fiction of sovereignty," 274). *Sovereignty in Fragments*, ed. Hent Kalmo and Quentin Skinner (Cambridge: Cambridge University Press, 2010) is a useful introduction to current debates. Not everyone agrees the classic theory is in trouble. See, for instance, Charles Chatterjee, *International Law and Diplomacy*, rev. ed. (London: Routledge, 2010), 36.

sassy inferior. They became rough synonyms for *rudeness* after we abandoned—officially, anyway—the background commitments to hierarchy that made sense of them.[11] But sometimes we discard concepts. Once people thought burning objects were shedding phlogiston. Now we know they are gaining oxygen. Bye-bye, phlogiston. You needn't know a thing about it unless you are a historian of science.

One difference between phlogiston and sovereignty matters. Plenty of legal texts with current authority are flecked with appeals to sovereignty, and we need to continue to make sense of them. Happily, many of those appeals are prefatory, decorative, hortatory: they don't do any real work. Again, that's what I think of the United Nations Charter's language ("The Organization is based on the principle of the sovereign equality of all its Members"), reiterated in countless UN documents. Now I've already confessed that I'd like to change some of those legal texts: the ones, for instance, enshrining the doctrine of sovereign immunity. Still, there and elsewhere there have been occasional bashing of and frequent chipping away at the classic theory, attempts to whittle it down to benign impotence. That chipping away has been sometimes surreptitious, sometimes unconscious, but often effective enough.

Were this right, would I be the first to notice? Of course not. I'm happy to concede—no, delighted to boast—that in this general way my thesis is in fact relentlessly, outrageously, unoriginal. (Less generally, I have wanted to be concrete about the political struggles first breathing life into sovereignty, second sticking in the dagger. That's where the action is. And I think my rendition of the classic theory—social order requires a locus of political authority that's unlimited, undivided, and

11. See my *Poisoning the Minds of the Lower Orders* (Princeton, NJ: Princeton University Press, 1998), 210–17.

unaccountable, with exalted dignity and law as command trooping dutifully along—is crisper, more faithful to the historical trajectories, than much of what's been written.) We've seen obscure, even anonymous, figures clearly articulating at least big portions of my thesis. Recall St. George Tucker, American editor of Blackstone, calmly noting that neither part nor whole of American government enjoyed "supreme, irresistible, absolute, uncontrolled authority." Recall the *Charleston Courier*, revealing that Blackstone "makes sovereignty synonymous with despotism," ridiculing "the old politico-metaphysico theory" that sovereignty is indivisible as obviously out of touch with the facts. Recall Jonathan Shipley bemoaning Parliament's imperious stance against the American colonies: "We pursue a vain phantom of unlimited sovereignty, which was not made for man." Recall the San Francisco newspaperman who despaired at the juvenile thought that either the League of Nations would be sovereign or the United States would be: "The whole 'either or' should belong to the high school debating society, unless, as is likely, present-day high school students have risen intellectually above it." Recall the Tennessee newspaper aghast at the state legislature's thinking of using sovereign immunity to renounce its debt: "Honest men can only hold down their heads in shame and hope for better times." Recall Louis-Sébastien Mercier's narrator reporting back from an imagined future: "The laws reign, and no man is above them, which was a horrid evil in your Gothic government." We've seen luminary politicians shredding sovereignty, too: Lincoln, John Quincy Adams, and more.[12] I want to review some theorists who've grasped the case against sovereignty.

12. For a stylized sketch of state-building as a tactic for securing social order followed by drives to limit the state, see Franklin D. Roosevelt, "Speech to the Commonwealth Club," in *American Speeches: Political Oratory from*

Here's Harold Laski, writing during World War I, briskly matter-of-fact: "We have only to look at the realities of social existence to see quite clearly that the State does not enjoy any necessary pre-eminence for its demands." Laski's interest is in social differentiation. The state is one social institution among many. So another problem with imagining that some state actor is the sole locus of authority is that authority surfaces in all those other social institutions, too. Parents exercise authority over children, teachers over students, bosses over employees, and so on. "We prefer a country where the sovereignty is distributed," Laski suggests. So he cautions, "We seem in genuine danger of going back to an ancient and false worship of unity, to a trust in an undivided sovereignty as the panacea for our ills."[13]

Laski was willing to characterize himself as something of a pragmatist,[14] and the great pragmatist John Dewey already had insisted on the importance of social differentiation. "It is only a false abstraction which makes us conceive of sovereignty, or authority, and of law and of rights as inhering only in some supreme organization, as the national state. The family, the school, the neighborhood group, has its authority as respects its members."[15] Then too, globalization had undercut the cogency of older views. "Something that is wholly unreal in the present state of the world called national sovereignty

---

Abraham Lincoln to Bill Clinton, ed. Ted Widmer (New York: Library of America, 2006), 385–86 (23 September 1934).

13. Harold J. Laski, *Studies in the Problem of Sovereignty* (New Haven, CT: Yale University Press, 1917), 15, 273, 284. Compare Jacques Maritain, "The Concept of Sovereignty," *American Political Science Review* (June 1950).

14. *Studies*, 284.

15. *Outlines of a Critical Theory of Ethics* [1891], in *The Early Works of John Dewey, 1882–1898*, ed. Jo Ann Boydston, 5 vols. (Carbondale: Southern Illinois University Press, 1969–72), 3:348.

is appealed to and employed as if it had significance."[16] "The unique and supreme position of the State in the social hierarchy . . . has hardened into unquestionable dogma under the title of sovereignty."[17] It's the trademark pragmatist or historicist clarion call, just the sort I am making here, cautioning against being in the clutches of concepts that might once have been helpful but now are obsolete, confused, pernicious.

Hannah Arendt cast a baleful eye on sovereignty because of its image of plenary control. That's not just antidemocratic, it's also antipolitical.[18] She too summoned up changes in our political arrangements: "National sovereignty, that is, the majesty of the public realm itself as it had come to be understood in the long centuries of absolute kingship, seemed in contradiction to the establishment of a republic."[19] Nor did she congratulate the American revolutionaries on assigning sovereignty to the people. Instead she congratulated them on discarding it: "the great and, in the long run, perhaps the greatest American innovation in politics as such was the consistent abolition of sovereignty within the body politic of the republic, the insight that in the realm of human affairs sovereignty and tyranny are the same."[20]

16. "Between Two Worlds" (20 March 1944), in *The Later Works of John Dewey, 1925–1953*, ed. Jo Ann Boydston, 17 vols. (Carbondale: Southern Illinois University Press, 1983–90), 17:455.

17. *Reconstruction in Philosophy* [1920], in *The Middle Works of John Dewey, 1899–1924*, ed. Jo Ann Boydston, 15 vols. (Carbondale: Southern Illinois University Press, 1976–83), 12:195. More generally, *Reconstruction* at 12:194–97 takes up both differentiation and globalization.

18. Hannah Arendt, *The Human Condition*, 2nd ed. (Chicago: University of Chicago Press, 1998), pt. 5.

19. Hannah Arendt, *On Revolution* (New York: Viking, 1963), 16.

20. *On Revolution*, 152. Patchen Markell, "The Rule of the People: Arendt, *Archê*, and Democracy," *American Political Science Review* (February 2006), sharpens Arendt's rejection of conventional notions of ruling.

Finally, H. L. A. Hart dismantled the command theory of law. But along the way he also demolished the thought that to make sense of law, we need some sovereign who can't be legally bound. The classic theorists worried that if a sovereign could be legally bound, there must be some higher authority issuing laws to bind him, and then that higher authority would be the sovereign. Hart deftly undoes the worry: "legal limitations on the legislative authority consist not of duties imposed on the legislator to obey some superior legislator but of disabilities contained in rules which qualify him to legislate."[21] Hart is relentless, too, in dismissing the attempt to save the classic theory of sovereignty by saying the people are sovereign. Which people, acting in which ways? Those questions can't be answered without an appeal to rules, rules that we might as well call law. In the American case, there are quite obviously laws governing voting rights, referenda, the calling of constitutional conventions, you name it.[22] Once again the idea that sovereign command or will has to be in some sense prior to law is a mistake.

21. H. L. A. Hart, *The Concept of Law* (Oxford: Clarendon, 1961), 69. See generally 64–76.

22. Consider the attack on the Staunton Convention in "The Crisis," *Richmond Enquirer* (2 August 1825). On Massachusetts's 1814 bid to call a convention of six states, see Henry Adams, *History of the United States of America during the Administrations of James Madison* (New York: Library of America, 1986), 909–13. On the Harrisburgh Convention, "Imposts on Woollens," *Evening Post* (3 December 1827). For a heated complaint about a "political club," with worries about *imperium in imperio* and insurrection, see Anti-Guillotine to Governor Hamilton, *Charleston Courier* (15 August 1831). For a popular convention bidding against the Tennessee legislature's impending vote to secede, see "Proceedings of the East Tennessee Convention, Held at Knoxville, May 30 and 31, 1861," in *The War of the Rebellion*, 70 vols. (Washington, DC, 1880–1901), 52:154.

Anyway, the dilemma I've posed to patrons of sovereignty is that either they forswear all the classic concept's criteria, in which case the concept is meaningless; or they cling to one or more of them, in which case the concept is pernicious. Let's examine three attempts to escape the dilemma by reframing the concept.

Popular Sovereignty

It's commonly said that the genius of the American revolutionaries was to transfer sovereignty from the government to the people.[23] In fact, it was already being said just after the revolution: "The rejection of British sovereignty therefore drew after it the necessity of fixing on some other principle of government. The genius of the Americans, their republican habits and sentiments, naturally led them to substitute the majesty of the people, in lieu of discarded royalty."[24] Yet I have pretty ruthlessly squelched references to popular sovereignty, though I let a few slip through. Why?

From the outset, I suggested that sovereignty is supposed to be held by some government actor or actors or institution. However fond you are of popular sovereignty, we still rely on that feature of the concept all the time. If someone is defending,

23. See, for instance, Larry D. Kramer, *The People Themselves: Popular Constitutionalism and Judicial Review* (Oxford: Oxford University Press, 2004), 54–56.

24. David Ramsay, *The History of the American Revolution*, 2 vols. (Philadelphia, 1789), 1:350. For an elaborate rendition of popular sovereignty, see Noah Webster, *Sketches of American Policy* (Hartford, 1785), 3–10. Governor Hutchinson must not have been pleased by Charles Turner, *A Sermon Preached before His Excellency Thomas Hutchinson, Esq.* (Boston, [1773]), 18–19.

say, the right of the state of Michigan not to answer to a lawsuit in federal court on the grounds of state sovereignty, it would be baffling to suggest that actually the people are sovereign. It would feel like changing the subject. Which is exactly what it would be.

Popular sovereignty has its place in a different debate. It's an answer to the question, what makes the government legitimate? As a foil to political authority's descending from God, it's plenty attractive.[25] Recall, for instance, the face-off between Charles I, invoking "a trust committed to me by God," and the lord president of the court, asserting that they could try him "in the name of the *People* of England." Accountability to God provided a reason for Charles to assert he couldn't be held legally accountable by any earthly power. If or insofar as popular sovereignty means rejecting that pose, I'm rabidly enthusiastic about it, even though it will often be not just tricky but also politically controversial to decide who qualifies as the people or who gets to act in their name. When the lord president made his grand assertion, Lady Fairfax's voice rang out from the gallery: "it was a Lie . . . not half, not a quarter of the people." Attending soldiers were ordered to shoot her.[26]

Not everyone is rabidly enthusiastic, though. Not even in the United States. Not even recently. Justice Scalia invoked

25. The classic source on the historical unfolding of the distinction between authority descending from God or ascending from the people is Walter Ullmann, *Principles of Government and Politics in the Middle Ages* (London: Methuen, 1961).

26. [Hineage Finch], *An Exact and Impartial Accompt of the Indictment, Arraignment, Trial, and Judgment (According to Law) of Twenty Nine Regicides, the Murtherers of His Late Sacred Majesty of Most Glorious Memory* (London, 1660), 186–87; and see 189–90 for one witness's startling (and startlingly implausible) claim: "I saw the Prisoner at the Bar, cry out, Down with the Whores, shoot them."

not just "the majority's ability to express its belief that government comes from God"—I confess that I doubt the majority believes that—but also "the fact that government comes—derives its authority from God."[27] Sounds like James I's lofty nod to "CHRIST, in whose Throne I sit in this Part of the Earth."[28] If it's a fact, it's one that the revolutionaries, as we usually imagine them, didn't miss, but flouted.

So it's one thing, and an exceedingly good one, to say that the legitimacy of political authority has to ascend from the people, not descend from God. It's another thing, and a weirdly contentious one, to say that in fact the people govern. Mostly they don't. One can point to moments in American history—popular ratifying conventions, referenda, and the like—to undergird the claim that popular sovereignty sounds in the actual exercise of political authority, not just legitimating it.[29] But even a painstaking search won't reveal a lot of that. If you are enamored of direct democracy, if you think there

27. Transcript of Oral Argument at 17, 16, *Van Orden v. Perry*, 545 U.S. 677 (2005), available at http://www.supremecourt.gov/oral_arguments/argument_transcripts/2004/03-1500.pdf (last visited 23 July 2018).

28. *Journal of the House of Lords* (19 February 1624). See too *The Soveraignty of Kings* (London, 1642), n.p.: "our gracious and Religious Soveraign King *Charles*, gracious as being like unto God whose Vice-gerent he is"; Richard Baxter, *A Call to the Unconverted* (London, 1658), preface, n.p. Contrast [S.H.], *The King of Kings: or The Soveraignty of Salus Populi, over All Kings, Princes, and Powers, Whatsoever* (London, 1655), 93, addressing foreign rulers on the importance of "happifying the People under you" (italics removed).

29. Consider, for instance, Gordon Wood, *The Creation of the American Republic, 1776–1787* (Chapel Hill: University of North Carolina Press, 1969), chap. 9. Compare Edmund S. Morgan, *Inventing the People: The Rise of Popular Sovereignty in England and America* (New York: Norton, 1988), 153, on popular sovereignty: "To sustain a fiction palpably so contrary to fact is not easy." For his hesitations on his use of fiction as an organizing category, see 14–15.

should be lots more, you'll run into the same sensible concerns about limits, divisions, and accountability; likewise for invocations of the people's "unlimited sovereignty" and the "unlimited obedience" they're owed.[30]

Here's another way to see that "popular sovereignty" is a different notion surfacing in a different debate. If there's a catalogue of Americans from the founding era onward embracing popular sovereignty, there's another catalogue of those not reformulating but simply rejecting sovereignty. We've seen, for instance, James Wilson. Consider too John Taylor, staunchly opposed to sovereignty in 1820: "I do not know how it happened, that this word has crept into our political dialect, unless it be that mankind prefer mystery to knowledge; and that governments love obscurity better than specification." "Our constitutions, therefore, wisely rejected this indefinite word

30. Thus Senator Littleton Tazewell (Democratic-Republican–VA), *Gales & Seaton's Register* (21 January 1825). Note the sharp response in *National Advocate* [New York] (14 February 1825): "we now deliberately ask Mr. Tazewell if this doctrine, a doctrine equally wicked and detestable, was not the precise doctrine both in terms and purport for which Lord North and his colleagues contended during the great war of the revolution?" More pointedly, in his inaugural address of 1841, William Henry Harrison urged "the limited sovereignty possessed by the people of the United States": *A Compilation of the Messages and Papers of the Presidents*, ed. James D. Richardson, 11 vols. (n.p.: Bureau of National Literature and Art, 1910), 3:1862. For a response, complaining that Harrison didn't believe in state sovereignty, see Jefferson, "To the Democracy of Ohio" no. 9, *Ohio Statesman* (7 April 1841). Finally, consider "Strict Construction Our Only Hope," *Georgia Telegraph* (17 August 1847): "our government is a restricted, limited, sovereignty of a free people and not a lawless majority mob"; "Judicial Expenses," *Connecticut Courant* (25 June 1853): "In a Representative Republic, the people have only a limited sovereignty"; "The People," *Augusta Chronicle* (27 July 1876), affirming popular sovereignty but adding, "it must be limited . . . an unlimited sovereignty would be but a wretched tyranny"; "Limited Sovereignty," *Atlantic* (February 1879).

as a traitor of civil rights, and endeavored to kill it dead by specifications and restrictions of power, that it might never again be used in political disquisitions." "Far from discerning any glimpse of the powers of sovereignty in our constitutions, I see nothing but long catalogues of limitations, restrictions, balances and divisions of power." Yes, Taylor was happy to embrace popular sovereignty and the people entrusting state actors with their roles as "obvious truths," but that doesn't begin to take back or qualify his staunch rejection.[31] Popular sovereignty is not his preferred answer to the questions people asked about the sovereignty of the state. Another writer denied the cogency of all sovereignty talk, whether applied to the government or the people.[32]

"Whatever it may be elsewhere," Charles Sumner instructed the Senate, "Popular Sovereignty within the sphere of the Constitution has its limitations."[33] Sumner was adamant that Kansas couldn't decide for itself whether it wanted to be a free or slave state in joining the union. Pursuing that same cause, Lincoln elicited laughter on the campaign trial by mocking "Popular sovereignty! everlasting popular sovereignty!"[34]

31. John Taylor, *Construction Construed, and Constitutions Vindicated* (Richmond, 1820), 25, 26, 31–32, 52. *Construction*, 143, insists that neither the federal government nor state governments are sovereign; contrast Taylor's treatment in *New Views of the Constitution of the United States* (Washington, DC, 1823), sec. 13.

32. "Supreme Court! Bashford vs. Barstow! More Delay Asked For! The Court Refuse It: Argument of Mr. Ryan," *Wisconsin Patriot* (8 March 1856).

33. *Congressional Globe* (4 June 1860).

34. "Speech at Chicago, Illinois," 10 July 1858, in Abraham Lincoln, *Speeches and Writings, 1832–1858*, ed. Don E. Fehrenbacher (New York: Library of America, 1989), 441. See too his pointed attack on Douglas's wanting to inherit the mantle of "genius of 'popular sovereignty'" from Clay, "Speech at Springfield, Illinois," 17 July 1858, in *Speeches*, 476.

Whatever commitments Americans have to the idea that popular sovereignty means actual governing authority, however frail or robust those commitments are, it's worth remembering they are parochial, by no means part of the common currency of Western politics today. Recall the *Economist* in 2018: it's "crystal clear" that sovereignty "does not lie, thank God, with that dangerous abstraction, 'the people.' It lies with Parliament, and ultimately with the House of Commons."[35]

A vintage eighteenth-century thesis is worth noting. Hume puts it this way: "As Force is always on the Side of the Governed, the Governors have nothing to support them but Opinion. 'Tis therefore, on Opinion only that government is founded; and this Maxim extends to the most despotic and most military governments, as well as to the most free and most popular."[36] Madison puts it this way: "Public opinion sets bounds to every government, and is the real sovereign in every free one."[37] With or without Madison's refinement of Hume, the basic view is sensible enough in a world of limited state capacity, though even there not beyond challenge: Montesquieu

35. Contrast "The Guardian View on May's Brexit Deal: It's Over, but What's Next?" *Guardian* (15 January 2019): "The country now faces a situation without precedent in its constitutional history: how to reconcile the sovereignty of the people with the sovereignty of parliament." Good luck with that.

36. David Hume, *Essays, Moral and Political*, 2nd ed. corr., 2 vols. (Edinburgh, 1743), 1:49.

37. "Public Opinion" (19 December 1791), in James Madison, *Writings*, ed. Jack N. Rakove (New York: Library of America, 1999), 500. Weber's thesis that domination invariably appeals to legitimacy is deeply continuous with this earlier view: see Max Weber, *Economy and Society: An Outline of Interpretive Sociology*, ed. Guenther Roth and Claus Wittich, trans. Ephraim Fischoff et al., 2 vols. (Berkeley: University of California Press, 1978), 1:212.

staked out the position that despots rule by fear.[38] And leaving aside how powerfully the government can shape the very opinion it is supposed to respond to, many of today's states have surveillance and repressive capacities that would have amazed Hume and Madison. Call it the Tiananmen effect: I think the eighteenth-century thesis has passed its sell-by date.

Regardless, as a quite general matter, the people don't exercise authority, don't rule, don't govern: they are governed.[39] Another fine old phrase—the consent of the governed—has the same central normative thrust as popular sovereignty, but on its face broadcasts what we need to hear loud and clear. We have good reasons to want government to be democratically responsive, though also good reasons to be skeptical of untrammeled majoritarianism and to want to make room for leadership.[40] Embracing democratic responsiveness is a far cry from saying the people actually govern, still less that their authority is unlimited, undivided, and unaccountable. No

38. Montesquieu, *The Spirit of Laws*, 2 vols. (London, 1750), 1:37–38.

39. For the American context, consider Sanford Levinson, "Popular Sovereignty and the United States Constitution: Tensions in the Ackermanian Program," *Yale Law Journal* (June 2014).

40. Round up the usual suspects (an instruction to you, not a reminder to me); but also consider James Bryce, *The American Commonwealth*, 3 vols. (London, 1888), 3:14–33 on "Government by Public Opinion" and "How Public Opinion Rules in America," and note 3:22: "The duty therefore of a patriotic statesman in a country where public opinion rules, would seem to be rather to resist and correct than to encourage the dominant sentiment. He will not be content with trying to form and mold and lead it, but he will confront it, lecture it, remind it that it is fallible, rouse it out of its self-complacency." Compare "Free Speech Address Delivered at Tremont Temple, Boston," 11 December 1860, in *Speeches of Carl Schurz* (Philadelphia, 1865), 225: "the all-powerful sovereign of this country, the *freedom of inquiry*."

amount of swooning over the originary or constituent powers of the people should let us ignore that.

Ubiquitous critics sometimes find popular sovereignty risible, but sometimes decry it as pernicious. "A Catholic Priest" surveying the wars of religion could see it only as incipient carnage.[41] A lawyer and Oxford professor offered a typically foreboding, forbidding warning in 1800:

> To inculcate unqualified notions of *popular sovereignty*; to hold forth the monarch as *the servant of his people*; to accustom the multitude to consider itself as "the root and father of kings"; to teach *the majority* to consider their sovereign as wearing a diadem which it was their good pleasure to confer, and wielding a scepter which at their bidding he must resign,—is to familiarize their minds to opinions, of all others, the most hostile to their own repose, and utterly to extinguish those allegiant sentiments of affection and courtesy, without which no government, no commonwealth, no modification of civil authority, can ensure its existence for a day. To greet the chief of the empire with the compellation of "servant of the people," is neither generous nor wise.[42]

41. A Cath. Priest, *Adelphomachia, or The Warrs of Protestancy* (n.p., 1637), 152.

42. James Sedgwick, *Remarks, Critical and Miscellaneous, on The Commentaries of Sir William Blackstone* (London, 1800), 160. For a similar earlier complaint, see William Dugdale, *A Perfect Copy of All Summons of the Nobility to the Great Councils and Parliaments of the Realm* (London, 1685), preface, n.p., denouncing the "pernicious Doctrine" "that the *Supreme Power*, and absolute *Sovereignty* doth totally reside in the *People*," so that "the *King* is to be no other, in effect, than a Ministerial Officer to the *Multitude*, and

Were those the only alternatives, I'd snicker at this late-breaking effusion of Hobbesian panic and side with popular sovereignty. Incredible that American government has lasted longer than a day, no? But they're not the only alternatives. We don't have to locate sovereignty somewhere and we needn't pride ourselves on our genius in assigning it to the people. We can instead abandon it. We don't need sovereignty to insist that the legitimacy of government depends on the consent of the governed, though if you want to use the word that way, I won't object.

Incidents of Sovereignty

Another approach to reconstructing the concept lies in focusing on marks (an older locution) or incidents of sovereignty. This approach could frame a more modest and up-to-date family-resemblance approach to the concept. Identify traits of ostensibly sovereign actors, or actions they routinely engage in that others don't, and then say, any entity exhibiting enough of them is a sovereign. No particular trait or action needs to be a necessary or sufficient condition.

It's not enough, of course, simply to use the word *mark* or *incident* or some synonym. Bodin himself discusses marks of sovereignty. But here's his opening bid, at which he hammers away: "This then is the first and chiefest mark of Sovereignty, to be of power to give laws and command to all in general, and to every one in particular," "to have power to give laws unto all and every one of the subjects, & to receive none from them,"

to give an Account to that confused Rout, when and as often as they shall require it." And consider the clashing views of John Thomson, *The Presbyterian Covenanter Displayed* (Dublin, 1765), 11, and John Thorburn, *Vindiciae Magistratus: or, The Divine Institution and Right of the Civil Magistrate Vindicated* (Edinburgh, 1773), 62.

"power to give laws unto all his subjects in general, & every one in particular, and not to receive any law or command from any other, but from almighty God only."[43] And he suggests that all the other marks can be spun out of this one. So far, there's no serious departure from articulating criteria for the concept, in the usual necessary-and-sufficient-conditions way; rather it seems merely another way to describe what I've called the classic theory.[44] Still, Bodin's list includes control over the country's currency.[45] From one point of view, that's a simple lemma of the sovereign's unlimited authority. But the motive to pick it out specially does sound in the alternate approach to the concept I'm considering here.

43. Jean Bodin, *The Six Bookes of a Commonweale: A Facsimile Reprint of the English Translation of 1606 Corrected and Supplemented*, ed. Kenneth Douglas McRae (Cambridge, MA: Harvard University Press, 1962), 162–63 [161–62]. That's also the first of four marks of sovereignty in [Thomas Palmer], *An Essay of the Meanes Hovv to Make Our Trauailes, into Forraine Countries, the More Profitable and Honourable* (London, 1606), 108–9; the first of nine in [Philippe de Béthune], *The Covnsellor of Estate: Contayning the Greatest and Most Remarkeable Considerations Seruing for the Managing of Publicke Affaires*, trans. E.G. (London, 1634), 15; with less emphasis on how sweeping it is, the first of nine in [John Wilson], *A Discourse of Monarchy* (London, 1684), 70–109. Philip Warwick, *A Discourse of Government* (London, 1694), 6–11, has thirteen marks of sovereignty. Also wobbling between unaccountable supremacy and incidents is John Bouvier, *A Law Dictionary*, 6th ed. rev. (Philadelphia, 1856), s.v. "sovereignty."

44. See too Tho[mas] Hobb[e]s, *De Corpore Politico: or The Elements of Law, Moral & Politick* (London, 1650), 69–71; Francis Wharton, *Commentaries on Law, Embracing Chapters on the Nature, the Source, and the History of Law* (Philadelphia, 1884), 212–29. See John Alexander Jameson, *The Constitutional Convention* (New York, 1867), 20–21 on the "*attributes* of sovereignty," including "indivisible," "indefeasible . . . incapable . . . of being defeated or abrogated."

45. So too, for instance, James Bayard, *Brief Exposition of the Constitution of the United States* (Philadelphia, 1840), 72: "The coinage of money, and the regulation of its value, have always been considered as incidents of sovereignty."

Here's a proposed list of incidents of sovereignty. I want to sidestep the question of whether we should see the incidents as descriptive or normative, abilities or rights: you can spin the approach either way. Still, there is something aspirational about it. For all its realism, this suggestion is debunking: "Worldly Princes often fancy Tyranny and Oppression to be the chief marks of Sovereignty, and think their Scepters not beautiful, till died in blood, nor the Throne secure, till established upon slain Carcasses."[46] I'll deploy a word you can tweak descriptively or normatively. The incidents of sovereignty, let's say, are the powers to:

- Control the country's territory, with a monopoly on legitimate coercion;
- Control the country's borders;
- Raise and command armed forces;
- Control the money supply;
- Promulgate laws of property and other matters;
- Declare war;
- Negotiate treaties and other international agreements;
- Send representatives to international organizations;
- Punish criminals, including with the "power of life and death";[47] and
- Impose taxes.

46. Stephen Charnocke, *Several Discourses upon the Existence and Attributes of God* (London, 1682), 715.

47. William Wiseman, comp., *The Christian Knight* (London, 1619), 25. Consider John Locke, *Two Treatises of Government* (London, 1690), 219 (*Second Treatise*, § 3): "Political Power, then I take to be a Right of making Laws with Penalties of death, and consequently all less Penalties, for

Others might add or subtract particular items, but this approach to grasping sovereignty is decidedly casual about what does and doesn't belong on the list, allergic to thinking there are items that simply must appear.[48]

Surely these incidents of sovereignty redeem the concept? I'm unmoved, for two reasons. One: *sovereign* here is standing in for *state*. These incidents do a good job picking out characteristic powers of states. But nothing illuminating happens when you shift instead to sovereignty. It's not as though we had an important contrast between sovereign states and nonsovereign states, not as though the incidents distinguish the former from the latter. The fewer incidents some putative state features, the less likely we are to characterize it as a state in the first place.

Two: it's apparently easy to forget how many states don't in fact command one power after another on this list, even the ones that might intuitively seem central. Unless you massage the concept of coercion relentlessly enough to make it fit the designed conclusion, no state actually claims a monopoly on its legitimate use: at least as far as I know, every state agrees that you may use force in self-defense. Then too it is worth noticing how many states rely on private coercion, some of it relatively decorous, such as privatized prisons; some of it emphatically not, such as death squads. Some states don't con-

---

the Regulating and Preserving of Property, and of employing the force of the Community, in the Execution of such Laws, and in the defense of the Common-wealth from Foreign Injury, and all this only for the Public Good." Compare with Robert Filmer, *Patriarcha: or The Natural Power of Kings* (London, 1680), 13: "These Acts of Judging in *Capital Crimes*, of making *War*, and concluding *Peace*, are the chiefest Marks of *Sovereignty* that are found in any *Monarch*."

48. For a modern list, see *Corpus Juris Secundum*, 48:32–33 (*International Law*, § 22).

trol their borders: the U.S. border with Canada is notoriously porous; whatever the maps portray, Pakistan doesn't even pretend to control the Pushtun tribal areas of its—"its"—northwest.[49] After World War II, Japan's constitution—you know, the one whose contents and adoption depended a lot more on General MacArthur than on the Japanese, even if the text solemnly proclaimed the principle of popular sovereignty, thus stripping the emperor of his claim—prevented it from fielding any armed forces abroad. Article 9 of the constitution says, "the Japanese people forever renounce war as a sovereign right of the nation and the threat or use of force as means of settling international disputes."[50] Today the country's forces are officially reserved for self-defense, and it's too easy to dismiss that restriction as fig leaf or pretense. Plenty of little countries still have no armed forces. Forget the U.S. dollar's role in international banking: El Salvador, Zimbabwe, and more don't even have their own currencies; they use the dollar instead. (An obvious reason is that it persuades foreign investors that they don't have to worry about rampant currency inflation.)[51] Most countries, Russia included,[52] have abandoned the death penalty. You might think this is ordinary sovereign self-binding, with unbinding available at the drop of a hat. The International Covenant on Civil and Political Rights is one reason to think that's not entirely right.[53]

49. "A Wild Frontier," *Economist* (18 September 2008).

50. The official translation is at http://japan.kantei.go.jp/constitution_and_government_of_japan/constitution_e.html (last visited 24 July 2018).

51. See, for instance, "Using the Dollar to Hold the Line: U.S. Currency Becomes Ecuador's," *New York Times* (18 January 2000).

52. "Russia: Death Penalty Ruled Unconstitutional," *Global Legal Monitor* (1 December 2009).

53. ICCPR, art. 6, available at http://www.ohchr.org/en/professionalinterest/pages/ccpr.aspx (last visited 30 August 2018).

Depending on how you construe *power*, you can perhaps argue that all these countries still have the powers in question, but they aren't exercising them; or if they have chosen to abandon them, even to place them off limits, they could undo that choice. (Here again we diligently recite, the sovereign cannot bind itself.) Maybe, but think too about the less juridical ways in which incidents of sovereignty can be left tattered, even threadbare. Bodin and others insist on the sovereign's right to frame and adopt laws. What could seem a more robust instance of untrammeled state autonomy? But many left-wing countries dare not pursue the legislative or tax agendas they like. They are constrained not just by the stern dictates of the International Monetary Fund and the World Bank, but also by the threat of capital flight.[54]

Here's a diagnostic device. If you think, in the retail way I recommend, "Well, lacking or deliberately abandoning such incidents of sovereignty might or might not be a good idea for particular countries, and as long as they still boast enough of them, they qualify as states," then *sovereignty* is doing no work at all in "incidents of sovereignty." If, however, you think that these derogations of sovereignty are a problem—"inherently" or "essentially" or "necessarily" a problem—you are likely in the clutches of the maximalist logic of sovereignty, where any limits are a threat. But then you've surrendered the alleged alternative approach, on which having enough incidents is good enough to qualify.

54. Fred Block, "The Ruling Class Does Not Rule: Notes on the Marxist Theory of the State," *Socialist Revolution* (May 1977), is a classic form of the argument, though more perhaps should be said about why Marx thinks the executive of the modern state, specifically, is the ruling committee of the bourgeoisie.

It's hard to see how you can have it both ways—that is, forswearing commitments to the classic theory of sovereignty but still finding limits or division or accountability as such a threat. "Sovereignty may seem like an enormous abstraction, gauzy and hard to understand," purrs John Bolton. "Indeed, it has a huge range of definitions, complicated and often contradictory, thus ironically making it easier for some people to believe that sovereignty is less important than it actually is." But "for Americans, sovereignty is not simply an academic abstraction. For us, sovereignty is our control over our own government." International agreements are "unquestionably a formula for reducing U.S. autonomy and reducing our control over government."[55] But how could it make sense to proceed in this wholesale way? Are all international agreements created equal? Doesn't the United States *expand* its options by participating in some arrangements? As I write, the Trump administration is demonstrating what happens when we rubbish the World Trade Organization. If you fix your vision solely at the moment at which the WTO hears a complaint and rules against the U.S., you can fume that we've been constrained. But if various countries agree to take some options off the table, as they have in setting up the WTO, that will open up otherwise unavailable options. Compare: if we all agree you can't drive on whatever side of the road you feel like, we gain the ability to hurtle around in our two-ton steel death traps relatively safely. Yes, you can complain that you were ticketed for driving on the wrong side of the road. Yes, you can denounce that as an invasion of your freedom. You can rail against the municipal

55. John R. Bolton, *How Barack Obama Is Endangering Our National Sovereignty* (New York: Encounter Books, 2010), 2–4; and see 21, 42.

authorities to whom we have surrendered control. But doing so seems, shall we say, shortsighted.

Schmittian Exception

"Sovereign is he who decides on the exception."[56] Carl Schmitt's Delphic claim has recently inspired a lot of work in political theory on law, politics, and emergencies.[57] The general claim seems to be that some actor, the sovereign, can suspend the law by appealing to a "state of exception" or emergency; that this possibility is always in play, so the idea of constitutional or legal restraints on sovereignty is a nonstarter; that liberal commitments to the rule of law and constitutionalism are illusory, because they don't constrain pure political will, but hang on it. The lingo is different, but the echo of the classic theory is unmistakable: he who can bind himself can always unbind himself.

So far, so abstract—that is, so invidiously abstract. We'd like examples. Giorgio Agamben offers a shower of them. Take this one, about Lincoln: "On September 22, 1862, the president proclaimed the emancipation of the slaves on his authority alone and, two days later, generalized the state of exception throughout the entire territory of the United States, autho-

56. Carl Schmitt, *Political Theology: Four Chapters on the Concept of Sovereignty*, trans. George Schwab (Chicago: University of Chicago Press, 2005), 5. For Schmitt's response to Laski, see his *The Concept of the Political*, trans. George Schwab (Chicago: University of Chicago Press, 1996), 40–45. Schmitt complains that in Laski's "numerous books . . . one does not find . . . a specific definition of the political" (44). On what one might say to scratch that itch, see my *Household Politics* (New Haven, CT: Yale University Press, 2013), 123–28.

57. The special issue of *diacritics* (Summer 2007) remains a good starting point for the explosion of interest in Schmittian exception.

rizing the arrest and trial before courts martials of 'all Rebels and Insurgents. . . . ' By this time, the president of the United States was the holder of the sovereign decision on the state of exception."[58] The date Agamben supplies is that of the Preliminary Emancipation Proclamation. I see no way to describe it as suspending law at all, let alone all of law; no way to describe it as Lincoln acting on his own authority; no way then to cast Lincoln as a sovereign: the proclamation painstakingly cites one statute after another as authority.[59]

I have no interest in quibbling with an example, though Agamben's other examples are no more persuasive. But I do have an interest in getting in focus what Schmitt was up to. Schmitt is crystal clear that "not every extraordinary measure, not every police emergency measure or emergency decree, is necessarily an exception. What characterizes an exception is principally unlimited authority, which means the suspension of the entire existing order."[60] Bang on all you like about Lincoln's suspension of habeas corpus[61] or his treatment of Confederate soldiers, nothing he did comes close to meeting Schmitt's criteria. More generally, it is not a routine feature of modern states that there is some actor, whether officially called sovereign or not, who can suspend the legal order. It's probably right that Britain's Parliament can, because officially

58. *State of Exception*, trans. Kevin Attell, in Giorgio Agamben, *The Omnibus Homo Sacer* (Stanford, CA: Stanford University Press, 2017), 183.

59. Abraham Lincoln, *Speeches and Writings, 1859–1865*, ed. Don E. Fehrenbacher (New York: Library of America, 1989), 368–70.

60. *Political Theology*, 12.

61. Consider "Message to Congress in Special Session," 4 July 1861, in Lincoln, *Speeches and Writings, 1859–1865*, 252–53; Lincoln to Erastus Corning and others, 12 June 1863, in *Speeches, 1859*, 457, 459. For an explicit comparison between Lincoln's act and Charles I's appeals to sovereignty, see *Southern Review* (1868), 74–76.

it can do anything and everything. But that's no necessary feature of states, and again I'm inclined to take it as a British bug, not a feature.

Schmitt exegesis aside, we're always free to depart from his view, to think that in states of emergency, however understood, law is subjected to political stress in illuminating ways.[62] So let's replace the implausible thought that a sovereign can suspend the entire legal order with the plausible—true—thought that all kinds of state actors can in some sense suspend all kinds of laws. Laws are, ordinarily anyway, what philosophers call defeasible. They have indefinitely many *unless* conditions attached, so that they might not properly apply in given cases, even if on their face they seem to. Without venturing into the jurisprudential thickets on that one, I'll add that it is often unclear quite what a law does and doesn't cover, even when the wording is perfectly straightforward.

You are speeding through a residential neighborhood and a policeman pulls you over. Ordinarily you'd get a caution or a speeding ticket, and it's simply up to the policeman to decide which: so far we have everyday legal discretion, and we worry about its being used unjustly. (You get a caution because the policeman likes the politics on your bumper sticker. You get a ticket because you're black.) But now suppose you're driving your friend to the emergency room: he's vomiting blood and lapsing into unconsciousness. Now the policeman apologizes for pulling you over and escorts you to the emergency room, his lights flashing and siren blaring to speed you along and keep you and other drivers safe. Or, to recur to a

62. Bonnie Honig, *Emergency Politics: Paradox, Law, Democracy* (Princeton, NJ: Princeton University Press, 2009), 66–68, explicitly departs from Schmitt.

hoary example in legal theory,[63] suppose the law forbids vehicles in a public park. But there's your four-year-old, sitting in the sandbox with her three-inch toy trucks: has she violated the law? What about the man in his wheelchair? I think it best to say the law doesn't cover such cases. The obvious point of the rule is to keep the park reasonably quiet and park users safe, and even if someone staring at a dictionary would agree that toy trucks and wheelchairs are vehicles, it seems nutty to construe the rule as covering such cases. Whatever the best jurisprudential account is, a sane policeman doesn't write a ticket for these putative infractions; and if somehow he does, a sane judge immediately throws them out.

Once we surrender the apocalyptic image of a particular actor suspending the law across the board, we have to reckon with particular state actors suspending (or overlooking or not enforcing or interpreting or . . .) particular laws in particular settings. They might have good reason to do so or not; we might have effective legal recourse when they suspend the law for bad reasons or not. The rule of law is not an inexorable machine; sometimes deciding what the law means or whether it should be applied requires real judgment. No wonder discretion routinely inspires heated protests.[64] But I don't see any way to extract some interesting alternate account of sovereignty from that congeries.

Let me bring back onstage for a brief encore everybody's favorite fice dog with its tail cut, Joseph Earle, the guy battered by the imperious Governor Evans. Many years before, Earle was desperately trying to bring off a duel with his once

63. Kicked off by H. L. A. Hart, "Positivism and the Separation of Law and Morals," *Harvard Law Review* (February 1958).

64. For instance, Richard Burn, *The History of the Poor Laws* (London, 1764), 117.

collaborator[65] and now bitter enemy, John Dargan. We don't know what drove the two apart.[66] It was "an old feud," one paper reported. "One of the parties says the difficulty will not be settled until one or the other is killed."[67] You'd need a gifted choreographer and the Keystone Kops for an accurate rendition of their abortive *pas de deux*. The two planned to leave Sumter for Augusta, Georgia, and fight there, I suppose to evade the authorities. Dargan was arrested in Sumter, paid bond—and left anyway for Augusta. The Sumter authorities sent a telegram, the Augusta police arrested the two—and Earle escaped: "Jumping into a buggy standing in front of the hotel, he jerked the reins from the hands of the colored driver, lashed the horse into a gallop and made for the bridge, which he crossed at a rapid pace." A policeman on horseback gave chase, but couldn't catch him. Back in Carolina, Earle didn't have to worry about Georgia's arrest: chalk it up to the joys of state sovereignty. A Carolina trial justice issued a warrant, but Earle had disappeared.[68] A few days later, Dargan set off again, this time for North Carolina; again a trusty telegram secured his arrest.[69] Held in a hotel room and guarded by a policeman, Dargan escaped: "he let himself down from a third

65. For their work in breaking up a Republican convention and the federal government's response, "Political," *Chicago Daily Tribune* (7 October 1878); "A Scare at Washington," *Yorkville Enquirer* [SC] (10 October 1878); "Political Troubles in Sumter," *Yorkville Enquirer* (17 October 1878).

66. Henry F. Cauthen, *John J. Dargan: His Dares and His Deeds* (Columbia, SC: State Printing Company, 1975), 15–20.

67. "Carolina Duellists," *Daily Constitution* [Atlanta] (21 September 1879).

68. "Contemplated Duel," *Augusta Chronicle* (20 September 1879); "The Duelling Party," *Augusta Chronicle* (20 September 1879).

69. "The Duelling Party," *Augusta Chronicle* (23 September 1879).

story window."[70] Now the two tried to meet in Charlotte, but Dargan didn't show, so Earle returned to Sumter, where he was again arrested and faced bond of $5,000. Friends raised the money.[71] Dargan eventually returned and faced the same daunting bond, which he paid.[72] The next year, the governor appealed to the two to reconcile. Saving face, they left it to confidants to agree; the confidants did; then the two agreed.[73] Yet a decade later, Dargan snarled that Earle was "not a fit man to be governor" and "remarked that he would fight Earle to the bitter end."[74] That's the end of the trail. Earle would die not from a bullet shot by Dargan's pistol, but shortly after beating Evans in the election to the Senate.[75]

It looks like the authorities really tried to stop this duel, that Dargan and Earle were slippery rascals. I know of no contemporary complaining that the very idea of dueling is an insult to the sovereign: in republican America, it's any old legal infraction. (Riddle for libertarians: why shouldn't two consenting adults be allowed to shoot at one another?) But suppose some state actor—the judge who issued the warrant, the

70. "The Duellists," *Augusta Chronicle* (24 September 1879).

71. "The Sumter Duellists," *Augusta Chronicle* (26 September 1879). For a hilariously detailed account of the pair's movements, see "The Duellists," *Augusta Chronicle* (26 September 1879).

72. "Blessed Are the Peace Makers," *Augusta Chronicle* (28 September 1879).

73. "The Earle-Dargan Difficulty," *Marion Star* [SC] (19 October 1880).

74. "Colonel Dargan and Colonel Earle," also an untitled story, *Georgetown Times* (7 June 1890). See also *Watchman and Southron* [Sumter] (4 June 1890), and, shrugging off Dargan's claim that Earle had "knocked" a friend of his as "very naughty," "Col. Dargan's Letter," *Watchman and Southron* (11 June 1890).

75. "Death of Joseph H. Earle," *New York Times* (21 May 1897).

policeman giving chase—shrugged and decided to let the two fight. Would there be any point scaring up sovereignty or a state of exception? Wouldn't it be better to keep thinking about the uses and abuses of discretion?

So here's another dilemma. Schmitt's account of sovereignty is strongly continuous with the classic theory: the sovereign stands above the law and can always suspend it, so it exists in some sense only as a matter of his will. Think of this as salvaging some picture of the priority of sovereignty to law without relying on a full-blown command theory. But Schmitt's understanding is decidedly unhelpful as a guide to today's states. Again, in government after government there is in fact no actor who can suspend the whole legal order. If you set Schmitt aside for a broader understanding of emergency and exception, you uncover some features of law on the ground that raise intriguing questions about the rule of law. But it's hard to see how you uncover any account of sovereignty.

Coda

I'd posed a dilemma. If you discard all three criteria of the classic theory of sovereignty, you have a vacuous or nonsensical concept on your hands. If you cling to one or more of them, you have a noxious account. You can try to escape the dilemma by reinterpreting the concept. But I don't know of some other viable account—and I don't see why we need one. We can get by just fine with the concepts of *state*, *jurisdiction*, and *authority*. None of them will trip us up with the strangely maximalist commitments of sovereignty.

So it's time, past time, to bury sovereignty. If you admire the work it did as a weapon against the wars of religion, you can make the burial as solemn and affectionate as you like.

You can stage a procession through the countryside. But admiration for its historic role is no reason to keep the putrescent corpse around. Today sovereignty stinks: it doesn't orient us toward our problems and possibilities. Don't like the rotting corpse imagery? Feel free to substitute: sovereignty is a zombie concept, undead, stalking the world, terrifying people. We haven't just domesticated sovereignty, we've destroyed it: we've managed to make political authority limited, divided, and more accountable. For us, here, now—not everyone in all times and places, but a much broader group than citizens of today's United States—sovereignty is pernicious.

An aristocrat dryly commented on the mutual affection of Catholics and Charles II. Catholics "embraced him gladly, and lull'd him asleep with those Enchanting Songs of Sovereignty, which the best and wisest Princes are often unable to resist."[76] It's odder when democratic citizens, lawyers, and politicians can't resist those same lullabies; odder yet when the lullabies are not sweet overtures to beatific slumbers, but strident preludes to repulsive nightmares.

76. A Person of Quality [John Sheffield, Duke of Buckingham], *The Character of Charles II* (London, 1696), 3–4. Compare the more scandalous *The Secret History of the Four Last Monarchs of Great-Britain* (London, 1693), 61.

Index